The New Right
Politics, Markets and Citizenship

Also by Desmond S. King

The State and the City
(with Ted Robert Gurr)

The New Right
Politics, Markets and Citizenship

Desmond S. King

Department of Politics, University of Edinburgh

MACMILLAN
EDUCATION

First published 1987

Published by
MACMILLAN EDUCATION LTD
Houndmills, Basingstoke, Hampshire RG21 2XS
and London
Companies and representatives
throughout the world

Printed in Hong Kong

British Library Cataloguing in Publication Data
King, Desmond S.
The new right: politics, markets and
citizenship.
1. Conservatism
I. Title
320.'52   JC571
ISBN 0-333-42074-8 (hardcover)
ISBN 0-333-42075-6 (paperback)

Contents

List of Tables

List of Figures

Acknowledgements

A number of people have helped me in the production of this book. I have benefited greatly from conversations with John Holmwood. I doubt whether I have met all his criticisms, but through our discussions the text has been improved immensely. Henry Drucker and Malcolm Anderson also deserve special thanks as they both read through the entire manuscript and made many useful comments.

I am grateful to several other colleagues for reading and commenting upon various portions of the manuscript. They include Nigel Bowles, Alice Brown, Jerry Goldman, Robert Goodin, Richard Parry and Jeremy Waldron. My thanks also to Steven Kennedy for his patience and encouragement with this book.

The author wishes to thank Pergamon Press for kindly giving permission for the use of copyright material for an abridged form of Table 3.1, reprinted with permission from Anthony Heath, Roger Jowell and John Curtice (1985) *How Britain Votes*.

Desmond S. King

1

Introduction

This book is about the political and economic ideas which have influenced the governments of Britain and the United States during the 1980s. In Britain, these ideas are commonly referred to as those of the 'New Right' – hence its common currency. It is also commonly employed in the United States though its meaning differs. In the United States, the term 'new right' is more closely associated with moral rather than economic arguments; this book concentrates primarily upon the British usage. None the less, there are sufficient similarities between recent British and American governing experience to justify a comparative study based on the shared assumptions and policy objectives evident in both the Thatcher and Reagan administrations. The distinct personalities of the current British and American political leaders, Margaret Thatcher and Ronald Reagan, and their political abilities have been extensively examined elsewhere. This book's concern is different: it attempts to explicate the set of economic and political ideas upon which these two leaders have drawn. Whilst the policies of these two governments are shaped as much by pragmatic political calculations as by ideology, New Right economic and political ideas have exercised a peculiar influence upon the intellectual framework within which policy is determined; and, given the demise of the post-war Keynesian welfare state consensus, are likely to continue to influence the nature of political debate. Accordingly, this book discusses the impact of New Right advocates upon the intellectual and political agenda principally through their revival of market mechanisms for public policy and their challenge to citizenship rights. The success of these ideas regarding markets can be gauged partly by opposition parties' questioning of their traditional hostility to the use of market mechanisms. Such a change is profoundly important and requires careful analysis. This book attempts to provide such an account of these conceptual and

1

intellectual tools, which will enable the reader to judge whether they have formed a significant influence upon government policy. My central thesis is that New Right ideas are a passing intellectual fashion, but one with important consequences: some New Right policies implemented by the Thatcher Government will be difficult to reverse. Further, the difficulties which Keynesian policy encountered in the 1970s makes its simple revival improbable. It is much more likely that the post-Thatcher period of British politics will comprise a reworking of the Keynesian welfare state consensus within the legacy of certain New Right ideas. This is evident from policy debates within the opposition political parties. Neither New Right liberalism nor pure Keynesian principles will be dominant by the end of the decade; each will contribute to the content of political debate and public policy as a new consensus is forged. In the United States the future is less clearcut. The opposition Democratic Party has yet to formulate a precise response to the Reagan administration's policies, but judging by the positions of 1984 Presidential candidates these will incorporate elements of the Reagan Presidency's policies.

As the ensuing chapter will demonstrate, New Right political and economic theories are far from new. Rather it is their promotion to the centre of the political arena which is recent – as recent as the 1970s. That decade heralded in an era of economic difficulty in most Western societies which contrasted markedly with the prosperity of the preceding three decades. A key source of these difficulties was international economic crisis caused by, in part, the 1973 oil price rise which affected both the British and American economies. Into the turbulent conditions of the 1970s came conservative New Right ideas promoted by determined interest groups who won the support of leading politicians. These New Right ideas cover a wide, and far from homogeneous, range of concepts and policy prescriptions. Chapter 2 reviews and catalogues these diverse ideas and considers their relationship with each other. Two main strands are identified: liberalism, which comprises the restoration of the traditional liberal values of individualism, limited government and free market forces; and conservatism, which consists of claims about government being used to establish societal order and authority based on social, religious and moral conservatism. The contradictions between these two strands, and the accommodations which advocates of each have reached with the other are reviewed.

New Right advocates seek not only to revive the role of market mechanisms and to end collectivist state policy but also to dismantle the citizenship rights established during the last two centuries. 'Citizenship rights' refer to the civil, political and social rights established under the impetus of economic development in advanced industrial societies and the extent to which they are available to all members of such societies. Modern usage of the term originates with T. H. Marshall (1964) and is widely used in social science analysis of advanced welfare state countries. These latter represent the most complete form of citizenship rights, which were hitherto limited to privileged elites. Marshall distinguishes between three types of citizenship rights: civil rights, which refers to the rights associated with individual freedom (that is, freedom of speech, the right to own property, equality before the law, and so on); political rights, comprising the rights associated with democracy (participation through universal suffrage, for example); and social rights, which refers to economic and welfare rights (that is, guarantees of a certain educational level, economic security, public welfare and health provision, and so on). These three sets of citizenship rights have been established sequentially since the early nineteenth century, with the post-war period crucial to social rights, of which the welfare state is the key institutional expression. Citizenship rights reduce inequalities in the political, social and economic spheres of society, and move toward a genuinely egalitarian social order.

New Right politicians seek to reverse this historical trend toward the widening scope of citizenship rights and ending of inequality. As will be seen from subsequent chapters, New Right advocates believe that inequality is a prerequisite for societal development and 'progress'. Liberals seek to place property rights over and above other citizenship rights: the right to own property is more important than social citizenship rights. Conservatives deny citizenship rights in their entirety, arguing that authority and order are more important values for society. Either way, New Right advocates want to restrict the range of citizenship rights widely accepted by advanced industrial societies in the 1970s. This is central to the position of New Right theorists and important for analysis of their political and economic ideas.

The right to own property is one aspect only of citizenship rights according to Marshall's threefold schema: it is part of the first category of citizenship rights – civil rights. New Right theorists, however, accord this one element of citizenship rights exclusive status. But, in doing so, they ignore the historical basis of such citizenship rights, including the right to property ownership. Property rights are only one element of citizenship rights; the conferring of them implies the negation of other citizenship rights. Such an account can be found in some early writings of Karl Marx on the 'theft of woods': this concerned attempts by the estates' Diets to outlaw the poor's collection and use of wood and to give exclusive ownership of these woods and forests to one group. Marx analysed this issue in terms of opposing claims over property rights (Lubasz, 1976, p. 30) whereby the traditional rights of the poor to 'certain material goods, to certain products of the earth, were being set aside in favour of the exclusive property rights of the owners of woods and forests'. Lubasz continues by noting that the poor 'appeared no longer as the poor relations of civil society to be treated, at best, with charity and benevolence, but as fellow-members of human society whose rights were being trampled on . . . The poor were not 'naturally' propertyless; they had been made propertyless through the historical process which had transformed feudal into modern property'.

New Right theorists present an ahistorical argument for the primacy of property rights: that is, they fail to recognize the historical basis of any such rights and thus seek to deny the extension and maintenance of citizenship rights crucial to contemporary industrial societies. They promote property rights as the single most valid form of citizenship rights denying, in the process, other civil, political and social citizenship rights. This text will consider the extent to which New Right ideas necessitate the abrogation of social citizenship rights and its implications. The concluding section of the book argues that the successful expansion of citizenship rights to the civil, political and, most importantly, social spheres has issued in a set of institutions and societal beliefs which New Right advocates cannot easily erode.

As noted above, New Right ideas have achieved political success in the wake of the serious economic crisis of the 1970s: the so-called crisis of Keynesianism. The failure of Keynesian economic management, in terms of employment and inflation, has been highlighted and capitalised upon by conservative politicians: Keynesian economics, New Right theorists contend, is no longer an appropriate basis for national economic policy. In its place, these theorists advocate a return to pre-Keynesian economic principles, initially emphasising monetarism and supply-side economics as viable alternative economic theories. What such theorists forget is that Keynesianism itself was a response to crisis: the unprecedented economic crisis of the 1930s, when the accepted economic orthodoxy (an orthodoxy which featured the market mechanisms New Right advocates seek to re-establish) was unable to resolve the severe economic problems of that decade. In the context of the 1930s and ensuing decades Keynesian economics was extremely successful (though some scholars locate the source of this success in other factors). Thus, simply because Keynesianism appears less successful in the 1970s does not imply that we should automatically return to pre-Keynesian economic principles. The capacity of Keynesianism to produce a successful response to the conditions of the 1930s is instructive: it suggests that economic policy need not necessarily revert to earlier principles as the basis for progressing forward and successfully addressing the current economic crisis. New Right advocates appear unwilling to recognise this implication.

The ensuing chapters address these and related themes. Chapter 2 distinguishes between the liberal and conservative strands of the New Right and examines the relationship between them. It identifies the dominant ideas within each strand, which provide the framework for the book's subsequent chapters. Chapter 3 presents an overview of the key political values and beliefs of New Right philosophy: freedom, equality and their arguments against the welfare state and its social citizenship rights. Chapter 4 sketches the historical and political background to the rise of New Right arguments: the post-war consensus in Britain and the adoption of Keynesian economic principles combined with a commitment to the welfare state. In the United States similar historical developments can be identified, including the post-1963 Keynesian policies and the gradual expansion of the state's commitment to public welfare provision.

Chapter 5 discusses the primary role of the market in New Right theories and arguments. It is the desire to reduce the role of the state in British and American society and to maximise market processes which distinguishes New Right theories, and leads to public policies such as privatisation. Chapter 6 extends this discussion to the public choice theories which have been closely associated with New Right intellectuals in Britain and in the United States. Next, the text moves to a consideration of the influence of New Right arguments upon public policy. Chapters 7 and 8 outline the policy objectives, reflecting New Right theories, of the Thatcher Government and Reagan Administration respectively and assess their success in realising them.

Chapters 9 and 10 conclude the book by taking stock of the current situation and looking to the future. Chapter 9 analyses the Keynesian welfare state institutions arguing that these have been integrated into society in a way which makes their dismantling by New Right politicians extremely difficult; and, to a considerable extent, these politicians have failed to make the inroads sought into the welfare state. However, despite the resilience of these Keynesian welfare state institutions it is unlikely that the coming years will see a reversion to pure Keynesian economic principles. New Right ideas have partly displaced these economic management principles from the political and intellectual agenda. In their place have come markets, and Chapter 10 explores how these will be incorporated in future policy. The Epilogue emphasises the importance of citizenship rights as a counter to market forces for the least advantaged members of society: this role necessitates a commitment to their maintenance and expansion.

2

Liberalism, Conservatism and the New Right

INTRODUCTION

The 1970s were years of economic difficulty in most advanced industrial societies in contrast to the prosperity of the preceding decades. The widely accepted post-war Keynesian welfare state consensus (Jessop, 1980) was criticised and challenged. Academics coined terms such as 'ungovernability' and 'political overload' to describe the political system during this period of crisis (Rose and Peters, 1978; King, 1975; Crozier *et al.*, 1975; Birch, 1984). Criticisms of the political system were joined with attacks upon conventional economic policy orthodoxy. On the one hand, Keynesian policies were rejected as ineffective under the new economic conditions: the assumption that high unemployment and high inflation would not occur simultaneously (the Phillips curve) was the principal evidence of this redundancy. On the other hand, the competitive political party system was accused of placing excessive demands upon the political system to provide goods and services it no longer had the revenues to finance. At least these were the interpretations propagated by New Right advocates.

These circumstances facilitated a revival of conservative political parties, ideas and movements. Several polities, including West Germany (1983), the Netherlands (1982), Denmark (1981), Sweden (1976), the United States (1980, 1984) and Britain (1979, 1983) swung electorally to the right. In most of these cases, the victorious parties advocated and pursued right-wing economic policies to resolve the failure of the post-war consensus. In Britain and the United States these economic policies were associated with an eclectic collection of ideas commonly termed 'New Right' which denoted a range of economic, political, moral and social beliefs and principles. 'New Right' has alternately been applied to theories, to administrations and to government policies, both in Britain and the United States. Underlying this general application are substantial differences between New Right ideas in the United States and in Britain, and between the policies pursued by Ronald Reagan and by Margaret Thatcher.

The meaning of the New Right

Given this wide usage, a definition of the term 'New Right' is necessary. In this study it refers primarily to economic and political *liberalism*. Such liberal theories either support or underlie (however loosely) the public policies pursued by the Thatcher and Reagan administrations. Both political leaders offered solutions to their respective economies' problems by reference to liberal arguments. This was the central element of their electoral platforms. Liberal economic arguments for the free market were joined with political arguments about individualism and a reduced public sector. The second element of New Right arguments is *conservatism*, which arises from the pursuit of liberal economic policy. These latter have certain political consequences which are subsequently justified in terms of social and moral conservative principles. Alone these conservative arguments would not have been the basis for electoral success; rather they constitute residual claims addressing the political consequences of liberal economic policies.

So, it is liberal arguments which are the core element. Liberalism constitutes the policy substance of New Right arguments: the promotion of limited government intervention in economic and welfare activities (and the erosion of social citizenship rights in these spheres). Monetarism, as a political and economic doctrine, derives from liberalism. Liberals do not challenge the capitalist system but want to recast it in a purer form. Conservatives, on the other hand, are pre-capitalist in orientation but have been forced to reach accommodation with capitalism. But given this accommodation, conservatives seek a minimal form of capitalism and are distressed by the gradual extension of citizenship rights and reduction of inequalities which has accompanied capitalist development. Therefore, conservatives join with liberals in attacking socialist developments in post-war capitalist countries: conservatives cannot accept welfare as a form of citizenship rights and unite with liberals in seeking a retrenchment of the welfare state. Both liberals and conservatives fear the expansion of citizenship rights: the first because it increases the role of government in society and thereby limits individual liberty, the second because it extends rights to wider groups and thereby limits traditional hierarchical and authority relationships. Accordingly, it is not entirely illogical for liberals and conservatives to coalesce to combat such developments.

One example is the shared antipathy toward feminism found in both liberal and conservative thought and public statements. There are other reasons for overlap. Liberalism does not really have a notion of the state: economic commerce, as conceptualised by Adam Smith, is a universal activity not limited by national boundaries. Conservatism, in contrast, is fundamentally a theory of statehood: it has an organic conception of the state, society and individual obligations. This gives liberalism a more coherent conception of nationhood and of the capacities of government within a given state than it would have otherwise. Although both sets of New Right ideas are important, in the main this book is concerned with the first, liberalism. It is this that has the most decisive implications for the development of the political system and the economy and which is at the core of New Right ideas. The remainder of this chapter identifies the principal core elements of New Right liberalism and conservatism, the most important of which are the subject of subsequent chapters.

LIBERALISM

Traditional liberal values

The core New Right liberal political and economic tenet is the superiority of market mechanisms as a promoter both of economic prosperity (because of the supposed greater efficiency of the market in the allocation and use of scarce resources); and of the maximisation of individual freedom through the limiting of state intervention: freedom must be market-based freedom rather than state-imposed. By implication, the range of civil, economic and social citizenship rights accumulated during the last two centuries would be better provided through the market. There is an ideological preference for increased reliance upon market forces and *laissez-faire* policies consistent with the traditional liberal beliefs: an emphasis on the individual (usually understood to be a healthy, employed, educated, white adult male), a limited role for the state and a faith in untrammelled market forces (see Ashford, 1984 and 1985; Bosanquet, 1983; Harris, 1985 and Hodgson, 1984). These principles – a belief in competitive individualism, a reduced and controlled role for the state, and a maximisation of the market – derive from the classical political and economic liberal tradition. Contemporary New Right liberalism is consequently a restatement of the ideas central to the classical liberal tradition. The key principle is to allow market forces to operate to as great an extent as possible, coupled with the assumption that the social order will be largely self-regulating: thus there is no particular need for state intervention other than to minimise market distortions or to offset market failures. In the modern period these classical values have become associated with the economic doctrine of *monetarism* which accords a limited role to the government in economic policy. According to monetarists, government intervention into the economy should be restricted to controlling the money supply. If this is done, the economy will be largely self-regulating (see discussion in Chapter 4 below).

Liberalism accords a minimum role to the state in the operation of the economy and social order. It assumes these latter will be largely self-regulating, in a way reminiscent of the classical liberalism of Adam Smith (Carnoy, 1983, ch. 1; Laski, 1936). Smith shared the rationalist and individualist beliefs of the eighteenth century and argued in *The Theory of Moral Sentiments* that each individual is capable of judging his or her own actions. In the economic sphere the individual pursuit of wealth and self-interest generates a collective prosperity which could not be as effective if planned by an external agent. The spontaneous working of nature results in wealth and social order, and government intervention must be firmly limited. For Smith, the state existed to provide public goods which would not be provided in the market place, to provide a judicial system and to engage in educational activities. By far the most important of these functions is the provision of a 'legal framework' facilitating the operation of market forces. These issues are the central concern of Chapter 5.

New Right liberals argue that post-war government intervention has failed and should be substantially reduced. Ashford (1985, p. 44) contends that 'when the reality of government failure is measured against the reality of market failure, the former is much worse'. Ashford argues that government has limited knowledge for successful intervention, that public policy can have undesired and unanticipated consequences (such as welfare policies undermining the family), and that a 'new class' grows up around governmental institutions (especially those associated with the welfare state). He concludes: 'I would now favour the market even if it was less productive and efficient, because it is the only moral system based on a voluntary choice of individuals and therefore based on the recognition of the dignity of the individual' (p. 45). Individualism and market forces underpin the ideas and policies of New Right liberalism.

Public choice school

Public choice theory refers to the application of economic assumptions and techniques to the analysis of political behaviour. Public choice theorists work in the liberal tradition discussed above, as revealed in the publications of the Institute of Economic Affairs, London. Their central contention is that the *absence* of market mechanisms (principally, the lack of profit incentives and constraints) from the arena of politics is responsible for the growth of government. Thus politicians are viewed as rational actors with the primary aim of maximising votes (in Tullock's title: *The Vote Motive*, 1976; see also Buchanan *et al.*, 1978) while the primary objective of bureaucrats is the aggrandisement of their budget, personal prestige and income/retirement benefits. Niskanen (1973) identifies the following variables as factors entering 'the bureaucrat's motives: salary, prerequisites of the office, public reputation, power, patronage, output of the bureau, ease of making changes, and ease of managing the bureau. All except the last two are a positive function of the total *budget* of the bureau during the bureaucrat's tenure'. The absence of profit criteria in the public sector encourages its reckless expansion engineered by self-interested rational bureaucrats. This tendency is exacerbated by elections where politicians promise goods and services to voters in order to get elected, ignoring their cost or how the burden of that cost is to be distributed. Public choice theorists deduce from their arguments that appropriate political institutions can be designed which enhance individual liberty and freedom. As Barry (1983) writes:

> the libertarianism of (public choice theory) consists basically in its deeply individualistic approach to social affairs. Thus private property, the market economy and the capitalist order are acceptable if they result from the necessarily subjective choices of individuals. 'Goods' and 'bads' are the subjective experiences of individuals and there is no collective organic entity called 'society' or the 'public' which is not reducible to individual experiences. In the absence of intervention people will exchange to improve their well-being so that states of affairs may be called 'better' only in so far as they represent strict agreement, and 'worse' in so far as they represent the annihilation of one person's preferences by another. (p. 102)

Public choice theorists' contention that there are no 'collective organic entities' such as societies or classes converges with the liberal value of individualism identified above (see Nisbet, 1966). Both liberals and public choice theorists consider liberty and individualism fundamental values. And public institutions should be designed, it is argued by public choice theorists, to maximise individual freedom for libertarian reasons. Most importantly, these institutions must impose constraints on the scope for spending allocation (and hence taxation needs) by politicians, and minimise the monopoly of the public sector. Public choice theorists are strong advocates of constitutional government because this provides a means of limiting government activity through precise constitutional specification (see Hayek, 1979, ch. 17). Chapter 6 below expounds the assumptions of this public choice perspective and its policy implications.

Libertarianism

A more extreme form of liberalism is represented by libertarianism. This includes the work of Robert Nozick (1974), anarcho-capitalists such as Murray Rothbard (1978) and the novelist/philosopher Ayn Rand (1957). Libertarians share the liberal commitment to individual property-based rights but lobby for a radically reduced state. They are libertarian in believing that the state should not diminish liberty in any way and that individuals should have maximum autonomy and freedom. However, there is disagreement amongst libertarians about the state's appropriate role: anarcho-capitalists reject even a minimal government for the provision of basic public goods, believing that all services should be privately financed, including streets and defence. In contrast, Nozick (1974) argues for the minarchic night-watchman state, opposing any expansion of this minimal state (see Newman, 1984 and Barry, 1983 for reviews of these different strands of libertarianism). Nozick develops his arguments on the basis of moral positions: given certain inviolable human rights originating in the state of nature, including the right to private or personal property, there will be some basis for a protection agency or state to enforce these rights. But Nozick's entitlement theory of justice (whereby the justice of a given distribution of property derives from their initial acquisition, not their distributional patterns) disallows any redistributive government policy (and thereby most welfare state policies). The state exists, by agreement, to protect individuals' private property since this is an inviolable right but must not go beyond this minimal role. In novels such as *Atlas Shrugged* (1957), Ayn Rand proselytised capitalist virtues such as selfishness, self-help and market superiority over state welfare. But for libertarians, religious or social conservatism has no appeal since this is contrary to maximising individual liberty. Freedom is more important than order to libertarians, which contrasts with New Right liberals (see Chapter 3).

Less radical forms of these arguments share some assumptions with New Right liberalism: for example, Buchanan's arguments (in *The Limits of Liberty*, 1975) about the appropriate role of the state reflect libertarian influences. And in their essential commitment to capitalism and anti-statism libertarians and New Right liberals are closely tied. However, the free living and unfettered individualism of some libertarian thought has little correspondence with the views expressed by many adherents to New Right ideologies: on these, New Right conservatism is quite distinct from liberalism (see below). More fundamentally they adopt a wholly different view on government and the state: while all libertarians want a minimum state, and some seek its complete abolition, New Right liberals reject such a view arguing the need for a state to enforce indispensable laws (and indeed this has led to the promotion of a 'strong state' as discussed below). Aspects of these libertarian arguments are considered in more detail in Chapters 3 and 5.

The work of F. A. Hayek

Reference to Hayek is appropriate here. Hayek is a writer of enormous importance and influence for the New Right: his work (see, for example, *The Road to Serfdom* (1944), *The Constitution of Liberty* (1960) and *Law, Legislation and Liberty* (1973)) represents the most complete and coherent statement of the liberal principles of individualism, a limited, constitutionally specified role for the state and faith in the market. Hayek's lifelong intellectual project has been to articulate as carefully as possible the economic and political assumptions of liberalism, to attack the post-war trend toward state intervention whether in economic or welfare activities, and to oppose the extension of citizenship rights throughout society. His positions and arguments have remained remarkably consistent from their earliest formulation in *The Road to Serfdom*: subsequent books develop more sophisticated arguments but the principles (opposition to state planning of any sort, criticisms of a large welfare state, advocacy of market relations, centrality of liberty, for example) remain unchanged. Although occasionally included amongst libertarian writers (see Newman, 1984) Hayek is differentiated from the bulk of this work by his appreciation that some state intervention to offset hardship is justified: while clearly critical of the scope of the contemporary welfare state Hayek is not averse to some state measures for the relief of suffering. Like all liberals, Hayek also recognises the need for public goods and a state-maintained legal framework. Not that such state action should be substantial (see also Friedman, 1962). Hayek's contention that a 'spontaneous order' emerges from the unplanned interaction of consumers and producers in the market-place has the corollary that government must both minimise market distortions and intervene only under specified conditions. He further argues that the concept of 'social justice' is meaningless and therefore should not be a basis for government policy (see Ashford, 1984 and Bosanquet, 1983). The thought and writings of Hayek are considered in Chapters 3 and 5.

In sum, liberalism is at the core of New Right ideas: for economic principles, a belief in the superiority of market forces as the basis for the production and allocation of goods and services in society. Relying on market forces also creates the ideal conditions for individual and political freedom. Where there is a need for some state provision of services, as in public goods, the extent of such public provision must be carefully specified and deliberately minimised. Liberalism implies a minimal state whereas the post-war Keynesian welfare consensus requires (see Chapter 4) an interventionist state: while the latter does not amount to full state control of the economy (as practised in Eastern Europe) it does imply considerably more intervention than liberal economic principles indicate. Figure 2.1 sketches these alternative levels of state

FIGURE 2.1
Levels of state intervention

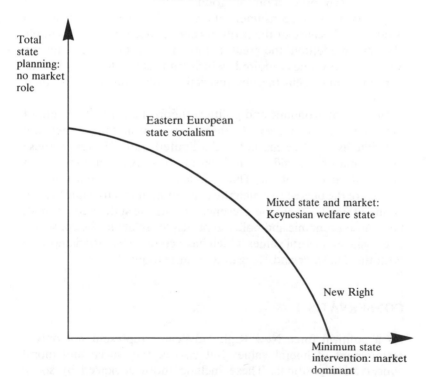

activity. This diagram presents a continuum stretching from minimal state intervention where the market is dominant to complete state planning as in Eastern Europe; the post-war Keynesian welfare state policies of the mixed economy lies in the middle of these opposites tending toward greater state activity.

The Thatcher and Reagan Governments have sought to push their respective political economies toward increased reliance upon the market sector. An obvious example of this is the Thatcher Government's vigorous pursuit of the privatisation of many areas of public ownership. It is a logical implication of New Right economic principles to reverse the post-war trend toward increased public (state-based) activity in place of private (market-based) activity. This implies also some erosion of those citizenship rights – namely social rights – associated with this post-war expansion of state activity. (However, the paradox here is that reducing the state's economic role actually requires increased action by the state.) The market-based production of goods and services ensures their responsiveness to consumer choice and greater efficiency in production because of the profit incentive, according to economic liberals. In addition, the greater state intervention the greater the amount of revenues required, which translates into a heavier tax burden upon citizens thereby restricting how individuals use their income.

New Right economic and political theories are a restatement of the values of *liberalism*. If there are central tenets they are individualism, a free market and a limited state. However, these ideas cannot be considered in isolation from two other important factors in analysis of the Thatcher and Reagan administrations. These are the degree to which the commitment to a free market can be maintained *without* the presence of a strong state; and, second, how these economic and political principles relate to the conservative social and moral values which have come to be associated with both the Thatcher and Reagan administrations.

CONSERVATISM

As a political force New Right advocates represent not only a restatement of liberal values but also certain social and moral conservative positions. These include those advanced by social authoritarians concerned to re-establish state power, moralists wishing to restore religious and pre-1960s values, and conservatives who fear the reduction of inequality and extension of citizenship rights. In this book these New Right arguments are collected under the rubric *conservatism*. Conservatism is secondary to liberalism in New Right ideology because it arises primarily in response to the consequences of liberal economic policies. Outside this context, conservative beliefs and objectives have a narrow appeal.

Social and moral conservatism: The erosion of social citizenship rights

Both the Thatcher and Reagan administrations have sought to retrench social welfare state programmes and policies: that is, they have sought to halt the post-1945 trend of increased state activity in the sphere of social citizenship rights. In pursuit of this objective, they have been guided both by economic principles (increasing the role of market forces necessitates reducing the benefits available to citizens from the state) and by social values (a fear of the effect of the welfare state upon family values and the shift in women's position in society). It is not just economic and political theories which have influenced these governments; there is an important social component reflected in these economic policies. New Right advocates' concern with the scope of the modern welfare state derives from its undesirable microeconomic consequences (for example, it weakens the incentive to participate in the market); and from the inroads it makes into traditional institutions such as the family, which is believed to be a key unit in society. The welfare state diminishes also the importance of self-help and self-reliance (which reflect individualist values). An important connection exists between the economic underpinning of the New Right, as sketched in the preceding section, and specific policy positions regarding the welfare state and a host of 'family' type issues: each reflects individualist (that is, healthy, adult male) assumptions; each seeks a reduced role for the state both in economic and welfare activities, and a restoration of the family as the main economic and social unit in society.

Both Thatcher and Reagan have sought to shift public spending away from public welfare services (though with limited success in the first case). The motivation for this objective lies in part with the social and moral conservatism with which both administrations are associated. Each has publicly stated its desire for a return to a greater reliance on private and philanthropic welfare, family support and self-reliance in a fashion reminiscent of the previous century. Such a trend would allow a reduction in the state provision of these services and is thus inextricably connected with the objectives regarding a shift in public/private activity: in accordance with liberalism, market provision of social services is the preferred option. Liberals also criticise welfare services. In particular, the welfare state is claimed to require a large tax burden with negative incentive affects. The government artificially distorts the market by providing insurance policies (in the form of social welfare policies) with harmful incentive affects. Lester Thurow (1983) summarises this argument:

> when government collectively agrees to insure its citizens against old age, illness, unemployment, poverty, and personal handicaps, government undercuts personal incentives to save and work to provide for one's own old age, illness, unemployment, poverty and personal handicaps. Individuals treat these programs as personal savings reducing their own private earnings, but because the programs are not savings in the aggregate they result in too little savings relative to what could be produced if preferences were undistorted. (p. 137)

Welfare state services are criticised further because they place unfair tax burdens on entrepreneurs and citizens (this point has obvious links with liberal economics discussed above); tax cuts also have a specific place in the supply-side economics embraced by Presidential candidate Ronald Reagan. New Right liberals consider progressive tax rates an unreasonable restriction upon entrepreneurs and risk-takers; this limits the founding of new industries and hence the level of economic activity. Progressivity in tax rates is viewed also as a disincentive upon hard work and productivity. The alleged detrimental effects of excessive taxes imply that state social benefits must be reduced; as Thurow (1983) notes, 'cuts in the social safety net are supposed to encourage individuals to work harder and save more to provide for their own old age, their own illnesses, their own unemployment, their own standard of living' (p. 129).

However, the conservatives' criticisms of the welfare state extend to a concern with its moral implications, in particular, with its impact on familial norms, traditional social values and its encouragement of feminism. New Right conservatives argue that the state provision of welfare erodes the family's traditional role as a provider of support against hardship: they believe that 'the health, welfare, and education of individuals . . . should be the purview of the family' (Eisenstein, 1981 p. 77). Equally important, conservatives fear that 'work once done in the home has been increasingly shifted to the market, and particular responsibilities of the family have been shifted to the state' (p. 89). Such arguments influence New Right policy proposals regarding welfare expenditures, though they are willing to use the state, especially in the United States, to promote pro-family legislation (see Peele, 1984 and Durham, 1985). Such arguments are taken to one extreme in the work of George Gilder (1982) (although published after Reagan's first electoral success many of the ideas in this text embody New Right beliefs and were promoted by Gilder in earlier books) where the author extends criticisms of the welfare state to include criticisms of working wives because of the affects on male authority and initiative: the father can 'no longer feel manly in his own home' (p. 114). Welfare services do not provide an escape from disadvantage: rather, Gilder contends, 'the only dependable route from poverty is always work, family, and faith' (p. 68). Such arguments are echoed in the religious movement associated with the New Right in the United States, personified by Jerry Falwell and the Moral Majority, though this is only part of a vast movement (see Peele, 1984, ch. 3). The Falwell movement emphasises the links between economic and political conservatism, patriotism and biblical teachings.

In Britain this social and moral conservatism has been less powerful. Proponents of such positions have certainly not yet influenced the political agenda of the Thatcher government as the American New Right has the Reagan agenda: there school prayers, anti-abortion, and defeat of the Equal Rights Amendment could claim support from the White House, reinforced by conservative federal judicial appointments (see Durham, 1985 and Peele, 1984). Social and moral conservatism is not irrelevant in Britain: it is plain that the frequent references to 'Victorian values' in Thatcher's rhetoric reflects in part a shared vision with the American New Right. For David Edgar (1984, 1986) the allusion to 'Victorian values' represents New Right advocates' deep antipathy to the social and sexual liberation of the 1960s. Thus Norman Tebbit, Conservative Party Chairman, attributes societal violence, not to unemployment, but to 'the era and attitudes of post-war funk which gave birth to the "Permissive Society" ' (*Guardian*, 15 November 1985). For many observers, including Edgar, the rhetoric and policy objectives of the Thatcher leadership combines these socially conservative values with the liberal economics of the New Right. Thus Stuart Hall (1983) writes:

> Thatcherite populism is a particularly rich mix. It combines the resonant themes of organic Toryism – nation, family, duty, authority, standards, traditionalism – with the aggressive themes of a revived neo-liberalism – self-interest, competitive individualism, anti-statism. Some of these elements had been secured in earlier times through the grand themes of one-Nation popular Conservatism: the means by which Toryism circumnavigated democracy, lodged itself in the hearts of the people . . . Other elements derived from the anachronistic vocabulary of political economy and possessive individualism. (p. 29)

For Hall, the New Right is synonymous with 'Thatcherism' – or, at least, it is the latter which is his primary analytical interest. Hall consequently combines several elements in his conception: Toryism, liberal political economy, traditional values upheld by the state and the family, and minimal government. Obviously these elements sit awkwardly but according to Hall this is central to 'Thatcherism'. This book divides these elements into liberal and conservative ones and argues that liberalism is at the core of the New Right: conservative arguments are developed to counter the political consequences of liberal economic policies.

The advent of the Gillick appeal (the efforts by Victoria Gillick to outlaw the provision of contraceptives to girls under 16 without parental consent) gave renewed energy to New Right moralists in Britain (see Shapiro, 1985), even though it remains a less-developed component of New Right ideology than it does in the United States. There are some organisations active in this area in Britain, such as the Society for the Protection of the Unborn Child, though they are less effective overall than in the United States. However, similarities may develop between the two countries on these issues. And indeed, David (1986) already sees many parallels between the two countries: 'the New Right in both Britain and the USA has long seen itself as developing a "new" morality through its approach to sexual and family matters. Its particular emphasis has been on redefining women's place within the family, especially as mothers' (p. 136). Attacking feminism, and reimposing traditional female roles within the family, is at the core of New Right conservatism.

This desire to restore traditional values both in the United States and in Britain is a powerful element of New Right rhetoric and relates to economic arguments about reducing the scope of the state. The two elements are connected in important ways. To date, most of the issues raised under the heading of social conservatism have shaped government rhetoric more than government policy in both countries, because economic liberals are not necessarily moral conservatives. The welfare state has not been destroyed in Britain; abortion has not been disallowed in either the United States or in Britain; the Gillick ruling was overruled by the Law Lords, and so on. Certainly, post-war welfare values have been challenged and institutions such as the trade unions have been substantially attacked (to some effect in the latter case, as will be discussed in subsequent chapters) but this is not equivalent to a complete historical break. A climate has been created whereby, for example, abortion clinics in the United States can be subjected to violent attack (which is outrageous) but as yet the state has not realised the New Right objective of outlawing abortion. What is of tangible consequence is the introduction of a programme of privatisation, efforts to curb the level of state intervention and thereby erode social citizenship rights. And it is measures like these which will have a more lasting effect than transient rhetorical promulgations. However, to pursue many of these conservative objectives an activist or strong state is necessary, thus violating the liberal desire for minimal government; this issue is treated below.

Social and populist authoritarianism

The quotation from Hall (1983) draws attention to the second issue for discussion in this section: the extent to which the political and economic arguments about a reduced state (and popular anti-statism) are contradicted in practice by the need for a strong state to maintain market forces. Linked to this is the influence of New Right conservatives who explicitly seek a strong state. Many commentators (including Gamble, 1985; Elliott and McCrone, 1985) have argued that the Thatcher Government, for example, has merely paid lip service to the notion of a free economy: in actuality, it has relied upon a strong and activist state both in the economic sphere and in non-economic areas. This derives from the conservative tradition presently associated with the Salisbury group (see essays in Cowling, 1978), with some supporters in the Conservative Party (see Chapter 7). While the Institute of Economic Affairs has been the powerhouse for the liberal economic and individualist principles of the New Right, it is the Salisbury group (and their journal *Salisbury Review*) which provides the energy behind the revival of conservatist beliefs. As represented in the essays (Cowling, 1978) these conservatives quite explicitly reject freedom as the most important value and put in its place order, authority and power.

This New Right conservative wing emphasises the importance of authority both of the state over citizens and of the father in the home. Scruton (1980) writes about the integral role of the family unit in the conservative world view:

> the family, then, is a small social unit which shares with civil society the singular quality of being non-contractual, of arising (both for the children and for the parents) not out of choice but out of natural necessity. And (to turn the analogy round) it is obvious that the bond which ties the citizen to society is likewise not a voluntary but a kind of natural bond. (p. 31)

Scruton considers the state's main role to be the maintenance of the social order: society 'exists through authority, and the recognition of this authority requires the allegiance to a bond that is not contractual but transcendent in the manner of the family tie' (1980, p. 45; see also Elliott and McCrone, 1985). The state's authority must be especially exercised to maintain property relations and the rights of property owners. Authority and discipline must also be reasserted in schools and in families. The egalitarian consequences of post-war social citizenship rights must be reversed: social hierarchy should be accorded its 'proper' role in society. Under the Thatcher Government conservative concerns with the weakness of the state have been linked with general concerns about the breakdown of authority in the home and schools and lack of discipline: 'the neo-conservative strand of the so-called New Right produced through the late '70s and early 1980s a series of critiques of the moral order in Britain. Matters of sex, race, family relations and religion were raised time and again [contributing to] the bases of populist appeals that Thatcher used in her bid for electoral support' (Elliott and McCrone 1985, p. 15).

Such concerns with the weakness of the state find no immediate parallel amongst the various elements of the American New Right, though concern about male authority and the family are important. American New Right supporters work with a stronger tradition of anti-statism and resistance to government expansion. But they do seek the restoration of familial relations and authority in a similar way to British conservatives. Also, the Reagan Presidency's set of radical policy objectives have necessitated the deployment of a strong state in direct contradiction to the avowed aim of cutting 'big government'. This and other contradictions within New Right ideology can now be addressed.

LIBERALISM AND CONSERVATISM: CONTRADICTION AND ACCOMMODATION

The contradiction between liberalism and conservatism concerning the role of the state is striking. Where liberalism implies a limited government, conservatism requires a strong state to maintain social order and authority. In his survey of the core ideas of sociology Robert Nisbet (1966) emphasises such differences between liberalism and conservatism: for the former the touchstone is 'individual freedom, not social authority' (p. 10). As outlined in the first part of this chapter, liberalism is premised upon individualism, 'acceptance of the basic structure of state and economy . . . and . . . a belief that progress [lies] in the emancipation of man's mind and spirit from the religious and traditional bonds of the social order' (1966, p. 10). Conservatism stands in contrast to this perspective:

> . . . the ethos of conservatism is tradition, essentially medieval tradition. From conservatism's defense of social tradition sprang its emphasis on the values of community, kinship, hierarchy, authority, and religion, and also its premonitions of social chaos surmounted by absolute power once individuals had become

wrenched from the contexts of these values by the forces of liberalism and radicalism . . . The conservatives began with the absolute reality of the institutional order as they found it, the order bequeathed by history. (Nisbet, 1966, pp. 11–12)

Arblaster (1984) reaches a similar conclusion: 'from Burke to W. B. Yeats and Michael Oakshott, conservatives have consistently expressed their mistrust of reason (or rationalism), and their faith in the virtues of tradition and custom. But the whole tendency of the liberal Enlightenment was in direct conflict with these celebrations of prejudice, custom and habit of thought unthinkingly inherited from the past' (p. 80).

Liberalism and conservatism thus contradict each other on a number of important issues including the role allocated to the state; the role of the individual; the nature and scope of freedom; and the importance of religious and familial values in society. On the role of the state, we find the New Right liberal Ashford (1985) attacking the New Right conservative Roger Scruton for the latter's conception of a strong state: Ashford writes that, 'it was Scruton's view that state and society have precedence over the freedom of the individual that I found so repugnant' (1985, p. 34). And liberals and conservatives differ in their perception of capitalism: the former value industrialisation as the basis of 'progress' and facilitator of increased happiness in society. Conservatives have an essentially pre-capitalist vision, as Nisbet makes clear: conservatism is 'the child of the Industrial and French revolutions: unintended, unwanted, hated by the protagonists of each, but the child nevertheless. What the two revolutions attacked, the conservatism of such men as Burke, Bonald, Haller, and Coleridge defended. And what the two revolutions engendered – in the way of popular democracy, technology, secularism, and so on – conservatism attacked' (1966, p. 11). Conservatives reject the order and prosperity produced by the Industrial Revolution preferring instead the pre-industrial social order based on strict hierarchy, inequality and authority. Where liberals emphasise the secularisation of society, conservatives desire the maintenance of the 'sacred' (Nisbet, 1966). In sum, liberalism and conservatism contradict significantly and appear mutually exclusive: liberals' concern with liberty, freedom and progress does not correspond with conservatives' emphasis upon the organic unity of society and the state, hierarchy and the negative consequences of economic activity. How, then, is their unity in political practice explained? Briefly, each strand gains something from joining with the other. Liberalism is the source of New Right economic and political theories and policy objectives; conservatism provides a set of residual claims to cover the consequences of pursuing liberal policies. For example, the liberal objective of reducing public welfare provision implies a traditional role for women and the family; conservatism provides an ideology justifying such outcomes from public policy. Conservatism provides liberals with a coherent theory of the state, absent from their own theories. Both ideologies fear the extension of social citizenship rights and therefore are united in their criticism of the welfare state.

There is also a tension between the liberal belief in a free market and limited government, and the conservative adherence to the maintenance of authority and public order through a strong state. How can liberal free-marketism be reconciled with the conservative authoritarian state? This is a contradiction which many writers have noted, particularly in relation to the Thatcher government (see Gamble, 1979, 1985; Levitas, 1985; Elliott and McCrone, 1985; Elliott, 1985 and Moore, 1985). Once in office, those administrations influenced by New Right liberal economics accept a strong state (as in their attack upon trade unions) despite the apparent contradiction. Gamble (1979, 1985) has argued that this transition reflects, to a large extent, the simple necessities of upholding the free market system (see Chapter 5 below). But there is more to it than this. First, a distinction can be drawn between a strong government and a weak state. New Right advocates seek the former: that is, the conservative desire to maintain social order and hierarchical authority, and to enforce familial values, requires strong centralised governmental authority but the liberal objective of limited government is reflected in the policy objective of a reduced state as manifested in the public sector. A strong government is sought by New Right politicians but in conjunction with a reduced state. Secondly, as noted above, liberals have a very modest conception of government: for political practice, New Right liberals need to join with the more trenchant conservative notion of government and its role as an enforcer of authority relationships. These contradictions and accommodations between liberals and conservatives will be alluded to in the ensuing chapters.

CONCLUSION

Despite the internal incoherence and inconsistencies of New Right ideas (and there are many, as later chapters will demonstrate), they have been a major intellectual and political force during the 1980s in Britain and the United States, even though many New Right policy objectives remain unrealised and many New Right supporters consequently are disillusioned. Be that as it may, the force of New Right advocates has been sufficient to displace effectively the post-war Keynesian consensus and to redefine the political agenda. The Thatcher and Reagan governments may not have destroyed the welfare state but they have succeeded in politicising a set of issues (for example, privatisation versus nationalisation, the role of markets and the inadequacy of public welfare services) long dormant in national political life. The evident failure of New Right-influenced economic policies in Britain has not resulted in a renewed statement of Keynesian principles: rather, the Labour and the Alliance of Liberal and Social Democratic parties have adopted many New Right assumptions, if only implicitly. New Right ideas will shape political debate and public policy long after the demise of the Thatcher and Reagan administrations. This makes a study of their ideas important.

The definition developed in this study is not intended to imply any exact correspondence between New Right theories and the public policy of the Thatcher and Reagan administrations. Rather, it acknowledges the existence of a set of broad ideas which has influenced these governments' policies; and it is these ideas with which this book is mainly concerned. By explicating the meaning and implications of these ideas, this study provides a basis for analysing contemporary political developments. As with any definition of a complex topic, this twofold categorisation may strike some as arbitrary; it is none the less necessary. It might be held that the exercise is not useful, that one should rather concentrate upon particular issues, policies and positions, exposing their strengths and weaknesses. However, this book's concern is with general patterns rather than with particular manifestations. The distinction drawn here between New Right liberalism and New Right conservatism serves this purpose, as others have sought to do.

For example, the contributors to Levitas (1985) generally share the assumption that the New Right refers both to a commitment to a free market and to a strong activist state in certain areas. In principle, these two elements are contradictory, as many commentators have noted, but this has caused New Right politicians little difficulty in practice. Analytically, the New Right is best considered as a coalition whose force has not been undermined by the diversity of its bases of support, intellectual and political. Further, any adequate conception of the New Right must be capable of moving between ideology and political practice since both are essential to a full understanding of its potency. New Right arguments about the superiority of market mechanisms are based on classical economics. In contrast, many New Right arguments about the detrimental economic consequences of the welfare state both for individuals and for economic activity are less grounded in theory than in rhetoric. Similarly, many of the morally conservative positions of leading New Right politicians can hardly be traced to testable hypotheses but rather derive from strongly held beliefs or prejudices. Definition and discussion of the New Right must take account of these elements and attempt to include them within a single study in a way which illustrates their connections, even if these do not cohere theoretically.

3

Politics and the New Right: the Primacy of Freedom

INTRODUCTION

New Right liberals achieved political prominence from the middle of the 1970s. They emphasised the failure of existing economic policy and the loss of individual liberty resultant from the post-war Keynesian welfare state and lobbied for a return to pre-Keynesian practices. By seeking to undermine the welfare state, New Right politicians favoured a reduction of those citizenship rights associated with post-1945 state expansion. They argued – unconvincingly – that the level of state intervention necessary for the social citizenship rights reduces individual freedom. For liberals, freedom, both political and economic, has a unique status: it is the single most important value which a social and economic order can provide and maximise. This chapter examines the liberal conception of freedom and other key political concepts of New Right liberalism. For the most part this exposition concentrates upon the writings of Hayek and Friedman, two writers at the centre of New Right liberalism, who have done much to propagate liberal arguments.

FREEDOM AND THE NEW RIGHT

The meaning of freedom

For liberals, freedom is first and foremost a political value. Economic freedom is a necessary corollary of political freedom, but liberty comes first. Hayek's conception is the most widespread amongst liberals: for him, freedom is a negative concept, defined

28

quite simply as the absence of coercion. In *The Constitution of Liberty* (1960) Hayek announces on the first page that the purpose of the book is an exploration of this condition. He writes:

> we are concerned in this book with that condition of men in which coercion of some by others is reduced as much as is possible in society. This state we shall describe throughout as a state of liberty or freedom ... The task of a policy of freedom must therefore be to minimize coercion or its harmful effects, even if it cannot eliminate it completely. (pp. 11–12)

It is important to record Hayek's full definition of coercion. It means:

> such control of the environment or circumstances of a person by another that, in order to avoid greater evil, he is forced to act not according to a coherent plan of his own but to serve the ends of another. Except in the sense of choosing the lesser evil in a situation forced on him by another, he is unable either to use his own intelligence or knowledge or to follow his own aims and beliefs. Coercion is evil precisely because it thus eliminates an individual as a thinking and valuing person and makes him a bare tool in his achievement of the ends of another. (pp. 20–1)

This last sentence is of vital significance: the individual, according to Hayek, must have as much control over her/his own behaviour and destiny as possible otherwise he/she is being coerced by another. Note that coercion is a personal attribute, manifested by other individuals, not an impersonal force such as the market. This is crucial to Hayek's arguments. The absence of coercion is narrowly conceived: Hayek's conception says nothing about the range of options available to the individual (or how real the choice is). Like other liberals, he contends that even where individuals are not controlled by others but have no real options they are still free. Hayek's own example of this instance concerns a rock-climber:

> freedom refers solely to a relation of men to other men, and the only infringement on it is coercion by men. This means, in particular, that the range of physical possibilities from which a person can choose at a given moment has no direct relevance to freedom. The rock climber on a difficult pitch who sees only one

way out to save his life is unquestionably free, though we would hardly say he has no choice. (p. 12)

How sustainable this conception of freedom is remains deeply controversial. An individual is free to starve in preference to taking a job in which he or she is obviously being exploited. Hayek maintains that such an individual is free because there is no coercion exercised by another individual and that there is a choice, however stark, between starvation or exploitation. Whether such a stark choice is the equivalent of freedom is debatable.

In the same volume Hayek rehearses alternative conceptions of freedom or liberty to explain why he thinks they are less cogent than his own. These alternatives are: political freedom; 'inner' or 'metaphysical' freedom; 'the ability to do what I want'/power; and liberty as wealth (pp. 13–18). Thus liberty or freedom for Hayek does not mean simply political rights (for example, the right to vote) or the physical or financial power to act just as one pleases. Nor does it refer to inner freedom, by which Hayek means 'the extent to which a person is guided in his actions by his own considered will, by his reason or lasting conviction, rather than by momentary impulse or circumstance' (p. 15). Of these alternative conceptions of liberty it is that which defines it as the power to do as one desires which Hayek considers most treacherous; here power is closely associated with material wealth, as Newman (1984) notes: 'Hayek seems most upset by our tendency to associate freedom with the possession of material resources. It is to this belief, which he deems erroneous, that he attributes the political demand for a redistribution of wealth' (p. 128). The concept of liberty must be returned to its classical origins, according to Hayek, and be restricted to a narrow, negative conception rather than a broad, positive one. It is negative in that it conceives freedom as the absence of constraints rather than in terms of the possibilities for positive and deliberate action. This is a distinction of major importance, and one which sets Hayek's concept of liberty (and other New Right liberals) strikingly apart from the conceptions of freedom dominant in the post-war industrial world (see Berlin (1969) for a formal statement of the distinction between negative and positive freedom). The Hayekian conception of liberty is thus a relational one, and that relationship is in terms of individuals, not impersonal forces. Newman (1984) summarises this conception:

Hayek would have us understand freedom not in terms of our capacity to act in the world but as an attribute of the relationship between mutually autonomous actors. All that this conception of freedom requires is that one be allowed to act for a purpose of one's own choosing; whether one achieves one's goal, or even has a selection of realizable goals from which to choose, is irrelevant from the standpoint of liberty. Freedom is abridged when one is forcibly coerced, deceived, or otherwise manipulated in such a way that one's conduct suits not one's own purposes but someone else's. (p. 129)

Freedom and the market

These latter inroads upon individual liberty – deception, coercion, manipulation – must be *intentional* and result from another individual's behaviour or actions. Hayek is quite candid about the negative status of his conception of liberty and equates it with concepts like peace and security: liberty 'describes the absence of a particular obstacle – coercion by other men. It becomes positive only through what we make of it. It does not assure us of any particular opportunities, but leaves it to us to decide what use we shall make of the circumstances in which we find ourselves' (1960, p. 19). Hayek believes that our liberty should be used for the generation and circulation of knowledge (see Bosanquet, 1983); and, as will be evident in Chapter 5 on the market, these latter processes are best undertaken in conjunction with a market-based economy. Liberty has the value for Hayek, accordingly, of creating and dispersing knowledge in a way which meets the needs of civilisation and progress. Liberty (of choice in the market) gives people the opportunity to pursue new ideas and methods, to respond to the unpredictable in the best way – unlike a planned command economy where unpredictability creates innate difficulties for the system. Freedom, for New Right liberals, is market-freedom: the maximisation of market processes will also maximise political and economic freedom. By inference, state activity through the provision of welfare or other types of economic security cannot provide freedom to the same extent: thus, citizenship rights are restricted to those which are compatible with the market for New Right theorists – the right to vote and *habeas corpus* rather than social and economic rights (see Chapter 9 below). But given the linking of liberalism and conservatism in New Right ideology, liberals do not shy away from using the state where necessary – for example, in strengthening the free market (through weakening trade unions) and the conditions for negative liberty to flourish.

But Hayek (1960) is adamant in his attack upon central planning:

> Freedom granted only when it is known beforehand that its effects will be beneficial is not freedom. If we knew how freedom would be used, the case for it would largely disappear... Freedom necessarily means that many things will be done which we do not like. Our faith in freedom does not rest on the forseeable results in particular circumstances but on the belief that it will, on balance, release more forces for the good than for the bad. (p. 31)

John Gray (1984) argues that part of the source of this argument lies with the work of Michael Polanyi (1951) whose observations about the inarticulate nature of knowledge (that is, that we cannot know its sources) leads to Hayek's juxtaposition of liberty and knowledge. Hayek's argument about individual liberty and freedom are thus intricately linked to his larger philosophical concerns about the nature of society, the processes of social change and 'progress'. It is important to appreciate this: Hayek is not presenting an abstract conception of liberty. Rather he consciously crafts that conception which both emerges from, and converges with, his philosophical framework.

For Hayek, the circumstances within which we receive and exercise our freedom derive not simply from the natural order but also from the economic and social order. That is, just as nature creates certain imperatives and boundaries for us, so does the social and economic order. Both reflect the outcome of 'circumstances no one intended to create. Even though these circumstances may drastically affect our lives, they do not affect our freedom' (Newman, 1984, p. 129). Thus, the market order may seem to repress some members of society and to reduce their liberty. But Hayek counters this claim by his definitional requirement that such coercion must demonstrably be the intended outcome of individual action which, in the case of the market, he argues, it is generally not. This is a controversial aspect of Hayek's arguments and is regularly questioned. To Hayek, the choice between starvation and exploitation is a real one; for many of his critics this is palpably not the case. Newman (1984), for example, argues that assuming our position in the social and economic order is a natural result of the market and therefore acceptable, this has dire consequences for a whole class. He writes: 'Hayek has not met the charge that the normal operation of the market systematically places an entire class of persons (wage earners) in circumstances that compel them to accept the terms and conditions of labor dictated by those who offer work. While it is true that individuals are formally free to seek better jobs or to withhold their labor in the hope of receiving higher wages, in the long run their position in the market works against them; they cannot live if they do not find employment' (p. 130).

There are systematic and consistent disadvantages and inequalities built into the market order. For Hayek these are both inevitable and acceptable outcomes; in particular, inequality is a necessary part of the process of achieving civilisation. As Hayek writes 'the case for individual freedom rests chiefly on the recognition of the inevitable ignorance of all of us concerning a great many of the factors on which the achievement of our ends and welfare depends... Liberty is essential in order to leave room for the unforseeable and unpredictable; we want it because we have learned to expect from it the opportunity of realizing many of our aims' (1960, p. 29). By implication, actions by the state to alter the bases of individual liberty and/or to alter the distribution of wealth, property, advantages and opportunities deriving from the market order are necessarily coercive and to be avoided according to this Hayekian conception of freedom and its understanding of progress and civilisation. The state does have some responsibilities, most notably the protection of property rights and the upholding of the legal system necessary for the market system to operate, but little beyond these; meeting these responsibilities may entail strong state action, however. And, in terms of the three types of citizenship rights identified in Chapter 1 – civil, political and social – New Right liberals question the need for state activity to provide the last. New Right advocates place certain citizenship rights over and above others as a consequence of the centrality of the market to their ideological principles. It is necessary for the state to guarantee the right of property ownership but not of a guaranteed job or health care. The former is a necessary element for the market to operate; the latter can be obtained through the market according to New Right critics.

Market outcomes

For Hayek's critics (and critics of liberalism generally), this acceptance of the naturally unequal distribution of wealth and advantages is largely indefensible. We have already noted Newman's criticisms and he has other cogent points (see 1984, pp. 130–1), concluding that ultimately 'Hayek's concept of negative freedom ("freedom from") legitimates degrees of positive freedom ("freedom to") that vary according to the wealth and resources at the disposal of the actors' (p. 137). Hodgson (1984), for example, highlights the consequences of inherited wealth for the notion that Hayekian liberty endows all with similar possibilities:

> Classic liberals and New Right ideologists are blind to the inherited or other inequalities present in the most 'voluntary' contracts. They stress only 'freedom of choice', in a current and limited sense, and the absence of more blatant forms of coercion in a 'free' market system. They rush headlong to the conclusion that it is within capitalism that freedom and liberty are maximized, ignoring the fact that in capitalist countries there is a very unequal distribution of wealth, even when house ownership and pension funds are taken into account. (p. 25)

Inherited patterns of wealth systematically distort people's liberty or freedom in market societies; they may conform to the terms of Hayek's negative conception of freedom but they impose limitations upon the capacity of individuals to exercise their liberty. Hayek and other New Right liberals argue that this distribution of wealth and income (either inherited or earned) is fair because the nature of the market system is one which intrinsically renders no moral priorities or claims of justice in its distributional patterns: 'the outcomes of free markets are *in principle* unprincipled' (Plant, 1984, p. 4).

Plant takes issue with these claims. He contends first that it is possible to make judgements about the unequal outcomes of the market system regardless of whether the Hayekian characterisation of it is accurate. As he notes, even if the causes of the naturalistic process are beyond our control this does not mean we should fail to respond to them. Where the natural order produces consistent inequalities we should act to offset them: 'while the market transactions are unintentional they may, like the weather, be predictable in that misfortunes are likely to fall heaviest on those least able to bear such burdens . . . The impersonal market does not distribute its benefits and burdens in a wholly random way' (p. 4). Plant thus challenges the moral acceptability of the natural order resulting from the market system: there are consistent patterns of disadvantage and bias built into that system which repeat themselves in such a way generationally that it is unjust to accept such a natural order.

There is a close connection between liberty and capitalism, the closest modern form of the market system, for New Right liberals like Hayek. Milton Friedman (1962) advances this close connection: capitalism maximises economic freedom which promotes political freedom, that is, the freedom to choose and make decisions about one's own life. He writes that:

> so long as effective freedom of exchange in maintained, the central feature of the market organization of economic activity is that it prevents one person from interfering with another in respect of most of his activities. The consumer is protected from coercion by the seller because of the presence of other sellers with whom he can deal. The seller is protected from coercion by the consumer because of other consumers to whom he can sell. The employee is protected from coercion by the employer because of other employers for whom he can work, and so on. And the market does this impersonally and without centralized authority. (pp. 14–15)

The language deployed here by Friedman is remarkably similar to Hayek's: a worry about coercion and an assumption that market transactions provide the means of maximising liberty through economic freedom. And there are clear parallels with Hayek's argument that the free market generates and circulates knowledge, the basis for economic wealth. Likewise, both Hayek and Friedman present the market as the key source of freedom and the state as the key force for coercion, tending to disregard the 'unfreedoms' generated by the market itself, noted above. Freedom in the market place (to sell, to buy, to own, and so on) has a critical relationship to private property and the ability to 'own' property, as Heald (1983) observes: 'these freedoms to use or dispose, which are extensive and very real under capitalism, generate a matching set of unfreedoms, whereby non-owners are precluded from either using or disposing. All property rules necessarily extend both freedoms and unfreedoms' (p. 60). New Right liberals value property rights more than other types of citizenship rights.

Freedom and the state

The contention that the state is the primary force of coercion threatening individual liberty has been powerfully taken up by those politicians influenced by, and eager to promote, New Right ideas. It is argued that the degree of liberty available in a society is a function of increased market relations and capitalism. The more activities and service provisions subsumed to the state, goes the argument, the greater the level of state coercion and diminution of individual liberty. This, of course, provides grounds for attacking the level of public spending and range of state activities. Hodgson (1984) argues that recourse to such arguments enables liberals to marshal support for its position which does not simply rely upon appeals to economic growth and the economy; rather they draw upon conservative arguments:

> attacks on trade union rights and the welfare state are part of a moral crusade. If there is massive unemployment and sustained economic recession 'Thatcherism' and 'Reagonomics' have not necessarily failed in their own terms. One of their central objectives is to maximize 'freedom', according to the New Right definition. Thus if market relations have been extended, and public enterprise privatized, then success is claimed whatever the economic repercussions. (p. 20)

As Heald (1983) notes, New Right politicians seek to 'change the relationship between the state, the market and the polity' (p. 68) in the interests of increasing liberty; however, in pursuing this objective they have had to utilise the full range of state activities available to it. Re-establishing the market has required the strengthening of the police force, curbing the trade unions and reducing welfare services: the achievement of liberty has required a strong state and a willingness to create unfreedoms. Liberals require conservatives, faith in a strong government to enlarge market activities. The ideal for New Right advocates, Heald suggests, is a free economy and strong state though this latter does not necessarily extend to the provision of welfare services (see Chapter 2 of this volume): 'public expenditure ... diminishes freedom because it substitutes judgements emanating from the state about the composition of output for unconstrained market outcomes and is a mechanism for coerced transfers of income between individuals' (Heald, 1983, p. 73). The state, therefore, runs directly counter to the interests of liberty and freedom (which are maximised in the market) by limiting the range of individual choice through the imposition of external preferences and decisions but is necessary for the achievement of some objectives.

New Right advocates continue to project their concept of freedom or liberty as the primary political value, more important than simple economic well-being (though this is believed to follow from liberty), and one which consequently justifies their political programme. It is a narrow conception of freedom which, like much New Right thought, begins with the individual as the crucial component both of social analysis and of prescriptive claims. Individualism is allied with market relations because these maximise liberty as voluntary choice and reduce coercion to a minimum, especially state-based coercion. There are additional problems with this argument to those raised above (coercion arises from impersonal as well as personal forces, individuals do not begin with meaningfully comparable positions in the market-place, and so on). First, the objectives we pursue and choices we make are socially determined, or at least reflect in part the social environment of which we are a part. The knowledge upon which people act is acquired through a social process which is not neutral, as Hayek's arguments would imply (see Hodgson, 1984, p. 30). To simply speak of the individual and individual choice without reference to this key social context is accordingly deeply problematic. Levine (1981), in his recent reformulation of economic theory, highlights the neglect of the social determinants of consumption and need as a serious weakness of most economic theory, including liberal theory:

A set of particular needs makes up an integrated pattern of need which establishes a person's pattern of consumption. This pattern expresses the uniqueness of the individual's personality. In this sense, needs are individual. At the same time, the individual discovers his personal consumption pattern in his relations with others. The necessity that other individuals recognize the pattern establishes its social determination. Furthermore, the means of consumption which satisfy uniquely individual needs, are provided by other individuals and by society. Individual determination of need which conforms to the requirements of recognition by others and provision by society is itself a social determination of need. (pp. 276–7)

Individualism cannot be abstracted from its social context (Hodgson, 1984). This social environment not only influences the development of individual purposes and ideas but fundamentally informs choices. Galbraith (1973) was one of the first to point to the key role of advertising in influencing our social and economic choices; this, of course, reflects the important role of large corporations in structuring our environment and our range of choices and desires. It is unreasonable to simply ignore the impact of these sorts of factors in shaping our perceptions and choices.

It is worth reiterating the problem of limiting coercion only to the intentional behavioural acts of other individuals. The market system deprives many individuals of real control over their lives and reduces their choices to a rather stark one between starvation and a possibly exploitative job. If freedom is a market-based and defined concept, however, such a conclusion follows. To what extent does a market system, despite its alleged neutrality and impartiality, generate an acceptable distribution of wealth and opportunity?

The necessity of inequality for market processes

Chapter 2 noted that inequality is viewed as a necessary element of market relations by liberal writers. The essential New Right position, including Hayek and Friedman, is that equality – whether defined in terms of material wealth or innate abilities – is not compatible with their notion of the free market and its operation. Liberals believe that the free market system of social organisation generates innovation and wealth in the most desirable fashion by maximising individual choice and liberty; a necessary element of this process is inequality. Hayek argues that inequality in remuneration is a necessary condition for some members of society to invest and innovate with new products, the ultimate basis of wealth accumulation; and, he contends, that those goods now only available to a rich minority will soon be available to all social groups. It is an argument developed in terms of a consumer goods-orientated society. As Newman (1984) observes, 'the gap between rich and poor is justified by the fact that even the poorest wretches are better off in a free-market system, where they benefit from all the improvements in the quality of life it makes possible, than they would be any place else. That the rich and the poor do not share equally in the enjoyment of these improvements is of no consequence' (p. 136). Thus inequality in the market system is a positive contribution to that system's long-term operation; also, the concentration of power in the state to reduce inequality is unacceptable to New Right liberals since this reduces individual liberty.

This is the essential New Right position on inequality: rewards in the market system cannot be equal across all individuals if that society is to prosper; and in the long run, all will eventually benefit in some way from the prosperity and progress initiated by the market system. Plant (1984) disputes the validity of these claims. He argues that the liberty available to all in the market system is seriously limited by the considerable disparities in material wealth and abilities of market participants. He writes that:

> while it may be that a structure of negative rights does secure equal liberty in that it defines the same limits of noncoercion in the same way for all, it does not secure an equal or even fair *value* of liberty. In order to live a purposive life shaped by my own values and not those of others I need opportunities and resources to choose my own way of life and values... The positive resources which individuals need to be able to live their own lives in their own way cannot be secured by a set of negative or procedural rights, important though these are. They require rather the marshalling of economic and social resources to enable individuals to live the kinds of lives which they want to live. (Plant, 1984, p. 6)

The objective of individual liberty is meaningful only as a means to achieving other desired ends. But to achieve these latter, individual freedoms within a grossly inegalitarian context is insufficient. Rather it needs to be accompanied by some conscious efforts at reducing stark inequalities, thereby increasing people's realistic opportunities to participate within the market system. As Plant concludes, 'the libertarian's defence of liberty is disingenuous because it neglects the resources and opportunities which make this defence of equal liberty of equal value for all citizens' (1984, p. 8).

Equality and state policy

New Right liberals and libertarians dispute the validity of equality as a rationale for public policy for a number of reasons other than that inequality contributes positively to market activity. The libertarian Robert Nozick (1974) opposes such policies because they violate individual property rights. To pursue egalitarian strategies entails government expenditure which must be based on taxes levied from citizens. Nozick considers taxes collected for redistributive policies to be illegitimate: for him justice can only exist in the acquisition of property not in distribution. Taxation for such policies, therefore, is illegitimate. This is an extreme position. New Right liberals concede the need for some taxation and government expenditure. But they do oppose elaborate public policy measures underpinned by egalitarian objectives. Liberals do not consider people to be equal, or that public policy should pursue such an end. Such a position informs Hayek's attack on the notion of social justice.

THE HAYEKIAN CRITIQUE OF SOCIAL JUSTICE

For Hayek, the concept of 'social justice' is devoid of meaning and an inappropriate basis for public policy. It is necessary to explain his views on this issue in some detail and evaluate their plausibility. Hayek's critique derives to a considerable extent from methodological individualism; that is, the belief that all social and political analysis must work from the behaviour of individuals and not 'abstract' collectivities such as 'society' or the 'state'. In addition, the close association between social justice and distributive justice (that is, some redistribution of wealth and property in a society through state-directed policies) concerns Hayek, since he opposes such measures.

By 'social justice' Hayek means the joint actions of members of society, or those actions taken on their behalf, which purport to create or extend justice to members of society. He notes that 'the appeal to "social justice" has by now become the most widely used and most effective argument in political discussion. Almost every claim for government action on behalf of particular groups is advanced in its name, and if it can be made to appear that a certain measure is demanded by "social justice", opposition to it will rapidly weaken' (1976, p. 65). The difficulty for Hayek with this type of claim is that the concept of 'social justice' implies an agreed standard of need or worth upon which to base policy. Hayek disputes this claim. There is no agreed merit which can underlie such policy since each member of society will have a different opinion as to whom deserves what and on what basis. A free society (that is, one based on individual liberty and a market system) does not generate a consensus about what is a fair distribution of wealth and property (except for that distribution which results from the market system since this is deemed impartial in its nature and results). Hayek acknowledges:

> ... the general feeling of injustice about the distribution of material goods in a society of free men. Though we are in this case less ready to admit it, our complaints about the outcome of the market as unjust do not really assert that somebody has been unjust; and there is no answer to the question of *who* has been unjust. Society has simply become the new deity to which we complain and clamour for redress if it does not fulfil the expectations it has created. (1976, p. 69)

Given that liberals such as Hayek reject organic entities such as 'society' as meaningless, it is curious that such a meaningless entity is deemed capable of generating expectations. Hayek does accept that if the inequality and disadvantage resulting from the market processes were the consequence of intentional and deliberate individual behaviour then some recourse to state policy would be justifiable. But he denies that is so: rather, the benefits and burdens of the market system are:

> [the] outcome of a process the effect of which on particular people was neither intended nor foreseen by anyone when the institutions first appeared – institutions which were then

permitted to continue because it was found that they improve for all or most the prospects of having their needs satisfied. To demand justice from such a process is clearly absurd, and to single out some people in such a society as entitled to a particular share evidently unjust. (1976, pp. 64–5)

For Hayek, the market process of allocating wealth and property 'can be neither just nor unjust, because the results are not intended or foreseen, and depend on a multitude of circumstances not known in their totality to anybody' (1976. p. 70). An equally important part of his objection to public policy based on 'social justice' claims is its harm to the market process which is, he claims, at the core of civilisation and progress. Further, an impersonal process such as the market cannot be redressed by state policy because market outcomes do not derive from intentional behaviour. This is central to Hayek's whole philosophical schema.

However, this line of reasoning has difficulties. In the quotation above, Hayek writes that market institutions were 'permitted to continue' because of their capacity to generate wealth. But this admission abrogates the earlier argument that the outcomes of markets are unintentional and unknown: the outcomes were known and this is why the market was 'permitted to continue'. In the context of a reproducing system once it is known that actions have certain consequences, the formation of intentions must include knowledge of these consequences which cannot therefore be said to be unknown. Hayek, at a minimum, knows the consequences and identifies the mechanisms whereby the reproduction is the consequence of the intentional theory.

A second problem for Hayek with the concept of social justice concerns the concentration of power in the state necessary for policies based upon it to be realised. To the question 'is it possible to preserve a market order while imposing upon it (in the name of "social justice" or any other pretext) some pattern of remuneration based on the assessment of the performance or the needs of different individuals or groups by an authority possessing the power to enforce it' (Hayek, 1976, p. 68) he answers with a resounding 'no'. It can be noted in passing that Hayek suffers here from a similar problem to that discussed above concerning his knowledge of the consequences of the operation of the market system. He acknowledges that it is necessary to 'preserve a market', which makes the market system an object of choice; thus its consequences have been chosen and therefore are intentional. For example, allowing the market to operate freely is likely to result in high unemployment; Hayek and New Right advocates are aware of this likely outcome which negates the 'unknown' dimension of the market system so central to Hayek's contentions and his defence of the market order.

More generally, Hayek's second problem with social justice relates to the scope of the state and, he believes, the necessary diminution of freedom that accompanies state expansion. To implement effectively the principles of social or distributive justice would require enormous concentration of power in the state, a point Friedman also makes in *Capitalism and Freedom* (1962). Hayek claims that pursuing the imperatives of social justice requires standardisation, universalisation and central government determination of people's wants (rather than individually). Thus the state would be required to decide upon a satisfactory level of income distribution and this would weaken the role of the market, Hayek maintains. Remuneration and reward in society must reflect what others in the market consider the value of labour or goods, not politically-determined standards; if the latter, the market system declines in its capacity to achieve general property. Imposing state-determined income levels will distort prices, and hence undermine their function in the market process. Further, the nature of the spontaneous order and constant change and uncertainty makes the establishment of a set income level undesirable for its continuance:

> men can be allowed to decide what work to do only if the remuneration they can expect to get for it corresponds to the value their services have to those of their fellows who receive them; and that *these values which their services will have to their fellows will often have no relations to their individual merits or needs*. Reward for merit earned and indication of what a person should do, both in his own and in his fellows' interest, are different things. It is not good intentions or needs but doing what in fact most benefits others, irrespective of motive, which will secure the best reward. (1976, p. 72)

To attempt to reward people other than in terms of market value assumes that some authority can distinguish meaningfully between the worth of different occupations; this is impossible without resorting to different values, argues Hayek. Gray (1984) summarises this issue: 'the only principle of justice application to distribution in a free society is that of commutative justice. Attempts to impose any other principle on the free exchanges of free men involve imposing upon them a hierarchy of ends and goals, a ranking of values and a code of judgements regarding the weightiness of competing needs and merits, about which no consensus exists in our society and which there is no reason to assume can be achieved' (p. 74). Any such attempt at distributive justice necessarily places considerable power in the state, which, according to Hayek, leads to totalitarianism. One might object to the scope of the lack of consensus Hayek observes – that is, a society may be able to agree on certain broad parameters of need and income distribution which it considers desirable. Likewise, that totalitarianism is the ineluctable outcome of entrusting distributive policies to the state is contentious. In fact, the post-war experience of most Western industrialised countries stands in opposition to this argument: the extension of welfare rights to significant segments of the population has neither resulted in totalitarian states nor eroded individual liberty in favour of the state, but has increased considerably their economic and social rights. Also absent from Hayek's account of income distribution is the key issue of inherited wealth and its profound impact upon people's capacity to participate in the market on an equal basis.

For Hayek and other New Right advocates, the best we can hope to provide is just or fair rules established by the state which do not promote specific ends but offer procedural fairness concerning income. This would include property rights, conditions for transfer of property, and contractual security. Justice must be sought in the rule of law, which must treat individuals equally disregarding their material wealth or lack of it. Justice cannot be concerned with individuals' differing wealth and abilities since this itself would necessitate treating individuals differently.

Thus for Hayek the concept of 'social justice' is illusory and intellectualy dangerous, and it has been uncritically adopted as the rationale for state public policy. It misunderstands the nature of the market economy and the extent to which the outcomes of that market system cannot be the object of policy; the market system is a spontaneous and poorly understood process but is the primary basis of wealth generation and of progress. And, once again, he argues that the complexity and success of this process is such that we cannot have sufficient knowledge to implement policy which is not harmful to it.

DOES THE WELFARE STATE REDUCE FREEDOM?

New Right theorists criticise state intervention on the grounds that it is coercive and therefore diminishes individual liberty. Hayek, as early as 1944 in *The Road to Serfdom*, argued that state planning unavoidably leads to totalitarianism. More recently, politicians influenced by these ideas have alleged that the welfare state and public expenditure diminish individual liberty. The Conservative Party's 1979 electoral manifesto spoke of the shift from private to public and promised to reverse this development. Can these claims be sustained?

Robert Goodin (1982; see also Heald (1983, pp. 77ff)) identifies six main ways in which the welfare state is alleged to reduce liberty. The six claims are:

(i)   that the welfare state through imposing an increased burden on taxpayers encroaches upon property rights;

(ii) that the welfare state unavoidably tends toward uniformity and standardisation by limiting the range of services available;

(iii) that the welfare state is intrinsically paternalistic through its deliberate directing of citizens toward defined choices;

(iv) that the welfare state imposes bureaucratic and/or legal restrictions upon individuals;

(v)   that the welfare state results in dependency amongst many of its recipients, and militates against their pursuit of alternative options;

(vi) that the welfare state creates its own supporting interest groups amongst bureaucrats and beneficiaries who undermine any efforts to reduce the public welfare sector.

These claims are of varying cogency and validity. Few would now disagree that the bureaucratic mechanisms necessary for the operation of the welfare state are substantial and at times paternalistic. Indeed, New Right criticisms of this aspect of the welfare state, certainly in Britain, have many similarities with left wing analyses. But discovering bureaucratic elements in welfare state administration need not imply a public dissatisfaction with the welfare state *per se*; rather it can mean that there is dissatisfaction with aspects of the welfare state's current form and administration (see Taylor-Gooby, 1985). The alleged paternalism of the welfare state concerns how welfare services are provided by the state: are they universal benefits or selective/means-tested benefits? The former involves a significantly different type of paternalism (if any), whereas the latter generates hostility since it implies a lack of competence on the part of recipients compared to others (see Korpi, 1983 and Goodin, 1986). Thus the welfare state need not necessarily be paternalistic. It is not clear that welfare state policies unavoidably result in standardisation, as New Right critics suggest. Nor is it clear to what extent the tax revenues required for its support have constituted a real threat to individual liberty. On this and the related issue of property rights, Heald (1983) notes that 'the state and the market constitute different barriers to freedom, impinging upon different but overlapping groups of individuals. For example, the free rider problem means that the state must coerce individuals if there is to be an efficient level of supply of public goods or an optimal (however determined) scale of redistribution' (p. 77).

Heald does concede, however, that a complete redistribution of property rights might well encroach upon individual liberty. The other two alleged threats to freedom – by creating dependence and by spawning special-interest groups centred on the welfare state – are less clearcut. It is certainly true that for some individuals and families, both in the United States and in Britain, dependence upon the welfare state is considerable. But since many of these would not survive in the market-place without some sort of public provision this is a weak argument. Is dependence upon public assistance somehow less valid than dependence upon the arbitrariness of market processes, especially in a period of mass unemployment? Dependency, both economic and psychological, is evident amongst certain segments of welfare state recipients, but whether these same groups would realistically be able to exploit their liberty without state assistance remains doubtful. Finally, it does seem correct to maintain that the welfare state has generated special-interest groups within the bureaucracy responsible for its administration, who then constitute support groups for its persistence. But this is no less true of other areas of public policy, for example regulatory agencies in the United States. And the arguments about such groups forcing bureaucratic expansion (and hence increased public expenditure) are similar to public choice analyses of bureaucratic behaviour (see Chapter 6). Whether their diminution of liberty is greater in the welfare component of the public sector than elsewhere is not clear. These issues are considered further in Chapter 9.

The welfare state has enlarged individual liberty in important ways (see Heald, 1983, pp. 81ff). It reduces poverty, which increases an individual's capacity to pursue his or her own objectives in life. It also reduces the necessity to rely upon self-interest in the pursuit of those objectives; and it opens up the possibility of action being guided in certain areas by moral principles since they are removed from the market. Goodin (1985a) has considered further the inherent limitations of forcing people back upon 'self-reliance' as an alternative to public welfare provision. Reliance, Goodin argues, entails planning, a facility frequently absent in those doing least well out of the market economy: 'if the poor are not planners, then reliance (being quintessentially a planning notion) would be inappropriate as applied to them. People with no plans one way or the other can hardly be said to be "relying" on state aid' (p. 30). Goodin further contends that advocates of increased 'self-reliance' are confused about the notion of 'the self': self-reliance for the needy clearly implies greater reliance, indeed dependence, upon families, but this is problematic:

> it is morally undesirable to insist upon 'self-reliance', if the boundaries of the 'self' for these purposes include the family but exclude the state. The sorts of dependencies that occur within the family are morally more objectionable than the dependencies that occur between citizen and state, at least in so far as the citizen's entitlements come in the form of rights which state officials have no choice but to honour. (p. 39)

The promotion of self-reliance in the place of welfare is a confused and unappealing notion: it emphasises dependencies within family structures (ignoring other types of dependency) and draws more upon conventional beliefs about character-formation and family life than upon empirical evidence about the harmful effects of the welfare state.

CONCLUSION

This chapter has explicated the liberal conception of freedom. Liberals conceive freedom negatively, impinged upon only by the intentionally coercive activities of other individuals. Such a definition precludes any consideration of impersonal market forces as sources of coercion. For New Right theorists, inequality contributes to the progressive development of civilisation. Lastly, the claim that the welfare state constitutes an attack upon individual liberty has been addressed.

The welfare state has had profound implications for the division between public and private in advanced industrialised countries. It has created a set of institutions and practices which have extended the role of the state in society in important and novel ways. By the same token, the social citizenship rights which it embodies have been of significant benefit to many citizens poorly placed in the market system. New Right liberals want to change this, given their political arguments about liberty and economic arguments about market mechanisms. The extent to which they can succeed in this aim is considered in subsequent chapters.

4

The Decline of the Keynesian Welfare State Consensus

INTRODUCTION

This chapter sketches the historical and political background to New Right theories. This means examining the 'post-war consensus' or settlement in Britain, manifested in the adoption of Keynesian economic principles combined with a commitment to the welfare state. In the United States similar policies can be observed also (notably the post-1963 Keynesian policies and the expansion of the state's commitment to welfare services), though in a less developed form. This chapter also highlights some of the political differences between the United States and Britain.

The chapter begins with the nature of the post-war consensus in Britain: Keynesian economics and the welfare state; and comparable features of the post-war American polity. The importance of economic growth to the support and maintenance of this consensus is emphasised. This is followed by an account of the economic problems of the 1970s, the detrimental impact of these on the dominant economic orthodoxy and how their discrediting facilitated the rise of alternative liberal economic policies, specifically monetarism and supply-side economics. Finally, it is pointed out that by the mid-1970s in the US and Britain (that is, prior to the Thatcher and Reagan administrations) economic policies had changed in both countries in a way compatible with New Right principles. There is some policy continuity between the Thatcher and Reagan Governments and their immediate predecessors.

It is essential to discuss the Keynesian welfare state consensus both as the background to the emergence of New Right ideas and as a set of institutions and policies sharply criticised as a viable policy in the political arena. What is likely to emerge in the coming years will combine elements of the Keynesian orthodoxy and of the New Right challenge, an option discussed in Chapter 10.

THE KEYNESIAN WELFARE STATE: BRITAIN

The origins of the British post-war consensus lie with the Labour Government of 1945–51 which initiated the 'social democratisation of the political system' (Jessop, 1980, p. 28) by promoting a mixed economy, by adopting demand-level economic management techniques and by vastly expanding the scope of the state's public welfare provision. The most authoritative study of this period is Morgan (1984) which provides a detailed account of the policies and politics of the 1945–51 Administration (see Addison (1975) for the importance of the wartime coalition and the two Beveridge reports in the development of the welfare state).

The welfare state

In Britain there is an historical tradition of state intervention in the field of welfare provision dating back to the Elizabethan Poor Law, initiated in the 1601 Act. This was replaced by the New Poor Law in the Poor Law Amendment Act of 1832. Both pieces of legislation attributed penury to personal fecklessness, and state relief assumed charitable status. Welfare policies, as we now think of them, originated in Britain in the series of reforms enacted between 1906–11 by a Liberal Administration under Herbert Asquith. Major legislation of this period includes the Labour Exchange Act 1908 and the National Insurance Act 1911, which provided health and unemployment insurance to designated categories of workers, some of whom were victims of cyclical unemployment (Furniss and Tilton, 1977). The 1908 pension bill provided five shillings per week to those over seventy with an income below a certain threshold; this was extended by the 1925 Contributory Pensions Act which 'lowered the benefit age to sixty-five and placed funding in the familiar employer-employee-state pattern. Thus, by the mid-1920s Britain had a social insurance system covering health, old age and unemployment, based broadly on the prescriptions of social reformers' (Furniss and Tilton, 1977, p. 102). However, these social security measures were judged too narrow, particularly by the new Labour Party: eligibility was restricted and, because based on wants, excluded many people. There were other flaws: notably, the benefit levels were judged incoherent reflecting neither a specified level of minimum need nor based on past earnings. And a fundamental flaw was the failure to relate social welfare provisions to macroeconomic policy. This set the stage for the post-war reforms.

Having secured a loan from the United States, the 1945 Clement Attlee-led Labour Government believed it had the financial base from which to extend the scope of welfare provisions in Britain. That it had the political commitment and mandate to do so was undisputed (Morgan, 1984), although the state of the economy remained uppermost in this Government's mind. The experience of wartime planning had increased the legitimacy of state activity. The key planning document for its reform of the social services was the 1942 Beveridge Plan, contained in *Social Insurance and Allied Services* (Beveridge 1942), which advocated a comprehensive and mandatory system of social security for all from 'the cradle to the grave'. The report identified three main assumptions as necessary to a 'satisfactory scheme of social security' (p. 120). these were: '(A) children's allowances for children up to the age of 15 or if in full-time education up to the age of 16; (B) comprehensive health and rehabilitation services for prevention and cure of disease and restoration of capacity for work, available to all members of the community; and (C) maintenance of employment, that is to say avoidance of mass unemployment' (p. 120). The last of these is particularly striking: it reflects the widespread determination to avoid a return in the post-war period to the massive unemployment of the 1930s. This was integral to the Keynesian post-war consensus. As Morgan (1984) observes, 'henceforth, the main framework of the Beveridge proposals, including such novelties as family allowances, along with its ancillary assumptions of the need for full employment and a national health service, became the foundation of all detailed social planning and policy-making for the post-war world' (p. 21).

The Beveridge Report specified the following six principles of social insurance. First, *Flat Rate of Subsistence Benefit*: 'the first fundamental principle of the social insurance scheme is provision of a flat rate of insurance benefit, irrespective of the amount of earnings which have been interrupted by unemployment or disability or ended by retirement' (p. 121). Second, *Flat Rate of Contribution*, whereby the 'compulsory contribution required of each insured person or his employer is at a flat rate, irrespective of his means' (p. 121). Third, *Unification of Administrative Responsibility*. Fourth, *Adequacy of Benefit*. Fifth, *Comprehensiveness*, whereby 'social insurance should be comprehensive, in respect both of the persons covered and of their needs' (p. 122). And, sixth, *Classification*, meaning that social insurance 'must take into account the different ways of life of different sections of the community; of those dependent on earnings by employment under contract of service; of those earning in other ways, of those rendering vital unpaid service as housewives, of those not yet of age to earn and of those past earning' (p. 122). In sum, the Beveridge Report sought social insurance for the whole population and not selective benefits. These benefits were to be distributed, and contributed to, on a flat-rate basis, determined by the central government from estimations of subsistence and need standards. This element represented the creation of a minimum standard of need to be assured by the state. The Plan also required the provision of children's allowances regardless of parental income and ascribed responsibility to the state for the provision of certain basic welfare services, specifically a free and comprehensive health service and free education. Finally, the Beveridge Report concluded that these welfare measures should be linked with a macroeconomic policy commitment to the pursuit of full employment. This last element leads to Keynesian economic policies, of which more below.

The first four elements of the Beveridge Plan (those focused on the provision of welfare services by the state) were largely enacted in the course of the first Attlee Government. The 1946 National Insurance Act created a unified and universal insurance scheme to guarantee against ill-health, unemployment and old age. The 1946 National Health Service Act created the comprehensive health system. In 1948 Parliament passed the Industrial Injuries and the National Assistance Acts: the latter provided assistance to the very destitute with no personal income other than that provided by the state, while the former Act extended benefits to victims of industrial accidents. Likewise the Attlee Government extended the principles embodied in Butler's 1944 Education Act by raising the school-leaving age to fifteen and eventually pursuing free comprehensive secondary education, though the public schools remained intact. The resultant welfare state combined innovatory change in social insurance and comprehensive care in health with smaller changes in housing, education and other areas.

The fifth element of the Beveridge Plan – that there should be a policy commitment to full employment by the national administration – had been included in the 1945 Labour Party electoral manifesto, and the Attlee Government consequently pursued this objective, to a largely successful extent, for the 1945–51 period. Paralleling this policy was a gradual shift toward explicit reliance upon Keynesian policy prescriptions, especially when the Chancellorship moved from Hugh Dalton to Stafford Cripps. Cripps relied upon demand-management techniques rather than the 'planned development' policy of Dalton. As Morgan (1984) observes of the Cripps era, 'the broad intellectual presuppositions were Keynesian, with a reliance on budgetary policy and demand management that anticipated the "Butskellism" of the fifties' (p. 363) (see Williams, 1979, pp. 312–18) for a critique of 'Butskellism').

Keynesian economic principles

Given this shift to Keynesian policy prescriptions in the late 1940s and a similar shift in the United States in the 1960s under Presidents Kennedy and Johnson (indeed earlier, if one includes the 1946 Employment Act which supposedly committed the federal government to the role of providing sufficient stimuli to maintain full employment), it is necessary to explain the central ideas of Keynesian economics. These were set out in *The General Theory of Employment, Interest and Money* by John Maynard Keynes (1936). They focused on macroeconomic behaviour (that is, the behaviour of the economy as a whole) and not on microeconomic behaviour (that is, the behaviour of individual consumers and producers within the market-place) (see Olson, 1982, for a critique of this neglect). Keynes considered the signals (in terms of supply and demand) produced by market forces to be sufficient for microeconomic activity to proceed smoothly *if aggregate effective demand was properly sustained*. Ensuring the latter was the lot of government economic policy. In particular, for aggregate demand to be sustained it is necessary that full employment, or a close approximation, be maintained. The government does this through providing the necessary fiscal stimuli by way of government spending *but* it has to avoid creating more demand than can be met by the economy as this will lead to inflation. Government economic policy thus becomes a matter of fine-tuning aggregate demand to generate full employment. The essential role for government implied by Keynesianism is responsibility for maintaining a sufficient level of aggregate demand. Of the four components of expenditure in the economy – personal consumption, investment, exports and government spending – it is the last over which government policymakers have greatest influence and can control to some degree. Pursuing a Keynesian fiscal stabilisation policy (that is, influencing the level of aggregate demand) means manipulating government expenditure and/or altering tax rates. Alt and Chrystal (1983, p. 60) explain thus:

> Government expenditure is a direct demand for goods. For any gross income, higher income taxes reduce private spending by leaving individuals less to allocate. Income taxes reduce the 'disposable' income available for consumers to spend. Aggregate demand in the economy is increased by either lowering taxes (and thus raising disposable income and consumer spending) or increasing government expenditure. Both increase national income through the famous 'multiplier', so named because in theory an increase in exogenous expenditure can lead to a larger increase in income. (p. 60) (See also Grant and Nath, 1984.)

The association between employment levels and prices was later formalised in the *Phillips curve*, which alluded to an historical study of this relationship demonstrating an inverse relationship: that is, high unemployment was associated with low prices and vice versa, though this curve has been questioned in subsequent re-analyses.

The two instruments of government fiscal policy are tax changes and government expenditure. But, as Alt and Chrystal (1983) point out, it is over tax changes and tax rates that government economic policymakers have the greatest control. It is much more difficult to alter government expenditure levels (as both current regimes are discovering) than to make changes in the tax rates. The key period at which policymakers influence these fiscal instruments is during the Budget: through Budgets, governments can stimulate aggregate demand by deliberately running a deficit in the short-term balanced by surpluses in other years. The nineteenth-century assumption of the annual budget as something to be balanced is discarded under Keynesianism as the Budget becomes a key instrument of government economic policy. Careful budgetary fine-tuning should enable the government to offset, or partially control, the impact of the business cycle on employment, prices and production levels.

As the core elements of the welfare state were enacted this provided further leverage for the government in its control of the aggregate economy, since it necessitated increases in public spending, taxation levied and public employment. The government could now alter its current and capital public expenditure as well as altering tax rates. Further, the government could vary the money supply through 'orthodox open-market operations in government securities, the Bank rate, reserve requirements, etc.' (Jessop, 1980, p. 29). Jessop also suggests that since Keynesian policy focuses on the behaviour of the macroeconomy it avoids direct confrontation with capital or labour: consequently 'when the Labour government was defeated in the 1951 general election, the incoming Conservative government was careful to retain the institutional basis of the post-war settlement and to maintain the commitment to full employment and welfare state' (1980, p. 29). That Keynesian demand-management techniques did not require direct interference with the status of capital or labour is critical to understanding its success: the government is essentially able to pursue its economic policies in the context of a *private economy* without significantly diminishing established interests.

Nationalisation

Other elements of the post-war consensus are the series of nationalisations carried out by the Attlee Government. Always a traditional objective, nationalisation plans were relatively undeveloped within the Labour Party in 1945. However, legislation was rapidly enacted by the Attlee Administration between 1945 and 1949, establishing the bulk of that Government's public ownership. These included: in 1946, civil aviation, cable and wireless, the Bank of England and the coal industry; in 1947, electricity and railways; in 1948, gas; and in 1949, iron and steel (see Morgan 1984, pp. 97–8). Morgan argues that short-term expediency was the critical motive for most nationalisation – that is, these industries were failing in economic terms – rather than coherent socialist objectives. The importance of these programmes is that they resulted in a 'mixed' economy in Britain – that is, the economy now included both privately-based economic activity and industries, and publicly-based or controlled industries. Thus a formerly predominantly private economy shifted towards a mixed public/private economy in a way which Shonfield (1965) identified as one of the key institutional characteristics of 'modern capitalism': he notes that from the 1950s onward 'there is [a] vastly increased influence of the public authorities on the management of the economic system' (p. 66), and a cognisance of the importance of national economic planning. Pointedly, Shonfield's influential book, *Modern Capitalism*, was subtitled 'The Changing Balance of Public and Private Power'. The mixed economy blurred the boundary between the 'public' and 'private' sectors in the modern political economy. This is an important issue considered further in relation to the current administrations' efforts at retrenching the public sector. And the mixed economy appealed both to trade unions and to business because it provided increased economic stabilisation without harming either of their interests.

The welfare state and mixed economy, in conjunction with the use of Keynesian economic techniques to maintain full employment, constitute the basis of the post-war consensus in Britain. And it is attacks on the functioning of nationalised industries, the supposed expense of the welfare state, the alleged inefficiency of state provision and control of industries and social services, the supposed ineffectiveness of Keynesian economics in the long-run, the inexorable propensity for voters to demand more services, politicians to accommodate these demands and bureaucrats to share in these expansionary interests which formed the context within which New Right ideas were formulated, promoting alternative economic, political and social policies and evaluative criteria. Before turning to these in detail it is first necessary to review the development of the welfare state in the United States, and to consider some of the arguments about governmental overload and ungovernability which became popular explanations for the economic and political crises of the 1970s.

THE KEYNESIAN WELFARE STATE: THE UNITED STATES

American welfare provision

The United States is conventionally considered an anomaly amongst advanced industrial societies because of its modest range of public welfare services. Most notably, the American polity has never enacted a comprehensive national health service comparable to that commonplace in Western Europe. Nevertheless, American public welfare provisions are not as minuscule as many casual observers believe, though they were initiated later than elsewhere. This section identifies the main developments in American public provision and the circumstances of their adoption. Important to the American case is the federal structure of government which creates obstacles to the formulation, adoption and implementation of universal policies in a way distinct to the experiences of a unitary political system like the United Kingdom. Subnational governments may have insufficient funds to provide adequate welfare services, which contributes to the weaker welfare state in the United States.

Although some measures of social welfare were initiated during the Progressive Era (1890s–1915), the first real public social measures occurred under the New Deal (1932–37). In general, the New Deal marks a profound break with the historical experience of the American state in that it legitimised, to some degree, the appropriateness of an interventionist state, if of a limited kind. In 1935 the Social Security Act was passed which had three sorts of welfare measures. First, it instituted unemployment compensation, though implementation was left to the fifty regional states' discretion until 1938, by which date all had met federal standards. Second, the 1935 Act provided aid for dependent children. Third, old age assistance was provided in two ways, 'aid to states for pensions and compulsory old age insurance for qualifying groups paid for by a tax levied on employers and employees' (Furniss and Tilton, 1977, p. 158). This last marks the beginning of 'social security' proper in the United States. Running throughout American welfare services is a distinction between social insurance programmes, which benefit all, and social assistance programmes, means-tested and selective in benefits; this distinction is returned to in Chapter 9.

Like Britain, the experience of the Second World War provided a firmer basis for state-based activities, as did the New Deal. However, this wartime experience did not influence policy until the 1960s. But during the war period many trade unions succeeded in establishing welfare measures for themselves independently of the national state: these included unemployment compensation, health costs, pensions and paid holidays. This reduced the pressure on the American government to provide these services, especially since those workers excluded from trade unions have always constituted (and continue to) a much less effectively mobilised pressure on legislators.

Thus the post-war period in the United States did not usher in an administration committed to public ownership, Keynesianism and the creation of a welfare state. In fact, it is not until the 1960s and the Kennedy/Johnson Administration (1961–68) that we find the state willing substantially to enlarge its welfare provision. President Eisenhower (1953–60) maintained a rhetorical commitment to the principles of the New Deal and the role of the state initiated during that era, but in practice did not expand the scope of services provided by the state or embrace the type of macroeconomic policies prevalent in Western Europe. In 1964, in the midst of considerable prosperity and sustained economic growth President Johnson declared a 'national war on poverty'. Around 1960 there was an unwelcome rediscovery of poverty in the United States, as recorded in books such as those by Galbraith (1958) and Harrington (1962). This poverty contrasted starkly with the general level of prosperity. And unlike comparable societies, the American state welfare system was ill-suited to compensating for private misery; further, trade unions excluded large segments of the least well-off American workers, many of whom were black. It was to these circumstances that Johnson's initiative was primarily responding.

The welfare legislation enacted under the 'national war on poverty' era falls into two main groupings. First, there was major legislation extending welfare benefits to sizeable segments of the population, most notably Medicare-Medicaid which vastly enlarged the health services available to the poor and to the old. Second, there were a series of accompanying measures aimed at the needs of especially disadvantaged groups in society. These included the provision of food stamps, aid to schools located in educationally deprived areas, and the new mental health clinics (see Furniss and

Tilton, 1977, p. 163). These eventually included Old Age, Survivors, and Disability Insurance (OASDI), the federal-state unemployment compensation system, the Supplemental Security Income (SSI) for the aged, blind and disabled, and the important Aid to Families with Dependent Children (AFDC). Other measures instituted under the 'war on poverty' initiative aimed at increasing community participation of the so-called 'poor' in the formulation and implementation of the programmes intended to benefit them. Notably absent from these welfare measures is a comprehensive system of national health insurance. However, until the present Reagan Administration most of these programmes continued to grow in application despite rhetoric to the contrary; and many have also been rationalised. As Furniss and Tilton (1977) conclude, 'More people are being helped than ever before... As in the expansion of social security coverage after the New Deal, much of the welfare effort proceeded apace despite the Vietnam War, despite Nixon's preference for work over welfare, and despite the unsympathetic outlook of Gerald Ford' (pp. 163–4). By the 1970s Americans could claim that their welfare and social security services provided assistance at a level less anomalous to that in other advanced industrial societies. From the election of Ronald Reagan in 1980, however, this position has been increasingly eroded.

Keynesian Economics in the United States

Just as the welfare measures were initiated later in the United States than elsewhere so the adoption of Keynesian economic techniques occurred there two decades after they were adopted in Europe. American economic decision-makers first utilised Keynesian policy prescriptions during the Kennedy Presidency, though the appropriateness of such measures were implied in the 1946 Employment Act (see above). In January 1964 the so-called Kennedy/Johnson tax cut was enacted. It reflected the basic Keynesian principle of trying to stimulate economic activity and reduce unemployment by increasing incentives through tax cuts and running a budget deficit. The bill was proposed by Kennedy but by the time it passed through Congress Lyndon Johnson had succeeded him as President, following Kennedy's assassination. A key economic adviser of the period, Walter Heller (1967, pp. 1–2) (in Martin, 1973), summarises the importance of this innovation to American economic policy: 'we at last accept in fact what was accepted in law twenty years ago (in the Employment Act of 1946), namely, that the Federal government has an overarching responsibility for the nation's economic stability and growth. And we have at last unleashed fiscal and monetary policy for the aggressive pursuit of those objectives' (pp. 1–2) (though see Stein (1969) on the 1946 Act). Keynesian economics had arrived on the national agenda in the United States, if twenty years later than in the rest of the advanced industrial world (Tobin, 1986). The tax cut succeeded in 1964, Sundquist (1968) argues, largely because of the support of business, while as Martin (1973) observes, 'business support for the tax cut reflected a basic change in the prevailing attitude among business elites toward budget deficits as an instrument of economic policy. This is evidently what changed and what made the difference. As long as business elites generally remained opposed to the use of that instrument, it could not be used' (p. 49). In the United States, a tax cut (and hence budget deficit), rather than an increase in government expenditure, is more acceptable to the business community given its aversion to enlarging the public sector/state. Martin, amongst others, suggests that this is the fundamental reality of power in the American political economy: business preferences for tax cuts over labour and liberal preferences for greater government expenditure. And the post-1964 years confirmed this: thus the tax bills of 1965, 1969 and 1971 all reduced taxes, whether corporate, individual or excise. The undeveloped welfare state sector in the United States is further evidence of how Keynesian economic principles have been adopted in national policy; that is, there was an unwillingness to extend state expenditures.

Regulation

A final issue is federal regulation of business and industry in the United States. Regulation constitutes the American equivalent of British post-war nationalisation: public ownership has never been a viable policy option in the United States except in a very limited form. Therefore, the imposition of government control upon unfettered capitalism or industrial activity has occurred through regulatory agencies charged with responsibility for overseeing specific industries or businesses. Prominent examples are the Civil Aeronautics Board, Food and Drug Administration, the Environmental Protection Agency, the Occupational Safety and Health Administration, state-level regulation of electric utilities, the Federal Maritime Commission and the Federal Trade Commission (see Wilson, 1980) – though some of these have disappeared in the last five years. Also relevant is the federal government's pursuit of anti-trust legislation and litigation against monopolies, though once again these have been pursued somewhat less enthusiastically under the Reagan Presidency. Anti-trust legislation represents the success of anti-large business populism. The origins of regulatory agencies are diverse (see Wilson, 1980), though they usually have a coalition of supporters; it is widely argued that they have been 'captured' by those groups or industries whom they are intended to regulate. The 'captive' thesis means that agencies have become defenders of those industries whom they were established to regulate; the consequence of this is that regulation is much less effective or worrying to the industries or businesses concerned.

This overview of post-war developments in Britain and the United States in the fields of economic policy, welfare state provision, and the mixed economy indicates the main components of the Keynesian welfare state consensus. Clearly, this term applies more aptly to the United Kingdom than to the United States, though it is certainly not irrelevant to the American post-war polity. In terms of welfare state policies and Keynesian economic policy prescriptions American practice remained less developed than British, but of sufficient magnitude to influence fundamentally the nature of politics there.

Some general points need to be made about this consensus. One concerns the critical role of economic growth, and the assumption of sustained economic growth, to the sorts of policies inherent in the post-war consensus. The types of public provision entailed in extending the welfare state assumed a large, and expanding, budget. This resulted in what Lauber (1983) terms 'the growth consensus', that is, the post-war Keynesian or social democratic consensus is underpinned by the assumption of sustained economic growth, and a public commitment to pursue growth policies. That this was the case is illustrated nicely by two major books of the period. One, Anthony Crosland's (1956) *The Future of Socialism*, setting out the social democratic policy sentiments of the British Labour Party, is littered with assumptions about economic growth and its persistence: in fact, some of Crosland's observations are, in retrospect, fascinating. For example, he concludes that by the mid-1950s 'there are no such easy reserves waiting to be tapped. Employment could hardly be fuller than it has been since 1945; while the bulk of the population would not gain much materially from further redistribution. Improved living standards, or any other economic claims, can now be met only by higher production per head; and questions about growth and efficiency move into the forefront' (1956, p. 286). A few pages later, he adds: 'I do not see how anyone can avoid the conclusion that a rapid rate of growth will be an important objective for many years to come' (p. 288). Economic growth is not only central to Crosland's vision but relatively unproblematic to attain. It is also noteworthy that he believes redistribution to have reached its targets.

Another influential book, written ten years later, is Shonfield's (1965) *Modern Capitalism*, referred to earlier. Despite being published ten years after Crosland's, the analysis of contemporary capitalist societies rests upon similar assumptions both about the importance of economic growth and the assumed ease of sustaining growth. Shonfield writes that, 'the advanced industrial countries of the Western world have during the 1950s and early 1960s enjoyed an extended period of prosperity for which it is impossible to find a precedent . . . Economic growth has been much steadier than in the past' (p. 61). Shonfield attributes this success, in part, to the implementation of Keynesian policies and the pursuit of full employment.

A second point important to understanding the Keynesian post-war consensus is that these macroeconomic techniques did not impose direct controls upon either workers or industrial leaders; in other words, Keynesian prescriptions did not require direct intervention at the microeconomic level. Adhering to this requirement was considerably easier under conditions of economic growth and prosperity which generated an annually expanding national product – the basis for redistributive policies. However, it should be noted that one of the most successful post-war economies – Sweden – incorporated redistributive policies into its national macroeconomic framework to good effect (see Chapter 10). Thus Keynesian principles can be combined with direct efforts at redistributing income.

THE KEYNESIAN WELFARE STATE CONSENSUS UNDER ATTACK

However, as widely known, by the end of the 1960s and certainly after 1973, commonplace assumptions about the persistence of economic growth changed, the core inverse relationship of unemployment and inflation (the Phillips curve) no longer held, and political satisfaction declined. The post-war Keynesian consensus was challenged: in Heald's (1983, p. 3) phrase the consensus became 'tarnished'. This is the context within which New Right liberalism developed. Two sorts of critique appeared in the 1970s. First, some political scientists characterised the polity as 'ungovernable' or 'overloaded'. A second series of criticisms focused specifically on the policy prescriptions of Keynesianism, arguing that they were fundamentally flawed and responsible partly for the economic problems of the current era; monetarism and supply-side economics were cited as alternatives in Britain and the United States respectively. When these latter joined with liberal criticisms of the consequences of state intervention for economic prosperity and individual freedom in modern capitalist societies the core New Right ideas are revealed.

Political overload

The literature on 'overload' contains two main propositions (King, 1975; Douglas, 1976; Rose and Peters, 1978; Brittan, 1975 and Crozier *et al.*, 1975). First, that modern governments have assumed vastly increased responsibilities, whether this is perceived as 'inevitable' in representative democratic political processes (compare Brittan, 1975) or the necessary corollary of maintaining capitalism; and, second, that governments no longer have sufficient resources to meet this enlarged range of activities (see King, 1975, for the original statement and Huntington in Crozier *et al.*, 1975, for similar arguments in the United States). Much of this enlarged range of state activities refers to the types of public provision associated with the welfare state, so 'overload' reflects the developments in the post-1945 political systems. Rose and Peters (1978) characterise this condition as 'political bankruptcy': working from the equation that national product is the function of the costs of public policy and take-home pay, a political economy is overloaded when 'the national product grows more slowly than the costs of public policy and the claims of take-home pay and there is not enough money in hand to meet both public and private claims' (pp. 29–30). (Note this definition of overload indicates the absence of a commitment to redistribution.) Thus the cost to the state of providing public services has outstripped the rate of growth of the GNP, beyond a threshold where it consumes more than the annual rise in national income. Consequently, the state has insufficient fiscal resources to meet its responsibilities. For some writers, especially those promoting New Right ideas, a central source of these difficulties lies with the activities of special interest groups. Thus, Brittan (1979) writes that 'the two great obstacles to the effective functioning of markets are (a) inflation and (b) the behaviour of coercive monopolistic groups, of which the unions are now the most important' (p. 48). He also advocates political reform to lower the electorate's expectations about what can be accomplished through political means.

Several writers on the overload theme suggest that it raises serious difficulties for the governability of these polities: declining political confidence, a state unable to meet its commitments or to expand public services necessarily loses support and legitimacy. The degree of this loss remains, however, controversial. For many neo-Marxists such as O'Connor (1973), Habermas (1975) and Offe (1984), delegitimation of the state is a profound problem for these societies and one capable of undermining them. This remains speculative (see Birch, 1984), but clearly these conditions and political developments opened up the political system to challenges to which New Right theories offered one powerful response, as Parsons (1982) notes: 'the development of the "crisis of democracy" as an idea offering an explanation to the tensions facing low-growth, inflation-ridden capitalism came from two main sources: (i) disillusionment with government intervention and the subsequent challenge to the political dominance of the managed economy; (ii) and related to this, the reemergence of conservative-libertarianism' (p. 424). The equivalent Marxist explanation of overload is not pursued in detail here since that would require a separate chapter. But the economic critiques raised of Keynesian economics must be treated.

Criticisms of Keynesian Economics

Keynesian economics fell into disrepute on empirical grounds; critics claimed it no longer offered successful policy solutions for macroeconomic problems. The advent of 'stagflation' (the combination of high unemployment and high inflation) contradicted a central Keynesian policy tenet (the Phillips curve): pursuing inflationary policies (that is, deficit-budgeting) to increase employment was no longer perceived as effective or politically acceptable since it generated substantial inflation, though Mukherjee (1972) argues that this reflects the failure by governments to intervene directly in labour markets. As Eltis (1976) wrote in the mid-1970s: 'inflation has accelerated throughout the world, and it must be particularly disturbing to Keynesian policy-makers that the countries where their influence was greatest are those which have suffered most. These countries, and Britain and Italy can be singled out, have suffered from faster inflation, slower growth, larger budget deficits and severer international currency collapses than their principal competitors where out-of-date pre-Keynesian methods of thought are still influential' (p. 1). For other countries, notably Sweden, Norway and Austria, Eltis's scenario is quite inappropriate: Keynesian influence there was considerable, as has been economic performance (Therborn, 1986).

The empirical failure of Keynesian policies, in combination with arguments about systemic overload, facilitated the promotion of alternative policy prescriptions, of which monetarism became the most influential in Britain. As Dean (1981) observes, economists had three sorts of responses to the problems of Keynesianism: a reversion to pre-Keynesian principles, the improvement of Keynesian models (by expanding the range of factors included and complexity of their interaction) and, a variant of the second, searching out a more complete microeconomic foundation of Keynesian principles. It is the first which entered the political arena most consequentially, through the doctrine of monetarism in Britain.

Monetarism

Monetarism rests upon pre-Keynesian economic principles, and as its name suggests, centres on the level, and supply, of money in the economy. Its principal advocate, Milton Friedman, contended that inflation results from an excessive growth of the monetary level, and that effective government economic policy should adhere to what he called the 'fixed monetary growth rule' (see Friedman and Schwartz, 1967). Monetarists argued that expanding demand in the Keynesian fashion, resulted over the long run in higher prices. Thus both Keynesian and monetarist economists are concerned with the level of demand for the economy's products but differ over how the government should influence it and over the consequences of different approaches. As Olson (1982) notes, 'monetarists argue that changes in the quantity of money are the only systematic and important sources of changes in the level of nominal income, whereas Keynes's theory also attributed a large role to budget deficits and surpluses and fiscal policy in general in determining the level of demand in the economy as a whole' (p. 185). Friedman further criticised the assumptions of the Phillips curve. He contended that there is a 'natural' rate of unemployment, evident from examining unemployment figures historically; this implies that policies stimulating demand, and hence employment levels, lead to higher prices. If government policy keeps unemployment below its 'natural' level then inflation will inevitably result – this is the acceleratist hypothesis (see Alt and Chrystal, 1983, p. 65, fig. 3.2). Friedman focused on the *expected* rate of inflation:

> There is no longer a single Phillips curve. For any level of demand in labor markets, higher expected inflation means higher increases in money wage rates and thus higher prices. If the current inflation is greater than expected, expectations will be revised upward. Only at a level of unemployment where expectations are fulfilled is the rate of inflation stable. This is called the 'natural' level of unemployment. Because of expectations, inflation *accelerates* at any level of unemployment below the natural rate. Above the natural rate of unemployment there is decelerating inflation. Only at the natural rate does existing inflation persist. (Alt and Chrystal, 1983, p. 64)

Two important policy implications follow from monetarism (and have been adopted by various governments). First, stimulating aggregate demand, which drives the economy below the natural rate of unemployment, is harmful since this will eventually result in serious inflation. But this has not been the universal experience: for example, both Sweden and Japan have pursued demand-management policies without generating massive unemployment (Therborn, 1986). Second, the monetary supply is critical, and governments must pursue a fixed level departing from it with great caution. In contrast to Keynesianism, monetarism implies a less active government fiscal and monetary policy, a greater concern with inflation than unemployment and a focus on the long rather than the short term. Monetarism thus disapproves of the fine-tuning associated with Keynesian policy techniques, which includes governments adjusting their level of spending. Increasing government spending usually involves increasing the money supply and borrowing, two unacceptable measures for monetarists. This naturally has implications for the size of the public sector, which concurs with New Right ideas. Also liberal and monetarist ideas about the individual, role of the state, market forces and public sector overlap considerably, as Chapter 5 will demonstrate (see Heald, 1983).

A further set of criticisms of the consequences of Keynesian economics have been developed by James Buchanan and Richard Wagner (1977). As public choice theorists, they focus on group behaviour and the pursuit of self-interest of politicians and voters in a Keynesian environment. Buchanan and Wagner argue that the nature of political life, including the imperative for elected politicians to ensure their survival, ineluctably results in deviations from Keynes' original assumptions. In particular, Buchanan and Wagner contend, the swing between budget deficits and budget surpluses, which Keynes envisaged, will not occur. Politicians will become reliant upon deficits: 'while there is little political resistance to budget deficits, there is substantial resistance to budget surpluses. Hence, fiscal policy will tend to be applied asymmetrically: deficits will be created frequently, but surpluses will materialize only rarely' (1977, p. 18). A little later, the same scholars explain this outcome: 'deficits allow politicians to increase spending without having directly and openly to raise taxes. There is little obstacle to such a policy. Surpluses, on the other hand, require governments to raise taxes without increasing spending – a programme far more capable of stimulating political opposition than budget deficits'. Public choice theorists advance a similar analysis of the behaviour of bureaucrats and politicians in the modern polity. And it is also similar to Brittan's (1975) interest group critique of the internal contradictions of democracy: groups will seek to increase their budgetary allocation within a Keynesian framework. Similar points are made by Buchanan and Wagner (1977) who note that Keynes did not consider his ideas for economic policy in the context of modern democracy where 'government is tempted to yield to group pressures to retain or return to power' (1977, p. 16).

CONCLUSION

The free market ideas of Friedman and of Hayek were promulgated long before their political success. While Keynesian policies dominated government practice in the post-war decades, liberal arguments were promulgated outside policy-making circles. The Institute for Economic Affairs, founded in 1957 in Britain, issued a stream of pamphlets, research notes and papers developing monetarist, and what are now termed New Right, arguments, later joined by other institutions including the Centre for Policy Studies (1974) and the Adam Smith Institute (1979). Such interest groups play an important role in promoting and disseminating political and economic ideas in both the United States and Britain: they provide a welcome source of accessible information and policy ideas for politicians and bureaucrats. Politicians in opposition have a particular interest, as well as more time, in acquiring such information (see Keegan, 1984 on the conversion of leading Tories to monetarism).

A further point, particularly for British political history, is that the death of Keynesian ideas in policy-making and the triumph of monetarism occurred three years prior to the electoral ascension of Margaret Thatcher and the Conservatives. In 1976 the then Labour Prime Minister James Callaghan told his annual Party Conference that, 'we used to think you could spend your way out of recession and increase employment by cutting taxes and boosting government spending. I tell you in all candour that that option no longer exists and that in so far as it ever did exist, it only worked by injecting a bigger dose of inflation into the economy, followed by a higher level of unemployment as the next step. High inflation followed by higher unemployment' (quoted in Parsons, 1982). (In the United States, the second half of President Carter's administration was marked by efforts to reduce the public sector.) Occurring in the midst of a monetary crisis, Callaghan's renunciation of Keynesianism by the Labour Party was extraordinarily significant: in effect, it meant that the British political party closest to the social democratic tradition was giving public notice of its abandonment of a central tenet of post-war European social democratic ideas. This is of enduring importance: the problems of the Labour Party in the mid-1970s make a return to Keynesianism very difficult; and their experience with an incomes policy at the same time makes this also an unattractive option. The hostility of the trade union movement in Britain to any form of incomes policy continues to be a serious problem for the Labour Party, and precludes it as a workable policy option. However, the abandonment of Keynesianism needs two qualifications. First, the Callaghan government maintained a public commitment to reducing unemployment, but this objective was always coupled with that of reducing inflation, unlike the preceding decades when unemployment enjoyed primacy. Second, the Chancellor, Denis Healey, did provide a £2 billion stimulus to the economy shortly after this statement by Callaghan which harked back to Keynesian economics. The future of Keynesian policy is central to Chapter 10.

5

Liberal Economics 1: the Market

INTRODUCTION

The market is central to New Right thinking. Chapter 2 linked this reliance upon the market with the liberal foundations of New Right ideas. In this chapter the role of the market in New Right liberalism is examined in detail. Its relationship to political freedom – the subject of Chapter 3 – is examined.

Social co-ordination in complex socioeconomic systems can occur through one, or a combination of three, methods. These are a centralised command or authority system, a system of mutual co-operation or through the voluntary exchange of the market-place (Lindblom, 1977). Command systems are represented by Eastern European models of socialism where, in its pure form, all decisions about the allocation, production and distribution of resources are taken by the centralised state authorities. There is no voluntary exchange market system where prices guide decisions about allocation and production determinant of demand and supply patterns. There is little or no input from decentralised authorities or enterprises about the appropriate allocation and production of goods and services; these are all centrally determined. Several Eastern European societies have deviated from a complete reliance upon centralised planning, as has China (see Nove, 1983; Feuchtwang and Hussain, 1983). More fundamentally, some economists – notably von Mises (1935) and Hayek (1935) – have maintained that economic calculation is impossible under such a centralised system where market prices have no role.

Mutual co-operation is a system for the allocation and production of goods and services whereby individuals and groups agree on appropriate levels for these latter activities, usually within the context of a market system. Nineteenth-century co-operatives in Britain are an example of such mutually based production (Carr-Saunders *et al.* 1938; Carter, 1986), whereby groups of individuals sought to provide their collective needs at a reasonable price through systems of co-operative allocation and production. Such systems of mutual co-operation are more practical the smaller the social group to which they apply (Olson, 1965). Co-operatives based around socially-useful production have become important again in the 1980s and have influenced such undertakings as the Greater London Council's London Industrial Plan (Greater London Council, 1985). This chapter is concerned with the third system – voluntary exchange through the market-place – which arises from exchange relations.

THE MARKET IN ECONOMIC THEORY

The market acquired modern intellectual significance in the famous book *The Wealth of Nations* by Adam Smith (1776) which purported to describe the nature of contemporary economic activity in the eighteenth century. Smith's major contribution was to describe how the pursuit of individual self-interest in commerce resulted in collective prosperity for society. The voluntary exchange of economic transactions between buyers and sellers brought economic gain to each party. Such transactions are multiple and uncoordinated, that is, there is no central planning or directing authority. Rather, market exchanges are based on the price mechanisms which not only contribute to the social order (by providing value indicators for goods and services derived from their demand and supply) but also allow rapid changes and adjustments in the allocation of resources and production of goods in accordance with market signals. As well as introducing machines and technology into economic activity, industrialisation ensures the development of an integrated national (and later international) market system whereby all individuals' livelihood derives from participation in the market – most commonly through the sale of individual labour. Smith argued that, despite the lack of central co-ordination, the outcome of market transactions was mutually beneficial; this could not be achieved by a bureaucratic authority charged with accomplishing the same end. Society's resources are distributed by means of the thousands of exchanges between buyers and sellers in a way which benefits each. Smith argued that overseeing the pursuit of individual self-interest was an 'invisible hand' which produced the collective societal good:

> As every individual, therefore, endeavours as much as he can both to employ his capital in the support of domestic industry, and so to direct that industry that its produce may be of the greatest value, every individual necessarily labours to render the annual revenue of the society as great as he can. He generally, indeed, neither intends to promote the public interest, nor knows how much he is promoting it. By preferring the support of domestic to that of foreign industry, he intends only his own security; and by directing that industry in such a manner as its produce may be of greatest value, he intends only his own gain, and he is in this, as in many other cases, led by an *invisible hand* to promote an end which was no part of his intention. Nor is it always the worse for the society that it was no part of it. By pursuing his own interest he frequently promotes that of the society more effectually than when he really intends to promote it. I have never known much good done by those who affected to trade for the public good. (*Wealth of Nations*, Book 4, ch. 2, p. 199, emphasis added).

Thus collective prosperity can be attained from the workings of the market without government activity, by simply allowing people to pursue their own economic interests; that is, to allocate resources to particular production ends, and then to market these goods or services through a value system based on money would result in prosperity. As Joan Robinson (1962) drily observes, 'it is the business of the economists, not to tell us what to do, but to show why what we are doing anyway is in accord with proper principles' (p. 25). This is the system satirised by Mandeville in his poem *The Fable of the Bees* (1970, originally published 1714): when the bees are productive and pursuing their economic self-interest the result is general affluence; when they pursue virtue the result is widespread poverty, particularly for the poor who become unemployed.

Smith did recognise that the voluntary market system requires some government activity. First, it is necessary to have a set of rules – a legal framework – upheld by the state facilitating the operation of market exchanges. In particular, property rights must be guaranteed by the legal system. As Lindblom (1977) notes, 'in the form of laws on personal liberty and property, rules specify that people have authority to control their own labour and can claim certain assets as their own to withold from or grant to other persons. And exchange is possible only in a society in which a moral code and authority keep social peace' (p. 34). Further, the state has responsibility for defence and the provision of certain public goods (though the extent of these is controversial).

These are the core ideas of contemporary New Right liberal market economics. The modern counterpart to Smith's 'invisible hand' is found in Hayek's (1976) concept of a 'spontaneous order' or 'catallaxy'. He defines the latter as 'the order brought about by the mutual adjustment of many individual economies in a market. A catallaxy is thus the special kind of spontaneous order produced by the market through people acting within the rules of the law of property, tort and contract' (1976, pp. 108–9). Hayek argues that the term 'economy' is inappropriate to describe market relations and activities since its connotations are too narrow. Like Smith's market economy, Hayek's catallaxy produces collective good from the pursuit of individual self-interest; and like Smith, Hayek argues that no mechanism created by society could accomplish this as efficiently and impartially as the *laissez-faire* market system. That the catallaxy does this impartially is critically important for Hayek, since the outcome of the market order provides an allocation of scarce resources which is fair because it makes no assumptions about the priority of objectives: 'the task of all economic activity is to reconcile the competing ends by deciding for which of them the limited means are to be used. The market order reconciles the claims of the different non-economic ends by the only known process that benefits all – without, however, assuring that the more important comes before the less important, for the simple reason that there can exist in such a system no single ordering of needs' (1976, p. 113; for a similar account see Brittan, 1979, pp. 63ff).

Hayek is very impressed by how the spontaneous working of the market order provides a means for distributing information through the price mechanism. The importance of the economy is increased for Hayek because it is a learning process through which information is acquired and knowledge generated; as Hayek (1960) writes, progress is a 'process of formation and modification of the human intellect, a process of adaptation and learning in which not only the possibilities known to us but also our values and desires continually change' (p. 40) (see Hodgson, 1984). Such a process could not be effected as efficiently by a planning authority, in part because the sum of human knowledge could not be centralised. In fact, central planning would be quite harmful to the creation of the knowledge by which society progresses, since it would stifle individual initiative. An equally important feature of the market is its ability to deal with uncertainty and risk: market processes are sufficiently flexible to respond to changes in demand as well as to innovations (see Friedman, 1962 on this point also). While not precluding some state activity (see below) Hayek considers the spontaneous *laissez-faire* market order to be the most satisfactory means of organising society and of providing a basis for societal development through the efficient generation and transmission of knowledge; as Bosanquet (1983) observes, 'Hayek takes the view that public action will nearly always produce bad results while individual action will nearly always serve the interests of the "spontaneous order"' (p. 17). It is impossible to predict the nature of technological innovation or of consumer preferences, Hayek contends, so it is most effective to follow market forces. Relying upon central planning authorities is not only inefficient when compared to the catallaxy but also infringes individual freedom, as Hayek outlined first in *The Road to Serfdom* (1944). This book is Hayek's first sustained critique on socialism and socialist planning – a theme of all his work. Socialism is considered undesirable for two reasons. First it restricts freedom by limiting individual decision-making and imposing universal standards. Second socialism is inherently inefficient. This theme reflects the work of the 'Austrian school' of which Hayek was a member, most famously recorded in von Mises' (1935) arguments about the impossibility of socialist planning without use of market and price mechanisms.

New Right liberals such as Hayek and Friedman also endorse the distribution of income which results from the market order. Income earned in the market reflects effort and the utility (in monetary terms) of each individual's contribution. For Hayek 'civilization is progress and progress is civilization' (1960, p. 39) and inequality is a necessary element in the process of attaining progress. Incentives are necessary for this process to operate effectively. Consequently, individuals make their own judgements about the use of their resources: those who make the shrewdest judgements using market criteria will garner the greatest rewards; notions of merit will rarely effect these reward patterns. In Hayek (1960) he spells out the relationship between progress and necessary inequality: 'it is one of the most characteristic facts of a progressive society that in it most things which individuals strive for can be obtained only through further progress. This follows from the necessary character of the process: new knowledge and its benefits can spread only gradually, and the ambitions of the many will always be determined by what is as yet accessible only to the few . . . There will always be people who already benefit from new achievements that have not yet reached others' (p. 42). Material reward must reflect 'assessable merit'. Because the market is an impersonal institution the resulting distribution of income and wealth cannot be judged unfair *in principle*: as noted in Chapter 3, for Hayek injustice can arise only from intentional individual behaviour which excludes, he argues, the impersonal market. Friedman (1962) contends that the inequality associated with market societies is less than that found in alternative economic system of organisation. He argues further that the concentration of power necessary to achieve society-wide equality would reduce significantly political freedom and fail to achieve equality: thus the process of attaining equality requires unequal power. Hayek (1960) argues that 'in order for a planned society to achieve the same rate of advance as a free society, the degree of inequality that would have to prevail would not be very different' (p. 46). Inequality is a positive function of economic progress. Hayek further argues that the pursuit of egalitarianism actually contributes to the decline of society: the imposition of a universal standard negates the basis for progress (1960, p. 49). The existing distribution of property and wealth is acceptable to New Right theorists because it embodies the inherited working of the market system.

It will be recalled from Chapter 2, that conservatives are highly sceptical of 'progress'. This contradicts with the liberal thrust of Hayek's arguments. Conservatives value tradition, the status quo and fear social change; their political themes consistently emphasise the need to return to an earlier era and to restructure social rights and classes in fairly hierarchical terms. But conservatives have had to reach accommodation with capitalism despite being hostile to its values, including that of 'progress'.

As this summary indicates, Hayek's thought is undoubtedly rich and constitutes a well worked-out account and defence of the market order as the basis for organising complex socioeconomic systems. Unlike many economic theorists, Hayek has a conception of society, of the role of individuals in the social order, and of how the social order changes or 'progresses'. Hayek's philosophy derives from his central propositions about individual behaviour, the nature of the spontaneous order and the role of knowledge in facilitating social change and advancement for the lot of humanity. These central propositions are all based upon the market nature of modern society which produces the 'spontaneous order'. Hayek believes we are unable to understand fully the processes at work in this order, which is further reason to accept its power in producing a social order and progress. While the spontaneous order is intimately linked to freedom it is its capacity to provide a system for generating and transmitting knowledge for collective benefit which gives it such a critical role.

The perfect competition model

The market economy described by Adam Smith (and elaborated upon by David Ricardo and James and John Stuart Mill) is incorporated into modern economic theory as the *perfect competition model*. According to this economic model, under certain assumptions, the free operation of the market economy results in an optimal (that is, most efficient) allocation of societal resources (see Alt and Chrystal, 1983; Lindblom, 1977). There is debate about whether these necessary conditions can ever hold, with some considered highly unrealistic – for example, the assumptions that all firms have achieved a perfect point of production whereby increasing the prices of its product would not improve its profit and that information is perfectly distributed (see Brittan, 1979, however). The perfect competitive model also assumes very few commodities and that 'each commodity is homogeneous and capable of complete description' (Hodgson, 1984, p. 72). This classical model concerns microeconomic behaviour; it emphasises the role and activities of individual markets in the production and consumption of goods and services. A balance is obtained between the supply of goods and the demand for goods by the price system which adjusts to achieve equilibrium between the two. It is important to emphasise, however, that many dynamics in the economy (for example, monopolistic tendencies) constitute attempts to create imperfections, an issue ignored by the perfect competitive theory.

Economists recognise that there is no single market but rather three main ones. First, there is the labour market where individuals offer their services, assets and labour-power in order to attain money for their own use; second, there is the consumer market where the money earned in the labour market is used to attain goods and services which the individual desires; and, third, there is an intermediate market where firms 'buy and sell with each other . . . from which both individual consumers and individual suppliers are excluded' (Lindblom, 1977, p. 37). The classical model originating with Smith, Ricardo and the Mills maintains that 'market clearing' is achieved by the price mechanism that is, prices for those goods too expensive are supposed to fall while those for underpriced goods in heavy demand rise. There is controversy about how efficiently this clearing process works: the instance of persistent involuntary unemployment is an obvious indicator of its problems. Alt and Chrystal (1983) outline the theory regarding the labour market:

> the classical system presumed that the wage rate adjusted to clear labor markets, just as prices adjust to clear commodity markets. If there are unemployed workers, wages adjust downward until the supply is just equal to the demand. Firms will hire more workers if they can pay them less. There is one wage at which everyone who wishes to work *at that wage* will be able to find a job. Any involuntary unemployment must be because wages are too high, but in that event wages could be expected to adjust downward. (p. 58)

In fact, it was the failure of the labour market to regulate itself in this theoretically predicted fashion in the 1930s which prompted Keynes to reconsider the nature of economic theory, as discussed in Chapter 4. He advocated that governments should use fiscal policy to sustain economic activity. Keynes' theory, however, was macroeconomic in focus whereas the classical model is microeconomic. The only macroeconomic aspect of the classical tradition concerns money in the economy, arguing that shifts in relative prices (that is, the price of commodities) would have consequences for the economy though such changes are not believed to occur. This theory, of course, has been greatly refined and developed by monetarists.

The perfect competitive model has a number of other unfulfilled assumptions. First, if the market economy is allowed to operate freely, as Adam Smith desired, it will not fully use all the economic resources available. Second, and more fundamentally, prices do not always reflect the scarcity of particular goods and services, as Smith maintains. Large corporations (monopolies and oligopolies) in the market can control the supply of goods and services thereby artificially distorting the prices sought. This point has been familiar to economists for most of the twentieth century (see Galbraith, 1973); and it is striking that those promoting the market model largely neglect this problem. The assumption of small firms interacting is seriously belied both by observation of contemporary economies and by empirical research: monopolies are an integral part of these market economies and exercise proportionately more power in the market-place as a consequence.

A third problem with the model is the assumption that consumers know exactly what goods and services will fulfil their needs. There are two problems with this: most consumers do not know their exact needs in that they do not have a sufficient range of detailed information and knowledge from which to reach consumption decisions. Further, as Galbraith (1973) and others have pointed out, advertising by large corporations represents a powerful distorting feature of Western market economies which further erodes 'consumer sovereignty'. This latter concept is central to New Right arguments: a large part of the appeal of a return to the classical economic model is the allegedly increased capacity it gives to individuals as consumers to express their own interests and preferences, rather than accepting state-determined ones as the post-war Keynesian welfare state is purported to entail. It is assumed that markets facilitate the exercise of consumer sovereignty: so, for example, New Right liberals such as Friedman (1962) advocate the use of vouchers in education, rather than the provision of state schools, since this will allow parents as consumers to make their own decisions in accord with their own preferences; rather than having to send their children to a school allocated by the state parents can use the voucher to decide which school is most appropriate for their children. The same principle could be extended to other areas, New Right supporters argue. But there is a serious difficulty with this argument: to what extent can the goods and services provided by the state, such as education, be equated with other goods and services provided in the market-place, and can the same standards be used to evaluate them? Thus in relation to education, the voucher argument equates parents as consumers of educational services with consumers of oranges. By this logic, parents should be happy if the number of students per class is raised from thirty to sixty since this must imply higher teacher productivity and more efficient services. But this is unlikely to be desired by parents. New Right arguments like these fail to allow for the different types of goods and services in the private and public sectors to which different evaluative criteria will be applied by consumers themselves.

The market economy also fails to ensure an effective allocation of resources between future investment and current consumption. Further, the market economy only produces goods and services that people want and can afford to pay for: however, since wealth is unevenly distributed the less urgent wants of the rich may well be supplied while the urgent needs of the less well off are ignored or undersupplied.

A final problem with the assumptions of the perfect competition model concerns profits. According to the model, the freely operating market, under the conditions of perfect competition, generates economic growth and general prosperity. The main motive of individual and firm participation in the market is profit: producers seek to profit from their engagement in market transactions; if they did not, there would be little reason to enter into market exchanges. But where the assumptions of the perfect competitive model are being met, as specified in the classical model, there is *no* profit. Profit is a function of disequilibrium in the competitive model, as Lachmann (1973) records: 'profits are earned wherever there are price-cost differences. They are thus a typical disequilibrium phenomenon, impermanent, continuously shifting as regards origin and magnitude, affected by contrived change (innovation) as well as by undesigned change emanating from population movements, shifts in demand and so on... The magnitude of profits, in each period, is shaped mainly by short-period forces. All the time a long-run force tending to eliminate these price-cost differences is at work' (pp. 31–2). Lachmann then notes that 'in long-run equilibrium, in which by definition the equilibrating forces have finally prevailed over all the forces of disruption, there are no profits. The persistence of profits in a market economy is due to the persistence of disequilibrium in some sector of the economic system' (1973, p. 32). Thus the optimal allocation allegedly produced by the liberal perfect competitive economic model precludes profit. Optimal allocation occurs under conditions of perfect competition, under which conditions there is no profit, the motivating force according to New Right liberalism. The imperfections (such as monopolistic tendencies) which liberals deplore are, in fact, key profit-generating dynamics in the economic system. In other words, market imperfections are the main source of profit in the economy. If liberals want a freely-operating market economy and profits, then market imperfections are likely to persist regardless of government action.

These are the unmet assumptions of the perfect competitive market model. There is also a need for the state to offset market failures, notably externalities, and to provide collective goods.

PUBLIC GOODS, STATE INTERVENTION AND THE MARKET ORDER

According to classical microeconomic theory, if the free market economy is left to itself it will attain an 'optimal' level of resource allocation. This optimality is known as 'Pareto optimality' (after Vilfredo Pareto): under certain conditions, a free market economy will produce an allocation of resources whereby no individual can be made better off without some other individual being made worse off at the given levels of distribution. As noted above, Smith's 'invisible hand' generates and circulates knowledge, technology and attitudes, eventually settling upon a 'Pareto optimal' position. Whether the necessary assumptions can actually hold has long been disputed, as we have discussed above. In particular, the assumption that all firms are in perfect competition is no longer considered realistic: that is, that the firms in the economy are too small to shift the market price by themselves, have freedom to enter and leave the industry, and their consumers have perfect information about them. This is one example of how a freely-operating market will fail to attain satisfactorily its own optimum level. This failure has implications for state intervention into market economies.

While promoting a *laissez-faire* market economy in *The Wealth of Nations* Adam Smith (1776) recognised that there were certain functions the state must undertake in order, somewhat paradoxically, for the free market to operate. These fell into three main groups. First the provision of a legal framework guaranteeing property rights, which facilitates economic activity. In modern terms, Hayek (1976) emphasises the 'rule of law' as a necessary precondition for the spontaneous order. Second, Smith ascribed the role of national defence to the state, a function which is widely accepted. Third, Smith argued that the state had a responsibility for providing some public goods which the market would fail to produce. These three state functions are described by Smith as follows:

> According to the system of natural liberty, the sovereign has only three duties to attend to; three duties of great importance . . . first, the duty of protecting the society from the violence and invasion of other independent societies; secondly, the duty of protecting, as far as possible, every member of the society from the injustice or oppression of other members of it, or the duty of erecting and maintaining certain public works and certain public institutions, which it can never be for the interest of any individual, or small number of individuals, to erect and maintain; because the profit could never repay the expense to any individual, or small number of individuals, though it may frequently do much more than repay it to a great society. (Book 4, ch. 9, p. 311)

Commonly characterised as 'public goods', the extent of this third area of state intervention is central to modern economic arguments: New Right liberals, in particular, maintain that the scope of state intervention under this third area is excessive. Public goods are strictly defined as those goods and services which have the characteristics of indivisibility (that is, their use cannot be meaningfully divided amongst individuals or groups) and nonexcludability (that is, individuals or groups cannot be effectively prevented from using them) (see Laver, 1981). An additional area of state intervention concerns market failure: externalities, arising from the operation of market processes require addressing by the state. Externalities can be either positive or negative. A common example of a negative externality is pollution, whether from cars or factories: car owners do not necessarily intend to pollute the environment but their cars do, which is therefore a negative externality; the government can offset this by requiring that lead-free petrol is used. Likewise, government legislation can regulate the level of pollution emanating from factories. Friedman (1962) calls these 'neighbourhood effects'. Finally, market failure can also concern microeconomic behaviour, as noted above: when one or other of the assumptions of Pareto optimality are not being met and the state has the opportunity to counteract them.

Since Smith's writings debate has raged over the appropriate scope of government intervention. With the exception of some libertarians (see Newman, 1984), it is generally agreed that the state should provide defence and maintain a set of laws which incorporate the principles of property rights, contract and tort law, and provide a means of adjudicating between conflicting members of the community. State activity beyond this is the subject of disagreement. New Right theorists such as Hayek, Friedman and Brittan (1979) favour little additional state activity. The public goods provided under this rubric remain minimal, such as defence, lighthouses and streets. Because the state is seen as a threat to individual liberty and the free market economy is considered the most preferable system of socioeconomic organisation, it follows for New Right writers that public provision of goods and services must be minimal. Liberals accept that government has a responsibility regarding some market imperfections, particularly those arising from negative externalities, but the market-based provision of goods is always preferred. Nor should the adoption of public provision at one point in time be seen as permanent (see Tullock (1973). This narrow conception of the state and its responsibilities underlies James Buchanan's book *The Limits of Liberty* (1975), which develops a public choice account of the state and its activities.

Such an account is largely mirrored by Milton Friedman in his widely read and cited book *Capitalism and Freedom* (1962). Friedman is an ardent opponent of government, contending that while market failure justifies some state intervention, for the reasons already discussed, the very nature of bureaucracy and government activity makes it an undesirable alternative to market processes: 'in a rapidly changing society . . . the conditions making for technical monopoly frequently change and I suspect that both public regulation and public monopoly are likely to be less responsive to such changes in conditions, to be less readily capable of elimination, than private monopoly' (1962, p. 28). The rigidity of government bureaucratic arrangements are contrasted by Friedman and others (notably Hayek) with the intrinsic flexibility of the market, which is geared to uncertainty and shifting environmental conditions. This latter intrinsic market strength is considered by Friedman as sufficient compensation for its imperfections. Here we find Hayek's (1960) reference to the 'spontaneous order' generated by the market (already explained) instinctively responsive to change and capable of adapting to uncertainty in the most collectively beneficial way. And, of course, for both Friedman and Hayek it is the capacity of the market to maximise individual freedom which provides the basis for wealth-generation in society: for them, the market is intrinsically more efficient in these functions than is the state. Guaranteeing economic freedom equals the promotion of capitalism for Friedman because such freedom increases reliance on the market economy, and is ultimately a guarantor of political freedom: Friedman suggests that, 'historical evidence speaks with a single voice on the relation between political freedom and a free market. I know of no example in time or place of a society that has been marked by a large measure of political freedom, and that has not also used something comparable to a free market to organize the bulk of economic activity' (1962, p. 9).

Friedman identifies four legitimate areas of intervention paralleling those mentioned above: defence, a judicial system, externality problems, and responsibility for the insane and children. However, he warns against extending state activity beyond these activities and seeks careful control of government actions:

How can we benefit from the promise of government while avoiding the threat of freedom? . . . The scope of government must be limited. Its major function must be to protect our freedom both from the enemies outside our gates and from our fellow-citizens: to preserve law and order, to enforce private contracts, to foster competitive markets. Beyond this major function, government may enable us at times to accomplish jointly what we would find it more difficult or accomplish severally. (1962, p. 2)

Friedman continues by noting that 'any such use of government is fraught with danger'; we must ensure that there is a 'clear and large balance of advantages' before government is used (1962, pp. 2–3). And elsewhere in *Capitalism and Freedom* Friedman presents a set of criticisms of government programmes offered as evidence of the failure of state activity including the minimum wage, rent control, occupational licensing, consumer protection laws, protectionism and Keynesian demand-management. For Friedman America's economic progress is due exclusively to market-based activities, with government measures simply trammelling these developments: progress has been the 'product of the initiative and drive of individuals cooperating through the free market. Government measures have hampered not helped this development' (1962, p. 200). He continues by noting that:

the central defect of these measures is that they seek through government to force people to act against their own immediate interests in order to promote a supposedly general interest. They seek to resolve what is supposedly a conflict of interest, or a difference in view about interests, not by establishing a framework that will eliminate the conflict, but by forcing people to act against their own interests. They substitute the values of outsiders for the values of participants. (1962, p. 200)

Government intervention is largely unsuccessful and has the dangerous consequence of reducing the freedom to pursue one's own interests in the free market economy, according to Friedman. Where state programmes are necessary for the less fortunate, as in those associated with the welfare state, Friedman advocates replacing current measures with market-based ones. Thus, instead of providing subsidised health care, people should be given cash vouchers to use as they choose in the competitive market system. Competition increases the level of services attained, the diversity of services offered, and maximises individual choice which is at the heart of economic growth and political freedom under capitalism. But the provision of vouchers represents a distortion of the market-based Pareto optimal allocation of resources so favoured by New Right theorists. That is, on one hand, such theorists seek restoration of a free market economy which they claim will find its own equilibrium; but implementing voucher policies necessarily distorts this optimality in a redistributive way which is criticised elsewhere by the same theorists.

Like Hayek, Friedman believes that the state has some responsibility for assisting the less well-off but such efforts should be market-based rather than paternalistic. Friedman also supports the privatisation of services currently under the administration of the welfare state. Hayek recognises also a necessary role for government to offset the hardship of the poor, the unemployed, the elderly and disabled (Hayek, 1976), that is, chiefly those who 'cannot make their living in the market, such as the sick, the old, the physically or mentally defective, the widows and orphans' (1979, p. 54). But Hayek sees no reason why public provision should be monopolistic nor why such services should remain permanently within the public sector. However, as Newman (1984) observes, Hayek 'gives us no reason to believe that the social effects of private bureaucracies are any less disruptive' (p. 153) than the supposed impersonal and unsatisfactory rule of public bureaucracies.

Such assumptions lie throughout the positions and policies of New Right politicians who agree with Hayek and Friedman that the role of government must be carefully controlled in the interests of economic wealth and political freedom; and that much of the existing intervention by the state, including welfare and other policies have failed and could be more effectively accomplished by market-based solutions. However, what has been missing from the discussion so far is some reference to the reasons explaining the rise of the welfare state and expanded public sector.

THE STATE AND CAPITALISM: CAN THE MARKET OPERATE WITH A MINIMAL STATE?

The Keynesian tradition and the post-war experience of social democratic regimes in advanced industrial societies has extended vastly both the range of activities under the rubric of public goods and state functions. The range and diversity of goods and services denoted by the contemporary public sector leads Steiner (1970) to suggest a modern and broader definition: 'any publicly induced or provided collective good is a public good' (p. 25), which is a more satisfactory characterisation of the contemporary public sector. Thus public goods include not only those which arise from externalities and from market imperfections (that is, failures in information available, competitiveness and too high transaction costs) but also from what Steiner describes as a concern with the quality of the environment such as 'the distribution of income, the nature or quality of goods produced, or the patterns of consumption that markets produce' (Steiner, 1970, p. 31). This last category is different from the market failures which classical economics deems a legitimate source of public provision of goods and services; and Steiner's (1970) justification that 'even perfectly functioning markets for all goods and services would not eliminate the desire for market interference' (p. 31) has gone largely unchallenged until New Right advocacy of a greater reliance on *laissez-faire* liberal market economics. One might dispute whether 'perfectly functioning markets' have ever been approximated in reality, even during the eighteenth and nineteenth centuries, but be that as it may. Concern with income distribution and other undesirable outcomes of the market fuelled the expansion of the Keynesian welfare state during the post-1945 period. Hayek and Friedman accept the need for some of the public goods falling within this third category though they consider contemporary state intervention excessive.

The paradox, however, is that the free market needs the state. This has already been noted in the discussion of Adam Smith's original formulation of classical microeconomics. There must be a state-maintained and legitimated judicial system; and the state must address market imperfections, underwriting those vital public goods which the market fails to produce. The state must be perceived as necessary although this is denied in the economic sphere: New Right theorists argue that it is, in the main, illegitimate for the state to intervene in the market system, yet its intervention is accepted for certain activities. This is an unsettled problem for these theorists. However, several scholars argue that in fact the role of the state in facilitating the *laissez-faire* market order has been, necessarily, far greater than this indicates. Undoubtedly public expenditure and state activity is much greater in the 1980s than it was in the 1880s (though less so in continental Europe where the state played a major role in fostering economic development) but it was not insignificant in the nineteenth century. Polanyi's (1957) classic study of the evolution of modern society provides a vivid account of this state role:

> The road to the free market was opened and kept open by an enormous increase in continuous, centrally organized and controlled interventionism. To make Adam Smith's "simple and natural liberty" compatible with the needs of a human society was a most complicated affair. Witness the complexity of the provision in the innumerable enclosure laws; the amount of bureaucratic control involved in the administration of the New Poor Laws which for the first time since Queen Elizabeth's reign were effectively supervised by central authority; or the increase in governmental administration entailed in the meritorious task of municipal reform. And yet all these strongholds of governmental interference were erected with a view to the organizing of some simple freedom – such as that of land, labor, or municipal administration. Just as, contrary to expectation, the invention of labor-saving machinery had not diminished but actually increased the uses of human labor, the introduction of free markets, far from doing away with the need for control, regulation, and intervention, enormously increased their range. Administrators had to be constantly on the watch to ensure the free working of the system. Thus even those who wished most ardently to free the state from all unnecessary duties, and whose whole philosophy demanded the restriction of state activities, could not but entrust the self-same state with the new powers, organs, and instruments required for the establishment of *laissez-faire*. (pp. 140–1).

More recently, Hodgson (1984) has argued that the association between the state and capitalist economies is inseparable because the latter requires state support. As Polanyi contended, the creation of a free market economic order depended crucially upon state intervention, support and policies: most obvious is the need for a judicial system which guarantees property rights and contract law. Hodgson (1984) argues that 'it requires a legal machinery to enact these laws. It needs a continuous process of legislation to minimize anomalies and keep the system up to date with a continuously changing social and economic reality' (p. 78). Other important examples of the state's contribution to economic development include legislation restricting the length of the working day so that workers would not be too fatigued and thus incapable either of working effectively or of learning new skills; and the education system was similarly created by the state as a necessary condition for effective economic growth. Because individuals and individual firms are pursuing their own interest, in the way advocated by Smith, the collective outcome can at times be contrary to the general interests of capital; the state must address this imbalance which means overriding market mechanisms. The general point advanced by Polanyi and Hodgson is that the very existence of a *laissez-faire* market order (or Hayek's spontaneous order), which New Right liberals advocate as the most desirable means of socioeconomic organisation, necessitates by its nature the existence of a state which intervenes to promote and facilitate this desired order. Most notably, this intervention takes the form of ensuring a system of private property based on individual rights and the denial of other forms of rights in social resources.

Throughout the advanced industrial world (that is, those liberal-democratic states committed to a substantial private economic sector), there has been increased state provision of services. New right liberals and conservatives deplore this trend and seek its reversal. But apart from state welfare policies many of those countries, such as France, West Germany, Sweden, Norway and Japan, which have ascribed a central role to state economic planning, have enjoyed considerable economic success in the post-war period (see Shonfield, 1965). The New Right argument for a reduced state is contradicted by historical trends and evidence in both the provision of welfare and economic planning. In Chapter 9 the dynamics behind the foundation and expansion of the welfare state are examined: the relevant forces will not be easily demolished, it is argued. Aside from this, the general disruptive nature of the free market, when its self-regulating mechanism fails, as during the 1930s and in the incidence of business cycles suggests the need for state intervention directly into the processes of economic activity.

CONCLUSION

This chapter has set out the concept of the market economy central to contemporary New Right thought, which derives from the classical microeconomics of Adam Smith, David Ricardo, James and John Stuart Mill, and is formalised in economic theory as the perfect competition model. The most powerful contemporary New Right account of this classical position – namely, Hayek's concept of the spontaneous order – has been outlined also. The principal controversy of the free market model is establishing the degree of state intervention with which it is compatible; and the positions of two New Right thinkers, Hayek and Friedman, have been examined. The intrinsic nature of the *laissez-faire* model requires a significant level of state activity and intervention: in fact, it is state policy and institutions which create the necessary framework for the successful flourishing of the free market. Further, the pursuit of individual self-interest in the market will not ensure a minimum income for all members of society. This is acknowledged by Hayek and Friedman and each accepts the need for some state responsibility to offset the hardship of certain disadvantaged groups, but within strict limits. Beyond these limits the expansion of state programmes reflects simply the reckless promises of vote-seeking politicians and favours special interests. That this occurs in liberal democracies is in part accurate but as Newman (1984) nicely notes 'there is an ironic flavor to Hayek's critique of democracy. While he accurately targets a number of problems, Hayek fails to realize that the politics he abhors is in large part a product of the economic order he defends. The same motives that drive people to seek their advantage in the market encourage them to pursue their end by political means as well. Self-interest, that great engine of material progress, teaches us to respect results, not principles' (p. 158).

The next chapter will consider these rational choice arguments. One final point: the growth of the state's responsibility for social welfare has not been exclusively fuelled by these sorts of political ambitions and abuses of the democratic process. Rather, they reflect to no insignificant degree, the objectives of the electorate in these countries seeking state-based compensation for the undesirable economic and social outcomes of the market process. The description of New Right liberals' *laissez-faire* property rights-based social order, in part explains why Western democracies have found it necessary to increase the role of government as a regulator of economic power and source of assistance to their less well off members. It is in this context that the Keynesian welfare state must be considered. These issues are treated further in the concluding chapters of this book.

6

Liberal Economics 2: Public Choice Theory

INTRODUCTION

An important element of New Right economics is public choice theory (also known as the 'Virginia School', or rational choice theory, or the economics of politics; see Dunleavy, 1986), which has been especially influential amongst New Right intellectuals. However, the term 'public choice' or the 'economics of politics' has not gained the wide usage of other New Right terms like monetarism and privatisation. This reflects the complexity of rational choice analysis. But there is significant overlap between public choice theory and other aspects of liberalism. Also, the influential New Right Institute of Economic Affairs has devoted part of its publications to propagating public choice arguments in a highly readable form. This has increased their accessibility for liberal politicians. This chapter begins with a discussion of the meaning of public choice analysis and then considers specific contributions. These include rational choice arguments about the behaviour of voters, politicians and bureaucrats in liberal democracies, and issues such as the prisoners' dilemma and the problem of collective action. Technical explanation is eschewed in favour of qualitative exposition of the core assumptions. The chapter does not provide a comprehensive account of public choice theory (for reviews see Laver, 1981; Mueller, 1979; Barry and Hardin, 1983; Bonner, 1986). Rather this chapter illustrates the nature of public choice analysis and identifies the contributions most influential amongst New Right advocates.

THE MEANING OF PUBLIC CHOICE THEORY

The scope of public choice analysis

The common British characterisation, 'the economics of politics' (Buchanan *et al.*, 1978), conveys the essence of the public choice theoretic approach. This is to apply the methods of economic analysis to political activity (such as the nature of the state and the consequences of utilising different voting methods) and to political behaviour (politicians, bureaucrats and voters). Using the methods and assumptions of microeconomic analysis means assuming, first and foremost, that individuals are egotistic, utility-maximising, rational self-interested actors, and that these characteristics shape all political behaviour be it that of a voter, politician or bureaucrat. As Buchanan *et al.* (1978) observes, 'in one sense, all of public choice or the economic theory of politics, may be summarized as the "discovery" or "rediscovery" that people should be treated as rational utility-maximizers in *all* of their behavioural capacities' (p. 17). A similar definition is offered by Shaw (1985) (see also Frey, 1978; Laver, 1981; Mueller, 1979):

> public choice theorists look at government decision-makers as rational, self-interested people, just like the rest of us, who view issues from their own perspective and act in the light of their personal incentives. While voters, politicians, and bureaucrats may desire to reflect the 'public interest', that desire is only one incentive among many and it is likely to be outweighed by more powerful ones. (Shaw 1985, p. 78)

Public choice analysis is both empirical and normative. It is empirical in that its practitioners have analysed specific institutions and political processes. It is normative in some of its implications and in developing propositions for reorganising political practice; see, for example, the work of James Buchanan who presents proposals for rearranging constitutions, the scope of government activity and the budgetary process.

Modern public choice theory has evolved during the last three decades mainly in the United States, in such institutions as the Virginia Polytechnic Institute (hence the 'Virginia School') and the University of Rochester. Its lineage extends back to nineteenth-century economists (for example, Knut Wicksell and Erik Lindahl, though these did not draw right-wing conclusions from their work), and includes twentieth-century mathematicians (for example, Black (1958)). Interestingly, early public choice work, such as that of Wicksell on public finance, argued the necessity for increased government expenditure, in contrast to subsequent theorists. Public choice theorists have analysed decision-making procedures, highlighting their enormous complexity, and the problem of formulating collective social choices. With Joseph Schumpeter, the analysis of political institutions begins: in *Capitalism Socialism and Democracy* (1950) he argues that democracy consists of electoral competition between organised vote-maximising political parties. In 1957 Anthony Downs published *An Economic Theory of Democracy*, which analysed the behaviour of political parties as vote-maximisers in liberal democracies more comprehensively than Schumpeter (1950). Downs conceptualised political parties as the equivalent of profit-seeking firms in the marketplace and argued that parties' vote-maximising behaviour should be the core of political analysis. One of Downs' lasting insights was that in a two-party system there is a tendency for parties to converge ideologically toward the centre of the left – right political continuum. Each party has a stable constituency; consequently they are each seeking to attract the same undecided voters, which creates the tendency to move to the centre. Later studies have analysed the behaviour of voters in equal detail and Downs himself studied voters' motives. In 1962 Buchanan and Tullock published *The Calculus of Consent*, which developed an analysis of voting procedures in political institutions, specifically examining the implications of majority voting rules and alternative procedures. They concluded that the complexity and unpredictability of outcomes from differing rules makes it essential to have 'fair' constitutional or voting procedures: by 'fair', they meant decision-making arrangements that are judged as fair in procedure irrespective of their outcome.

In *The Logic of Collective Action* (1965) Mancur Olson provided a penetrating analysis of the nature and problems of collective action in society and in organisations. Olson highlighted the 'free rider' problem, that is, the tendency for people not to participate in groups or organisations if they cannot be included in the benefits accruing from those groups' activities. William Niskanen (1971) analysed the behaviour of civil servants assuming individual rationality; he concluded that their behaviour reflected rational incentives despite being in a non-market environment. Public choice theorists have also addressed the problems associated with deriving preference functions as the basis for collective social choice, given the diversity of preferences within the political community. The classic work here is Arrow (1951) in which he expounds his famous 'impossibility theorem': this demonstrates the impossibility of aggregating individual preferences to some general social welfare function. Such analysis has been linked to the work on decision rules: for example, the different outcomes of using a majority rule rather than unanimity in voting procedures. This area of public choice theory has important implications for institutional design; if political arrangements are to maximise individual preferences and avoid the tyranny of the majority, certain decision-making procedures must be implemented. Public choice theorists have also studied the behaviour of political parties, governments, bureaucracies and the sources of public expenditure. It is these which are most relevant to New Right arguments since public choice analysis of these institutions tends to support the objectives of New Right politicians. Analysts have examined both the demand-side and the supply-side of public expenditure. The former dominated earlier analyses, as in the purported consequences of the competitive electoral process, while more recent work has focused on the dynamics within political institutions responsible for the supply of public goods and services.

The assumptions of public choice analysis

The microeconomic assumptions of public choice theory overlap with those of liberalism, reviewed in earlier chapters. The most striking overlap is the common assumption of methodological individualism, that is, all phenomena are reducible to individual behaviour; organic entities such as 'society' or the 'state' are comprehensible only in terms of the activities of their constitutive individuals. This implies that the rules and procedures which underpin the workings of political institutions are very important, but only in their implications for individualist behaviour. Norman Barry (1983) emphasises especially the methodological individual-ism of the public choice school: 'the libertarianism of the Virginia

School consists basically in it deeply individualistic approach to social affairs. Thus private property, the market economy and the capitalist order are acceptable if they result from the necessarily subjective choices of individuals. "Goods" and "bads" are the subjective experiences of individuals and there is no collective organic entity called "society" or the "public" which is not reducible to individual experiences' (p. 102). Public choice theorists are more comfortable with liberals than with conservatives and share many of the former's differences with conservative beliefs.

Individualism is not the only assumption made by public choice theorists, however. Obviously, it assumes rational maximising behaviour by all individuals regardless of their level of political activity and/or participation. Further, each individual creates the basis for their behaviour from a calculation of the relative costs and benefits of each course of action, as in conventional rational-choice models. As in classical economics, the central assumption of public choice theory is that the pursuit of selfish individual utility generates a desirable social order, though some public choice theory (such as the prisoners' dilemma – see Figure 4.1 on page 97 discovers difficulty with this assumption. It is further assumed that each individual has sufficient information to calculate her or his most rational course of action.

THE CONTRIBUTION OF PUBLIC CHOICE THEORY

Preference aggregation

Preference aggregation is a very important element of public choice theory, given that 'all decision-making mechanisms are procedures to aggregate non-homogeneous preferences' (Frey, 1978, p. 68). Society is made up of a large number of people, most of whom hold different opinions and preferences about issues: for example, there will be enormous diversity of opinion about schools or about tax laws. To derive a universally agreed preference from this heterogeneity for public policy-making is immensely difficult. And, in fact, Arrow (1951) has maintained that it is impossible: his 'impossibility theorem' stipulates four necessary conditions for the satisfactory aggregation of individual preferences for a collective social welfare function. By 'necessary conditions' Arrow means values that would be widely accepted as being required for socially acceptable decision-making. His conditions (see Mueller, 1979, ch. 10; Frey, 1978, ch. 6; Bonner, 1986, ch. 4) are: unanimity or the Pareto criterion, that is, individual preferences unopposed by others are included in the social ordering; non-dictatorship, that is, no individual can dictate his or her preference over others; transitivity or unrestricted domain, that is, all feasible preference alternatives for a social welfare function must be provided; and independence of irrelevant alternatives, that is, the choice between any given two alternatives does not take account of other alternatives. Using mathematical analysis Arrow concludes that such a social welfare function cannot be aggregated: that is, if all individuals rank in order their preferences regarding any issue (for example, pollution laws or level of public health provision) without any restrictions about how they order their preferences (that is, Arrow's four necessary conditions hold) majority voting would fail to produce an acceptable social preference function. This is an important conclusion for representative liberal democracies seeking to implement voters' interests. It is impossible for such societies to determine, by logical means, an agreed-social preference function which can then inform public policy. This is a serious problem for democratic societies whose supporters believe are capable of accurately representing individual preferences in national policy. Arrow's work has generated a stream of subsequent literature, much densely theoretical and mathematical; Arrow's important analysis remains intact.

The aggregation of individual preferences is rendered difficult by other phenomena studied by public choice theorists – for example, log-rolling and strategic voting. The former refers to how participants in a policy process – for example, interest groups or legislators – trade with each other when voting on policy decisions. This can distort true individual preferences: for example, if there are three voters for two issues it might be the case that under majority voting neither issue would succeed if treated separately; this creates incentives for two voters to give each other support for the issues. There is vote trading to pass the issues but at the price of compromising individual preferences. Public choice theorists argue that such log-rolling can result, in the long run, in excessive public expenditure, as Dunleavy (1986) observes: through log-rolling 'sectional interests struggle to commit taxpayers' money to serving their own private purposes, and in which winning coalitions of groups can use the political process to exploit those left in the minority' (p. 383).

The prisoners' dilemma: the necessity of collective choice and the problem of collective action

Free market economics maintains that the pursuit of individual self-interest generates collective good: the benefits of mutual exchange guided by an 'invisible hand' are so great as to outweigh alternative means of social organisation. But public choice theory suggests that this pursuit of individual selfish interest may not in fact generate mutually beneficial exchange. This occurs when the outcome of each actor pursuing their rational interests is in aggregate irrational for the society as a whole. This is illustrated by the 'prisoners' dilemma' where two prisoners are separated and face a number of choices, as Figure 4.1 indicates. Each can remain quiet and receive two years' imprisonment; each can confess, receive one years' imprisonment and implicate the other who will then receive twenty years. The 'rational' decision is to confess, but if each prisoner does this then both receive ten years in gaol: individual rationality has not been

FIGURE 6.1
The prisoners' dilemma

Prisoner X

		Keep quiet		Talk	
		(Cell 1)	−2	(Cell 4)	−1
Keep quiet					
		−2		−20	
Prisoner Y					
		(Cell 2)	−20	(Cell 3)	−10
Talk					
		−1		−10	

most beneficial. This example can be replaced with the scenario of thief versus voluntary exchange in the market: if two individuals face the options of stealing from each other or trading fairly it will be rational on an individual basis to steal rather than trade even though this will make each of them worse off. This suggests that co-operation within a judicial system enforced by an external legitimate authority will be preferable to the freely operating market. If, however, the two individuals calculate their rational options in terms of recurrent activities and exchanges they may well consider it rational to co-operate without the assistance of an external agency.

Two important consequences follow from the prisoners' dilemma. First, regarding the provision of public goods, the prisoners' dilemma suggests the need for government and rule enforcement. As Mueller (1979) observes:

> the movement from cell 3 to cell 1 is a Pareto optimal move that lifts the individuals out of a Hobbesian state of nature. An agreement to make such a move is a form of 'constitutional contract' establishing the property rights and behavioural constraints of each individual. The existence of these rights is undoubtedly a necessary precondition for the creation of the 'postconstitutional contracts', which make up a system of voluntary exchange. Problems of collective choice arise with the departure from Hobbesian anarchy, and are coterminous with the existence of recognizable groups and communities. (p. 12)

The second implication is problematic for New Right arguments. The pursuit of self-interest as advocated by New Right liberals does not necessarily result in a socially optimal outcome as Hodgson (1984) summarises:

> the sum total of individually 'rational' actions is not necessarily optimal or rational for society as a whole. Self-interested behaviour may be collectively self-defeating. This undermines the idea of a benevolent 'invisible hand' in the market system, in which the sum total of individual and selfish actions leads to a socially desirable outcome. In exactly the same way as the prisoners' dilemma, the market system can produce a result which goes against the wishes of the majority. The New Right

claim that the same can be said of democratic voting procedures. However, there is an important difference: democracy involves some conscious overall regulation, and the possibility that mistakes will be debated and understood, leading to a guided change in direction; the market permits no overall guidance other than that of a shaky, erratic and untrustworthy invisible hand. (p. 45)

The prisoners' dilemma points both to the problems arising from the pursuit of self-interest and to the need for some form of government to provide rules within which economic activity can occur. The pursuit of rational behaviour results in widespread conflict; to create desirable social and economic conditions it is necessary to have negotiations in society preferably through an agreed authority, that is, the state.

The prisoners' dilemma also applies to the provision of public or collective goods as discussed in the previous chapter. Rational self-interest will ensure that no one individual provides these services. If public goods are provided privately it is almost impossible to exclude others from availing of them, which once again raises the need for a state (see Olson, 1965). This is known as the collective action problem: it is not rational for individuals either to contribute to or to participate in the production of certain goods and services if they cannot be excluded from using them despite not having contributed to their cost. For example, national defence benefits all members of a country regardless of whether or not they pay taxes. This is one of the reasons why taxes are compulsory: without them, public goods would not be produced and everyone in the community would be worse off. The prisoners' dilemma increases in significance the larger the group it is applied to: thus while it may be possible for two or three individuals to co-operate on mutually beneficial terms, such arrangements are logistically precluded for a modern political community. Thus the collective action problem increases with the number of people involved. At a national level, a good example of the problems associated with collective action is provided by car pollution: many people contribute individually to pollution with their car fumes but if only one or two people alter their cars to reduce the fumes released this will have little impact upon the problem. Meanwhile everyone in the community is made worse off as a consequence of continued car pollution. To resolve this problem requires the imposition of a solution by an external agency – most obviously the state.

PUBLIC CHOICE ANALYSIS AND POLITICS

Public choice theorists have expended considerable energy on the analysis of political institutions including the state, processes of representation, voting procedures, political parties, voters and bureaucrats. The focus of this chapter is on analyses which have been interpreted by New Right advocates as supporting their arguments. This concerns public choice analyses of voters, politicians and bureaucrats. It is the consequences of the behaviour of these groups which overlap with New Right criticisms of excessive government (that is, public sector) pandering to the desires of special interest-groups.

Political parties and voters

The economic theory of political party competition originates with Schumpeter (1950) and is formalised by Downs (1957). Downs' central hypothesis is that political parties develop their policy objectives in order exclusively to achieve electoral success rather than the other way around. In contrast with the conventional economic view that states and governments serve to maximise society's welfare, public choice theory 'regards the state and government as institutions composed of selfish individuals' (Frey, 1978, p. 90), with the government's takeover of an activity leading to an optimal outcome 'only if specific conditions are fulfilled' (p. 90) (the most important of these being that 'parties compete for votes on a perfectly functioning political market' (p. 90)). The emphasis is on the microeconomic assumptions of actors (egoism, self-interest) and context (a perfect political 'market'), with utility maximisation and rational action by the parties also assumed.

Similar rational egotistic assumptions are ascribed to voters by public choice theorists. Thus Tullock (1976) argues that, 'voters and customers are essentially the same people . . . There is no strong reason to believe . . . behaviour is radically different in the two environments. We assume that in both he will choose the product or candidate he thinks is the best bargain for him' (p. 5). Tullock is unequivocal about the extent to which self-interest or selfishness is at the core of human behaviour; he writes:

> Both the market and democratic government are institutional structures through which the bulk of us, as customers or as voters, try to achieve our goals. The bulk of us also, as producers, find ourselves employed either in the private or the government sector; and most of us in both are also primarily seeking personal goals. As a general proposition, we shall achieve the well-being of society for the most part only if there is some private benefit for us in taking action to that end ... The difference between government and private employment is simply that the limitations within which the individual operates differ. In general the constraints put upon people's behaviour in the market are more 'efficient' than those in government. (pp. 6–7)

Because voters are not immediately aware of either the costs or revenue source of government programmes the production of government goods and services is inherently less efficient than work in the private sector, according to public choice theorists; if voters related these costs more directly to the taxes they pay, support for government programmes will evaporate considerably. Tullock and others argue that there are really no constraints on what politicians can offer the electorate, and that the general propensity is for those politicians to get elected who offer specific goods and services rather than those with strong and well worked out policy proposals (though the two need hardly be mutually exclusive). One implication of this analysis has been developed by Brittan (1975), noted briefly in Chapter 2, that the continued demands of voters for public goods will inevitably have a negative affect on the political system since eventually demands will outrace resources. Interest groups, too, can affect the supply of public goods: the latter provide a stimulus for individuals to join interest groups.

Mancur Olson has written extensively about interest groups, collective goods, and collective action. In *The Logic of Collective Action* (1965) Olson argued that individuals only organise together when there is a specific benefit to be gained which could not otherwise be acquired, and from which individuals can be excluded if it is provided by others. This means it is easier for smaller groups and groups sharing similar characteristics to be formed: for example, it is easier for the leading industrialists in a particular industry to unite than for *all* consumers or taxpayers. Olson suggests that such groups can have a powerful effect on public policy harmful to other weaker and less effectively organised groups. In *The Rise and Decline of Nations* (1982) he refers to 'distributional coalitions' as such powerful groups including trade unions which have a disproportionate influence upon public policy. By implication, such interest groups or distributional coalitions are inefficient, largely uncontrolled by voters, require additional government regulation and resistant to change or innovation, the central dynamic of the market. Olson argues that the different economic performances of countries such as Britain and Germany, and within the United States, between the North-east and South-west, can be explained, to an important extent, by the presence or absence of these distributional coalitions. Thus, large effectively-organised groups have a disproportionate influence upon government and the economy compared to the unorganised voters. The former also encourage the growth of government programmes, uncontrolled by voters' preferences.

The behaviour of bureaucrats

Public choice theorists assume bureaucrats behave rationally, like voters and politicians, or like industrialists and consumers in any other area of society and economy. As Tullock (1976) asserts, 'like everyone else, bureaucrats presumably try to improve their own utility'. He continues thus: 'their utility, again like everyone else's, is partly based upon their immediate ability to consume goods and partly on their appreciation of good things happening to other people. In other words, they are partly selfish and partly public-interested' (p. 27).

These arguments have been most systematically developed by Niskanen (1971); he develops his arguments in mathematical terms but his thesis is straightforward enough. He is concerned with public goods production resulting from the quasi-independent activities of bureaucrats. Consequently he is interested in the nature of their environment, the sorts of incentives and inducements they work with and the rewards they seek. For Niskanen, the very essence of bureaucrats is that they are self-interested budget-maximisers, and the pursuit of this self-interest results in the expansion of government. His major substantive conclusion is that government is invariably oversupplied as a consequence of the nature of bureaucrats' behaviour in their particular environment. His major policy proposal is to introduce competition into government bureaucracy.

In Niskanen's model there are two types of actors: bureaucrats (the suppliers of public goods and services) and politicians (the sponsors of government production of goods). Their relationship is that of a bilateral monopoly, that is, the bureaucrats are the sole suppliers of public goods and services and politicians are the only buyers of bureaucratic outputs. Each has a distinctive objective: for bureaucrats, it is to maximise their agency or ministry budget, while for politicians it is to maximise votes. The outome of this relationship between bureaucrats and politicians is the oversupply of public goods and services when compared to what would be optimal according to citizen preferences. Niskanen argues that the bureaucrats' position of monopoly supplier also enables them to hold a monopoly of information about the production function of any given good. Bureaucrats consequently exaggerate the cost estimate for producing any given good or service. If the monopolistic nature of the bureaucracy was eliminated, or at least reduced, the supply of public goods and services would be more efficient, Niskanen contends. One might, of course, question whether profitability is an appropriate criterion for public goods.

Given that bureaucrats have no real financial inducements from their bureaucratic position, what are their incentives? Niskanen (1971) lists the following, 'salary, perquisites of the office, public reputation, power, patronage, output of the bureau, ease of making changes and ease in managing the bureau' (p. 38), all of which (except the last two) are a function of the size of the bureau's budget. By implication, bureaucrats attempt to maximise the budget of their bureau or department, within the constraint of politicians' budgetary control which is usually assumed to be fairly weak. The policy implications of such public choice analyses of bureaucratic behaviour are clear: public monopolies should be reduced to a minimum; budget requests and appropriations should be much more vigorously stated and defended; and competition should be increased within public bureaucracies to increase efficiency and productivity. Niskanen (1973) favours this last option: 'the most important change would be to increase competition among bureaus. Competition is generally regarded as undesirable or, at best, in deference to certain institutional traditions, as tolerable. The major structural changes in the US federal government since the Second World War have reduced the competition among bureaus' (pp. 37–8). More radical proposals entail reducing the public sector entirely or introducing private initiatives into whole sections of public services such as those pursued by the Thatcher Government in the National Health Service (see Dunleavy, 1986a, on public choice and privatisation). Niskanen's study is more provocative than cogent (Goodin, 1982). He attributes too much power to bureaucrats, unfairly reduces their motivations to personal ones, ignoring the possibility that they are committed to the realisation or maintenance of certain policy objectives (Goodin, 1982; Gurr and King, 1987). Niskanen also assumes that bureaucrats will instinctively exploit their position as monopolists of information, by relying upon the 'bare-faced lie . . . The problem with [this strategy] is that the liar must keep his lies down to believable proportions or he loses credibility, which costs him dearly in the future as people begin examining his claims far more critically than before' (Goodin, 1982, p. 26). However, such difficulties with Niskanen's thesis have never seriously concerned those New Right advocates who seized upon his central thesis to support their criticisms of bureaucrats and the size of the public sector.

THE NEW RIGHT AND PUBLIC CHOICE ANALYSIS: POLICIES FOR REFORM

It is plain that concern with the individual and individual rights is central to both public choice and New Right theorists; intellectually, each stems from the liberal political economy tradition. This leads each to a concern with the role of the individual and to analytically assuming individual rationality and behaviour as the basis of social action. And both New Right and public choice theorists are inherently conservative in their analysis and implications given the assumptions used in their work. Thus where New Right politicians have engaged in politics to seek a reduced state and increased privatisation as means of maximising economic growth and freedom, so public choice theorists produce models demonstrating the results of utility-maximisation by voters, bureaucrats and politicians with implications for change.

Most public choice prescriptions for constitutional and political institutional change have been formulated by Americans for the American polity. They reflect a fundamental concern with individual liberty: the public interest, for Buchanan (1975) at least, must maximise individual liberty. Political institutions must be designed to facilitate this by placing limitations on the activity of self-interested politicians and bureaucrats. As Barry (1983) observes of James Buchanan's work: 'he has been concerned with the *design* of institutions which reflect individual preferences more accurately than orthodox democracy does. Under simple majority-rule procedures, competition for votes encourages coalitions of minorities to form which violate individual property rights' (p. 103). Barry continues thus:

> Instead of limiting government by reference to morality, Buchanan hopes to achieve the same effect by reference to a *social decision procedure*. The market is obviously acceptable, because it is a process of uncoerced exchanges in which no one is harmed, but for those things that have to be decided politically ... his initial preference is *unanimity*, the political analogue of the Pareto-optimality principle of free market economics, in which no change is acceptable unless everyone agrees. This obviously puts the status quo in a privileged position because it is always superior to any change which *harms at least one person*. (pp. 103–4)

Other reforms include constitutional amendments to limit the budget to a specified percentage of gross national produce, insisting that precise revenue sources are identified for proposed government programmes, a constitutional amendment requiring a balanced budget by removing politicians' capacity to provide increased goods and services through deficit-spending.

Public choice theorists also seek changes in the structure of bureaucracies. This includes altering the incentive system for public servants, introducing competitive schemes into government by allowing several bureaucrats or groups of bureaucrats to provide the same service. In the American context, public choice theorists favour a greater reliance upon local governments since 'the existence of many governments allows the testing of many alternatives and provides a semblance of competition. People can point to successful alternatives or even "vote with their feet" when the government taxes them too much or is inefficient' (Shaw, 1985, p. 80). Greater use of referenda is also advocated by public choice theorists. In general, a preference for the decentralisation of decision-making is found in the writings of public choice theorists since they believe that this allows individual preferences to prevail over the tyranny of majorities. The popular movement against taxation in the state of California in the late 1970s (Proposition 13) confirms the public choice argument that subnational governments are more representative in the sense of maximising the expression of individual preferences; in this instance, tax rates were reduced. As Sugden (1981) notes, 'the market system ... is a particularly decentralised procedure for decision-making. For this reason it provides a particularly effective defence of the interests and freedoms of individuals and minorities against the tyranny of majorities' (p. 198).

An important caveat must be attached here. The market does not maximise individual choice and preference satisfaction for those who cannot participate in it (for example, the sick, the handicapped, some unemployed people). Thus, much hangs on the distribution of property rights underlying the market system and shaping individual participation in it. It might well be argued that the market prevents the tyranny of majorities by institutionalising, through the system of property rights and ownership, the tyranny of minorities – private property owners. Private property ownership is central to the market system and is thus the basis for success and power; this means that those weakly placed in the distribution of property are less well favoured.

In *The Limits of Liberty* Buchanan (1975) seeks to construct a constitutional contract specifying the bases of social organisation which will promote and protect individual preferences. His account of the state begins with the assumption of 'property rights', and hence private property, naturally distributed between individuals (the 'Constitutional Contract') which provides the basis for agreement on state institutions (a 'post-constitutional contract'). The state provides the institutional structures and rules for the social and economic order derivative of property rights, which also define the nature of exchange – competitive and co-operative – in the economy at large. The state takes two main forms, moving from a minimalist 'protective state' which guarantees private property and the enforcement of contracts and agreements to a 'productive state' which actively intervenes in the market through the production of public goods. Active intervention by the state has social benefits for the population: the state can provide those public goods not likely to be generated within the market and it can offset market failures by improved information flows. Buchanan would prefer the state's operation to be based on unanimity but recognises the impracticality of this in large polities and accepts constitution-ally specified majority rule. Buchanan is searching for a state form which lies 'between anarchy and leviathan'. Therefore, he argues for state institutions built upon a constitution specifying the primacy of property rights, which places careful limitations on the role of the state distinguishing between its different branches. And, individual rational utility functions imply a preference for a state which 'minimises the maximum tax share which can be extracted from the economy' (Alt and Chrystal, 1983, p. 30).

Thus, where public choice assumptions underlie a concept of the state, certain implications follow. The state exists to protect and promote private property rights (the narrow 'protective state' conception) initially, but expands to provide certain public goods which produce net social benefits (the broader 'productive state' conception). The extent of the latter should be constitutionally based and regulated. But it is quite evident that public expenditure should not go much beyond the more narrowly-defined public goods and services of economists resultant principally upon externalities, market failures and some narrowly conceived social needs.

It further follows from Buchanan and others that tax levels should be strictly controlled since they constitute both a reduction of individual freedom (to dispose of one's own income as one chooses) and may be used recklessly by elected representatives. The need to place limitations and constraints upon politicians and bureaucrats motivates many of the proposals of public choice theorists. Buchanan (1978) summarises this point:

> because people will tend to maximize their own utilities, institutions must be designed so that individual behaviour will further the interests of the group, small or large, local or national.

The challenge to us is one of constructing, or re-constructing, a political order that will channel the self-serving behaviour of participants towards the common good in a manner that comes as close as possible to that described to us by Adam Smith with respect to the economic order. (p. 17)

An obvious problem with this schema is that it takes little account of the power and role of large organised groups in the political system. Given that many New Right analysts (see Chapter 2) excoriate the effect of organised groups on government expenditure, this is an extraordinary oversight. Coercion does not just arise from the market place but results also from large organised groups and corporations exercising disproportionate power in the marketplace. New Right writers disapprove of this phenomenon but remain short on solutions to the problem. Not all public choice scholars are necessarily conservative in their policy preferences. For example, Mancur Olson, despite writing about the power of organised interest groups, remains an advocate of a strong role for government in addressing those social needs created and ignored by the market, as does Anthony Downs (see Shaw, 1985).

CONCLUSION

Public choice theory has useful insights to offer in the areas of collective choice and the behaviour of political institutions and actors – bureaucrats, politicians and voters. It would be churlish to ignore these analyses or to overlook their implications, and public choice arguments now influence a wide range of social science work (McLean, 1986). But equally, many aspects of public choice theory can be queried, while the policy prescriptions which they offer are neither the most obvious nor helpful. Concerning assumptions, the major debate must revolve around public choice's dependence on rationality and utility-maximisation (be that of votes, budgets or individual preferences). For example, ascribing rationality to the activity of voting is dubious, given the marginal impact of any single vote (though empirical evidence does indicate more obviously rational behaviour when the outcome is close), how can people's willingness to vote be explained? Barry (1970) suggests alternative reasons: 'it may well be that both the costs and the (suitably discounted) benefits of voting are so low that it is simply not worth being "rational" about it. Thus habit, self-expression, duty and other things have plenty of room to make themselves felt' (p. 23). Such criticisms do not concern New Right liberals greatly since they are mainly concerned with the outcomes of the political process, namely, expanded bureaucracy. It is, of course, the lack of a budget constraint upon voters which partly contributes to this situation. But in many other areas of political and economic behaviour the appropriateness of the utility-maximisation assumption must be challenged (see Sen, 1982, for an extended critique). It is also the case that many of the reforms suggested by public choice theorists, especially those concerned with constitutional clauses, are neither particularly practical nor necessarily likely to succeed in their stated objective. Many of these proposals emanate from American scholars and have little direct applicability to the British political system, especially those concerning constitutional specification (see Dunleavy, 1983).

7

The Thatcher Government and State Activity

INTRODUCTION

This chapter, and the next, examine the experience of two contemporary governments influenced in different degrees by the New Right economic and political theories reviewed in this book. This necessarily implies considerable compression, but is allowable given the primary aim of assessing the influence of liberal theories upon the policies of the Thatcher Government: these concern reducing public spending and the public sector, adopting monetarist economic targets, privatising state enterprises, and weakening trade unions in the political economy. The main theme of these policy objectives comes, to some extent, from liberal precepts: reducing the government's role in the economy, giving greater power to market forces and limiting the public sector. Whether the Thatcher Government has succeeded in these aims is a different issue, considered subsequently. Concentrating upon the liberal sources of the Thatcher Government's public policy means neglecting other aspects of their policy: for example, foreign affairs and the pursuit of tougher law and order measures. These issues are important but the main interest here is with the influence of New Right liberalism. The chapter begins with the Thatcher leadership in the Conservative Party and concludes with interpretations of this Government produced in the academic literature.

The Conservative Party led by Margaret Thatcher has won two successive general elections, and the Thatcher government has now been in office for seven years – an unprecedented post-war record. It has been distinguished from previous administrations by its public commitment to a set of economic and political theories intended to initiate a radical break with post-war politics. Despite the enormous

110

unemployment generated by the pursuit of these policies, New Right liberal arguments have influenced profoundly the content of political debate in the British polity. However, neither the 1979 nor the 1983 elections represented more than partial mandates from the electorate, exaggerated by the first-past-the-post electoral system. Thus, in 1983 the Conservative Party won 42.5 per cent of the vote but 60 per cent of the parliamentary seats. Further, the 1979 election must be set against an unpopular Labour administration, while the 1983 election was contested by the Thatcher government after a successful military campaign and against a divided and weak opposition.

THE CONSERVATIVE PARTY

The February 1975 election of Margaret Thatcher as Edward Heath's successor brought a significant change to the political and economic ideas expressed by the Conservative Party. Under its new leader the Party espoused the superior virtues of the free market in contrast to the state interventionist policy characteristic of post-war policy. The economic doctrine of monetarism was adopted by the Party along with criticisms of welfare state institutions. The Conservative Party was committed also to individual liberty and to the support of traditional institutions such as the family, recalling the individualism of the pre-Keynesian welfare state era. How did the Thatcher leadership fit within the Conservative Party?

The three traditions of the Conservative Party

Like most political parties, the Conservatives are a coalition of diverse interests. Blake's (1970) major study of the evolution of the Conservative Party and Beer's (1969) account of the Party's formation provide a picture of the dominant strands within the Tory Party (see Moran, 1985). These include, first, a pragmatic tradition: the belief that the Conservative Party is not bound rigidly to any particular ideology but, rather, can adapt successfully to shifting cirumstances. The capacity of the Conservative Party to endure lends some credence to this view. Exponents of a second tradition explain the Conservatives' durability by their consistent support of certain key values. For example, Conservatives have steadfastly emphasised freedom and patriotism. However, as Moran (1985, p. 99) observes, this interpretation must be treated cautiously: the meaning of terms like freedom and private property have changed radically over the last two hundred years. It is probably better to recognise the Party's capacity for pragmatic response to shifting conditions, which may mean dropping cherished values.

The Party's third strand is very important. This is the mixture of the 'Tory' tradition of belief in a strong state and state authority as the basis for a durable social order with the 'liberal' tradition based on free market principles. This distinction corresponds to that between conservatism and liberalism established in chapter 2 of this book. And the contradiction between these two elements is important in analysis of the Thatcher Government. For example, the disagreements within the Party about legalising Sunday trading derive from this contradiction: liberal free marketeers want to exercise every opportunity to lift restrictions upon market forces, while conservatives express concern about the threat to family values presented by Sunday shopping. Moran (1985, p. 100), amongst others, warns against expecting too literal a manifestation of this distinction; rather, all Conservatives and Tory Governments must reach some accord between these two propensities. However, during certain periods the relationship between these two strands becomes particularly strained, which is reflected in policy. Under the Thatcher Government this has been apparent: this Government draws upon liberalism for policy and conservatism for the affects of such policies, despite the contradictory relationship between them. And Government critics, especially those of its record on civil liberties and on law and order, have stressed the increased reliance upon the non-liberal tradition of the Conservative Party despite the avowed pursuit of liberal principles.

There are then diverse strands within the Conservative Party. However, while the rhetoric of the Thatcher leadership has drawn upon both liberalism and conservativism, it is the former which has been the dominant influence on policy. As advanced in Chapter 2, liberal theories provide the policy substance and electoral appeal for New Right arguments; conservatism is a secondary doctrine concerned with the problematic consequences arising from liberal policies. It is the third tradition within the Tory Party which is the most relevant for analysing the Thatcher Government. Other elements of the Party – such as the moderate Reform Group and

Francis Pym's new Centre group – remain very critical of the Thatcher leadership but, as yet, exercise little influence upon policy decisions.

THE POLICIES OF THE THATCHER GOVERNMENT

Monetarism

Economic crisis was endemic throughout the 1970s, affecting electoral outcomes and Government policy. The crisis assumed its most vivid form in the International Monetary Fund's 1976 intervention (through the provision of a loan on strict terms) in James Callaghan's Labour Administration. In order to reduce the balance of payments deficit, control inflation and lower public sector borrowing that Government was forced to increase its foreign debt and to cut public expenditure. In a famous 1976 Conference speech Prime Minister James Callaghan announced the end of 'borrowing and spending' as a viable policy solution to economic crisis: 'We cannot now, if we ever could, spend our way out of recession'. This position was anticipated by the Chancellor, Denis Healey, in his January 1975 East Leeds speech which expounded Friedmanite monetarism. So by 1979, and the election of the Thatcher government, Keynesian policies were already long abandoned – formally by at least three years. Under Thatcher's leadership the Conservative Party had made monetarism an explicit cornerstone of its election platform. In contrast to the Labour government's reluctant adoption of monetarist policy the Thatcher Government wholeheartedly embraced monetarist doctrine (Riddell, 1983). Several studies (Keegan, 1984; Loney, 1986) have discussed the conversion within the Conservative party under the Thatcher leadership to monetarist policy.

The principles of monetarism were explicated in Chapter 4. The central belief is that the money supply is the cause of inflation: careful control and monitoring of the rate of change in the money supply is claimed to be sufficient to control inflation. The doctrine is closely associated with the work of Milton Friedman, who has also been an active publicist of monetarist policy. In a major study of money supply levels in the United States and changes in prices, Friedman claimed to find a meaningful correlation: he argued that the rate of change in the money supply determined the latter; that is, increases in prices followed temporally upon increases in the money supply. Government monetary policy should aim, therefore, to control the rate of change in the money supply to ensure it remains within specified levels; this would lead to a reduction in inflation, the major problem according to the Tories in the mid-1970s. Monetarists, including Friedman, are highly critical of government economic policies derived from Keynesianism: they consider that 'fine-tuning' the economy (see Chapter 4 above) has damaging long-term affects. Friedman further disputed the Phillips curve (that is, the alleged inverse relationship between unemployment and prices), arguing that government policy to maintain full employment pushes unemployment below its 'natural' level which leads to inflation; (the term 'natural rate' of unemployment is very controversial). For monetarists government economic policy should be minimal, concerned exclusively with controlling the money supply over the long run rather than with short-term efforts to maintain full employment or with stabilisation policy. Such monetarist principles appealed to the new Thatcher Government. In contrast to the discredited Keynesian economics, monetarism promised a solution to the perennial problem of inflation.

Ideologically, monetarism was attractive because it implied a small role for the Government in the economy, which fitted well with the Thatcher Government's liberal free markets ideas. Most monetarists, however, want a smaller state role than do Mrs Thatcher and her associates. The minimal state, prescribed by many monetarists, has responsibility for controlling the money supply (conventionally defined as notes, coins and bank balances). This requires the specification, and adherence to, a fixed rate of money supply to the economy, and eschewing unplanned, short-term government interventions into the money supply. Government policy should address inflation: its eradication facilitates economic growth and employment. If inflation was reduced and the Government removed market distortions and imperfections, the framework for economic growth would prevail. The Government should undertake no more than this according to monetarism.

Monetarism implemented   The Thatcher Government translated this theory into two policy objectives, the first of which reflected most directly monetarist policy prescriptions: a controlled money supply – that is, a government policy which set a fixed annual monetary target and ensured that the growth of money did not exceed this. Thus, as recorded in their expenditure plans, the Government planned 'to bring down the rate of inflation and interest rates by curtailing the growth of the money supply and controlling Government borrowing' (HMSO, 1980; p. 3). The 1979 Government established a medium-term financial strategy embodying the fixed monetary growth rate principle with targets for the annual growth of the money supply over the ensuing four years: the definition of money was sterling M3, cash plus bank deposits. The targets were 7–11 per cent for the financial year 1980–81, 6–10 per cent for 1981–82, 5–9 per cent for 1982–83, and 4–8 per cent for 1983–84. The Government also reduced standard taxation levels: basic rate of income tax dropped to 30 per cent from 33 per cent and the tax on unearned income dropped to 60 per cent from 83 per cent. The second element of the Thatcher government's monetary policy was to reduce the public sector borrowing requirement (PSBR); this would in turn cut public spending and hence state activity. The objective of reducing the PSBR comes only very indirectly from monetarist principles; most obviously, reducing the role of the state ties with monetarism. But in strict Friedmanite monetarist theory the size of the PSBR holds no causal relationship with inflation. The PSBR reflects the growth of public expenditure which reflects partly the pressures of inflation; also if the PSBR is increasing this can be associated with a rise in the money supply (defined as £M3). The PSBR consists of the amount borrowed by central government, local authorities, and public bodies from the private sector and overseas, netting out transactions internal to the public sector; it is thus a net measure of borrowing. Therefore, in order to control the money supply it is necessary to reduce partly the PSBR. In the terms of the Thatcher Government 'medium term financial strategy', reducing public spending would reduce both the PSBR and the money supply, in order to lead to a reduction in inflation (Whiteley, 1985). Reducing the PSBR was viewed also as a means of freeing market forces.

For Mrs Thatcher, the connection between the PSBR and inflation was very clear and important; replying to the 1977 Budget statement she argued that 'the increase in inflation . . . has not come about in any way through wage inflation but, indirectly, through the level of the public sector borrowing requirement and public spending' (Hansard, 1977, col. 291). Some commentators have disputed the relationship between inflation and the PSBR but for the Thatcher Government there was little uncertainty about the connection.

The failure of monetarist policy   The monetarist targets set by the Thatcher Government have by now been abandoned, and the Government has failed to adhere to these targets in its public policy (see Table 7.1). As Whiteley (1985) concludes, 'monetarism in practice had not worked in the way described by Friedman . . . . The government had failed to control the money supply in line with targets, and at the same time there was a huge loss of output and employment resulting from the policies which it had pursued' (p. 11). Unemployment has reached unprecedented levels under the Thatcher Government: inflation has been dramatically lowered but the cost in unemployment has been enormous. Economic growth has not been as abundant as predicted by the Thatcher Government, given its policy course: by 1984 neither manufacturing output nor investment had reached their 1979 levels. In his 1985 Mansion House speech the Chancellor Nigel Lawson effectively acknowledged the Government's abandonment of monetarist economic targets. The Thatcher Government can no longer be viewed, in a strict sense, as adhering to monetarist economic doctrine: it has consistently failed to meet its own money supply

TABLE 7.1
Economic indicators under the Thatcher Government

	1977	1978	1979	1980	1981	1982	1983	1984	1985
Foreign public debt/GDP (%)	0.99	1.36	1.98	2.99	3.64	3.76	3.60	3.56	2.96
Real GDP (%)	1.0	3.6	2.1	−2.2	−1.3	1.8	3.2	1.6	2.4
Consumer prices (%)	15.8	8.3	13.5	17.9	11.9	8.6	4.6	5.0	6.1
Money supply growth (%)	20.8	16.3	9.1	4.0	17.7	11.3	11.1	15.4	18.1
Unemployment		5.7	5.3	6.8	10.5	12.2	13.0	11.7	11.9

Sources: International Economic Statistics (Craig Gardner/Price Waterhouse Economic Consultants in association with the International Economic Appraisal Service of The Economist Publications Ltd), June 1986. For Unemployment figures: *Employer Gazette* (Department of Employment), January 1984 and October 1986. Note that the method of calculating unemployment totals has been altered by this Government innumerable times over the last seven years which makes comparison between years difficult.

targets and the Government has been much more interventionist than monetarism prescribes. Economically, the Thatcher Government has presided over a mounting crisis: unemployment has continued to rise since 1979. The Select Committee on Overseas Trade of the House of Lords presented a damning Report in October 1985 of the Government's failure to generate adequate economic growth or industrial development, and was pessimistic about long-term prospects: indeed, the Select Committee predicted balance of payments crises, increased unemployment and 'stagflation'.

The Report focused particularly on the collapse of Britain's manufacturing base since the late 1970s, which they argued to be a consequence, in part, of the Government's tight monetary policy. The steady decrease in North Sea oil revenues is also viewed very ominously by the Select Committee. On the credit side, inflation has fallen since 1979, economic growth and productivity have increased but the price in unemployment has been very high, with between three and four million being out of work depending on how the figures are calculated. The rise in productivity must be qualified: it has increased when considered in abstract from employment levels, since depression-induced unemployment necessarily increases productivity rates. The Government continues to offer sanguine budgetary predictions about economic growth, employment and inflation but there is little evidence either of a coherent economic strategy underpinning these objectives or of significant improvement in the economy. The Thatcher Government's monetarist convictions have dissipated without being replaced by anything else – and there has been no substantial improvement in economic conditions. In fact, economic conditions deteriorated from 1979 to 1986, most spectacularly in unemployment.

Monetarist critics of the Government frequently maintain that it is, in fact, not monetarism which has failed, but this Government's efforts to implement its prescriptions. For example, such critics attribute the failure to control the money supply to the Thatcher Government. Some, therefore, continue to believe in monetarist doctrines. But an alternative interpretation is that it is monetarist doctrines which are faulty rather than governmental resolve. It is the latter view which is supported by the experience of this Government's economic policies. If the economy was a 'pure' nineteenth-century capitalist one, then perhaps monetarist principles might have greater relevance; but no economy of the advanced industrial countries approximates this pure capitalist form.

The attack on trade unions A core part of the Thatcher Government's economic strategy was to weaken the position of trade unions in the British political economy. The 1970–74 Heath Conservative Government's conflict with the National Union of Miners remained particularly galling to the Conservative Party; in addition, New Right liberals such as Hayek had attributed an important part of the blame for Britain's economic problems to restrictive trade union practices in the mid-1970s. Hayek (1978) denounced especially 'wage rigidities' (that is, the inability of wages to respond sufficiently to market forces because of the capacity of trade unions to control them):

> it is generally accepted that the most severe difficulties of contemporary economic policy are due to what is usually described as the rigidity of wages, which means in effect that both the wage structure and the level of money wages have increasingly become impervious to market forces ... [Even by the 1920s] Britain had ... the oldest, most firmly entrenched and most comprehensive trade union movement in the world which by its wage policy had largely succeeded in establishing a wage structure determined much more by considerations of 'justice', which meant little else than the preservation of traditional wage differentials, and which made those changes in relative wages demanded by an adaptation to changed conditions 'politically unfeasible'. (pp. 109–10; see also Hayek, 1980)

To reduce the power of trade unions the Government introduced the Employment Act in 1980. This Act first attempted to limit the 'closed shop' practice by entitling non-union workers to sue the union concerned and employers for damages. It made the introduction of further closed shops dependent upon support from 80 per cent of the work-force in any work-place. The Act sought to encourage postal balloting for leadership elections by providing finance for the expenses of this arrangement. The 1980 Act also placed restrictions upon picketing both in the numbers of pickets and in their legal status; these restrictions were intended to limit secondary picketing. The objective of these measures was to weaken trade union power and to try to facilitate the election of 'moderate' leaders (Crouch, 1982; McBride, 1986). In 1980 the Government also altered the payment of social security benefits to strikers and their families, on the assumption (by no means always justified) that they received strike pay from their union.

These changes in trade union legislation were pressed further in 1982 with a second bill introduced by James Prior's successor at Employment, Norman Tebbit. It extended balloting provisions within unions, including secret votes for strike action; it also made union funds liable to actions for damages (up to £250,000) for unlawful strikes, and to sequestration for contempt. These latter remedies have been prominent in subsequent industrial conflicts under the Thatcher government, including the divisive and bloody 1984–85 miners' strike. The ferocity of this dispute, both verbally and physically, have left an indelible imprint upon British industrial relations. From the Conservative Government's point of view, the eventual 1984–85 failure of the National Union of Miners under Arthur Scargill's leadership and the emergence of an alternative miners' union was a major step in their efforts to weaken trade unions. Subsequent attempts as mass strikes – such as Jimmy Knapp's National Union of Railworkers' London underground strike in 1985 – failed to elicit support from union members, as did the ballots amongst British Rail engineers, guards and signalmen in 1985 and 1986. By its annual conference in 1986, the TUC had come largely to accept the requirements for postal balloting on strike action and elections. Also, several major unions, for example the Amalgamated Union of Engineering Workers, have negotiated 'strike-free' agreements, an unlikely decision ten years earlier (Bassett, 1986).

The Conservative Government's union legislation has restricted substantially trade union activity and limited leadership scope. Strikes must now be agreed by secret ballot (introduced in the 1984 Trade Union Act), while leadership elections are conducted by postal ballot. The scope of picketing – especially secondary picketing – has been sharply limited, and unions can be held liable for damages during strike periods. The closed shop must be given 80 per cent support every five years by the work force in each work place. The economic rationale for these measures is to subject wage levels to market forces and thereby to eliminate wage rigidities; certainly the latter have been weakened, but the economic consequence has been increased unemployment rather than prosperity. The political rationale has been quite explicitly to weaken trade unions as an interest group representing their members' interests in the political economy. The Conservative Party in particular has a legacy of hostility toward unions and a legacy of direct conflict with them over government policy. Thus, for the Thatcher Government a weakening of union power has been a central objective of its economic and political policies. The consequences of its monetarist policies – massive unemployment – has placed unions and their members in a vulnerable position, less capable of militant resistance to the Government's policies. Economic problems have weakened the position of unions while strengthening the power of the Government to pursue its anti-union objectives. The decline of full-time employment and rise of part-time work – where employees are predominantly women (see Chapter 10) – has further weakened the power of trade unions.

Rolling back the state: public spending and government priorities

Reducing public expenditure was a part of the Thatcher Government's economic strategy: 'the Government is determined not merely to halt the growth of public expenditure but progressively to reduce it' (HMSO, 1980, p. 5). While it was argued this would reduce the public sector borrowing requirement (PSBR), thereby lowering the money supply and inflation, the Government's commitment to cutting public spending also reflected its antipathy, based in liberalism, toward the public sector. For New Right liberals, public expenditure is an undesirable intrusion by the state into the market-place, which must be kept to a minimum; this view extends to welfare spending. According to New Right liberals the welfare state places unnecessary tax burdens upon the electorate, particularly entrepreneurs, and has disincentive effects amongst the work-force. In the Conservative Party's 1979 election manifesto, Margaret Thatcher observed that few could 'fail to be aware of how the balance of our society has been increasingly tilted in favour of the state'. But under the Thatcher Government, this liberal commitment to a reduced government role has been contradicted by its commitment to expanding defence and law and order public expenditures. Both reflect the ideological beliefs of the Thatcher leadership.

The objective of 'rolling back the state' promoted by the Thatcher Government disguises a number of different priorities. They want to reduce public spending on social welfare, health and education – in other words, to reduce the scope of the welfare state built up during the period of the post-war Keynesian welfare state consensus and to free market forces. Equally, there is a commitment to increase defence expenditure moderately and to increase the resources allocated to law and order: thus the 1980–81 to 1983–84 expenditure plans 'reflect the Government's policy to give greater priority to defence, and law and order' (HMSO, 1980, p. 6). A variety of motives underlie these aims. There are liberal economic reasons for cutting public expenditure: related to the monetarist policies, it should lower the PSBR thereby contributing to the attack on inflation; it should reduce the level of taxation levied on the electorate; and, by reducing the assistance available through the various institutions of the welfare state it should increase the potential for market forces to work. The last aim reflects also ideological motives as does the desire to increase the defence capabilities of the state and the domestic structures of law and order. Table 7.2 summarises public spending trends under this Government.

First and foremost, the Thatcher Government has not reduced the aggregate size of the public sector. As a percentage of GNP, total public expenditure has grown every year since 1979: as Congdon (1985) writes, 'the "planning total", the most comprehensive measure available, was 9.4 per cent higher in real terms in 1984–85 than in 1979–80. This increase was appreciably faster than the rise in national income' (see also O'Higgins and Patterson, 1985). However, this growth in total spending masks significant shifts in the composition of public expenditure, shifts which reflect the new priorities of the Thatcher government, as shown in Table 7.2. The most dramatic trend is the fall-off in spending on housing due to the Government's privatisation policy (see next section), though the fall in housing expenditure does continue a trend begun under the Labour Administration. Expenditure on defence and on law and order has increased, reflecting pre-electoral commitments; also, the Thatcher government implemented pay recommendations in these two areas from the Callaghan Administration. Concerning police pay and conditions, the Government quickly implemented the 1978 Edmund–Davies Report which added an immediate

TABLE 7.2
Public expenditure under the Thatcher Government

	1980–81	1981–82	1982–83	1983–84	1984–85	1985–86 (est.)
Programmes (£m current):						
Defence	11,182	12,553	14,366	15,476	17,191	18,222
Housing	4,452	3,118	2,652	3,102	3,204	2,742
Law and order	3,179	3,748	4,174	4,600	5,102	5,388
Education and science	10,899	11,841	12,750	13,433	13,953	14,461
Health and personal social services	11,405	12,734	13,868	14,723	15,768	16,681
Social security	23,444	28,570	32,448	35,186	38,148	41,224
Constant (1979–80 = 100):						
Defence	102.1	104.7	112.2	115.5		
Law and order	104.1	111.5	116.6	123.4		
Housing	83.2	53.1	42.3	46.5	45.3	
Education	102.7	101.5	101.5	102.5	101.0	
Health and social services	107.6	109.6	111.6	114.1	116.7	
Social security	101.8	112.9	120.1	124.9	128.4	

Sources: current expenditure statistics: *The Government's Expenditure Plans 1986–87 to 1988–89* (HM Treasury, Cmnd 9702–11 vol. 2 Table 2.11); constant figures: see calculations in King (1985). O'Higgins (1986), Robinson (1986).

£550m to public expenditure on law and order.

Spending on law and order and on defence also reflected personal commitments of the Prime Minister: in June 1985 Mrs Thatcher told the House of Commons that she was 'proud' of the Government's record on police spending. The other noticeable trend is the Government's evident failure to reduce the share of the public sector consumed by education, health, social services and social security as it had sought to do. Education, health and income support programmes all grew substantially more than planned; these services also had sharp increases in costs which inflated their expenditures (see Robinson, 1986; King, 1985). The close-to-doubling of social security reflects the increased number of beneficiaries, notably pensioners, and obviously the unemployed. This failure reflects both the nature of these expenditures (see Chapter 9 below) and the consequences of the recession over which the Thatcher Government presided, which made the implementation of cuts very difficult.

So, the Thatcher Government has not succeeded in controlling the rate of growth of aggregate public expenditure – one aim of its economic strategy and clearly derivative of liberal theory. However, the priorities of public spending have been altered – clearly challenging some of the major post-war consensus priorities by de-emphasising social welfare state provision and placing a new emphasis upon law and order expenditure. After five years of her Government, the Prime Minister believed she had induced significant change: 'I believe that five years ago the British people made me Prime Minister primarily because they sensed that socialism had been leading them a life of debilitating dependency on the state, when what they really wanted was the independence and freedom of self-reliance and responsibility' (*Financial Times*, 24 July 1986). The long-term implications of this shift are examined in Chapter 9. For the moment, it is necessary to turn to privatisation policy, the last element of the Thatcher Government's strategy of reducing state activity.

Privatisation: state revenues and market solutions

Privatisation was a relatively late discovery by the Conservative Party under Margaret Thatcher's leadership. The objective of privatisation is to alter the balance between the public and the private sectors in the British political economy in favour of the latter; and to subject the public sector to market pressures and practices to as great an extent as possible. Ideologically, privatisation follows logically from liberalism. New Right liberals stress the superiority of market mechanisms over public sector provision of services. In policy terms, privatisation covers the sale of state enterprises, the allocation of public sector services amongst private competitors, eliminating or loosening state monopolies, and the introduction of private companies into public-based or initiated investment projects. Privatisation allows the state under the Thatcher Government to dispose of previously acquired state commitments. Financially, the privatisation programme has also been useful for the Government; the funds accruing to the Treasury from these measures increases the Government's policy flexibility in other areas.

Selling off council housing was a 1979 electoral pledge but the success of this programme made privatisation a very attractive policy for the Government. The 1980 Housing Act set out provisions for the sale of council houses and provisions to overcome the resistance of Labour-controlled local authorities. By September 1986 a million dwellings had been sold to their occupants. The success of this policy transformed privatisation from a fairly low-key item in the 1979 manifesto into a major policy initiative. After council housing the most publicised privatisation measure has been the sale of British Telecom, where the Government engaged in considerable pre-sales promotion. In addition, the Thatcher Government has privatised British Aerospace, Britoil, Cable and Wireless, National Freight, Associated British Ports, Enterprise Oil and Jaguar. There are plans to privatise British Airways, British Gas, British water authorities (postponed indefinitely in July 1986), British Shipbuilders' warship yards, National Bus Company, British Steel, British Leyland, Rolls Royce, Short Bros., and some of Britain's airports (see Table 7.3). Many of the companies initially privatised (and some of those designated for privatisation in the future) were both relatively prosperous and/or had only recently been nationalised because of economic difficulties; in contrast, most of the 'traditional, immediate post-Second World War nationalised industries' have not yet been privatised (Thompson, 1984, p. 290; Webster, 1985).

Curiously, the Thatcher Government chose to replace public monopolies with private ones in implementing privatisation, which contradicts liberal free market principles. According to these principles, the way to increase efficiency in services (and in the economy) is by maximising competition. But, in fact, the Thatcher Government has not ended monopolistic practices: most glaringly in the case of British Telecom which has been transferred into the private sector as one large corporation rather than broken into separate units (the course followed by the Reagan Administration with the American Telephone and Telegraph Corporation); alternatively, licences could have been granted to competitors in the different areas of telecommunications. Similar practices characterise other areas of this Government's privatisation policy.

Overall, this is a very substantial programme and constitutes an important legacy of the Government. The Government has also ended monopolies in some industries to allow the entry of new competitors (for example, on bus routes), and it has reduced public subsidies to some nationalised industries. In the non-industrial public sector – such as hospital laundry and refuse collection – the Thatcher Government has introduced contracting-out to private

TABLE 7.3
Privatisation under the Thatcher Government

Major asset shares	Date		Percentage	£m raised
British Petroleum	June	1977	17	548
	Oct	1979	5	276
	Sept	1983	7	543
British Aerospace	Feb	1981	52	43
	May	1985	48	346
National Freight Corporation (now Consortium)	Feb	1982	100	5
Cable and Wireless	Oct	1981	49	182
	Dec	1983	28	263
	Dec	1985	23	600
Britoil	Nov	1982	51	627
	Aug	1985	49	425
Associated British Ports	Feb	1983	52	46
	Apr	1984	48	51
Enterprise Oil	June	1984	100	380
Jaguar	July	1984	100	297
British Telecom	Nov	1984	50	3,916

To be privatised (100 per cent in each case):
British Airways [early 1987]
British Gas [November 1986]
British Airports Authority
National Bus Company
Royal Ordinance Factories
Water authorities (England and Wales) [postponed indefinitely]

Sources: *The Economist*, 21 December 1985; *The Sunday Times*, 10 November 1985.

firms (Shackleton, 1985, p. 8). Between 1981 and the middle of 1986, fifty-six public tenders for refuse and street-cleaning services had been issued by district councils, twenty-nine of which were won by private contractors over the councils' direct-labour organisations. Most recently, in August 1986, Lincolnshire County Council awarded a £3.3m cleaning contract for its buildings to a private company – one of the biggest service contracts to be awarded by the public sector. By cutting hourly wages from £2.24 to £1.70 the private cleaning company will save the company £400 000 a year; such is the nature of private competitive servicing over public sector provision (*Financial Times*, 22 August 1986). Such contracting-out, and the introduction of competition in the state sector, concurs with the policies advocated by public choice critics of the public sector reviewed in Chapter 6 (see Dunleavy, 1985 and 1986). Young (1986) identifies additional privatisation measures instituted by the Thatcher Government: reduced subsidies and increased charges for welfare services (for example, in April 1985 the National Health Service stopped providing spectacles except to children, students and social security claimants); the extension of private-sector practices into the public sector, as in urban aid projects; private provision of services (for example, getting private companies to provide school meals); and private sector responsibility for investment projects.

To reverse the drift toward privatisation will be a sizeable task for any subsequent administration not sharing the Thatcher Government's anti-nationalisation aims. In terms of the general mix of public (state) and private (market)-based activities in the British political economy, the Thatcher Government's policy of privatisation represents a strong prod towards more of the second. But to implement privatisation, the Government has had to play a major role, as Young (1986) notes: 'at the heart of privatisation there appears to be a paradox. Its promotion depends on government playing an active and interventionist role on a continuing basis' (p. 248). To achieve the liberal objective of a minimal government and an expanded market through privatisation measures requires considerable Government activity not just initially but on a sustained basis. This is the paradox which Young correctly identifies. But this Conservative Government's privatisation programme has certainly challenged post-1945 Morrisonian styles of nationalisation as a public policy option; the response of Opposition parties and the Trades Union Congress challenge is developing slowly and is discussed in Chaper 10.

INTERPRETATIONS OF THE THATCHER GOVERNMENT

The main danger in interpreting the Thatcher Government and/or 'Thatcherism' is that of attributing too much homogeneity to the phenomenon. New Right ideas have many sources, as do the political movements, such as the Conservative Party, which propagate them. Furthermore, it is necessary to distinguish between New Right influence upon the policy objectives of the Thatcher Government, and the outcome of those policies. And like all administrations, this one has changed in the course of its incumbency: while early policy decisions may bear the influence of liberalism (as in its monetarist policies), subsequent policy may be much less affected by these sources.

The Thatcher Government and pragmatic politics

Peter Riddell cannot be accused of according too much ideological coherence or consistency to the Thatcher Government. For him, this Government is a pragmatic one despite its rhetorical commitment to liberal free market economics. It has not followed the rigid policy implications of its public statements. Riddell characterises Margaret Thatcher's leadership style as 'instinctual politics'. In *The Thatcher Government* (1983) he argues against an ideological interpretation of this Government or of its leader. For Riddell, 'Thatcherism is essentially an instinct, a sense of moral values and an approach to leadership rather than an ideology. It is an expression of Mrs Thatcher's upbringing in Grantham, her background of hard work and family responsibility, ambition and postponed satisfaction, duty and patriotism. Her views were "born of a conviction which I learned in a small town from a father who had a conviction approach"' (1983, p. 7). Riddell argues that consistent themes inform Margaret Thatcher's speeches, which provide the backbone of her political ideas. These include 'personal responsibility, the family and national pride' (1983, p. 7). Mrs Thatcher also harks back to a version of 'Victorian values' interpreted as central to the economic and imperial success of late-nineteenth and early-twentieth century. The relevance of these historical allusions have been challenged by many critics of the Thatcher Government but the appeal to Victorian values remains: for example, the Thatcher Government's criticisms of the welfare state and advocacy of self-reliance or the family as an alternative draw upon historical images (Levitas, 1986). Riddell (1983) also argues that 'there is no hint of traditional Tory scepticism in her approach' (p. 9).

The 'instinctual politics' interpretation of the Thatcher Government is a highly personalised one: it emphasises the distinctiveness of Margaret Thatcher's leadership of the Conservative Party; and acknowledges her espousal of deeply held liberal and conservative values. But Riddell's interpretation queries the degree to which these beliefs and values have shaped public policy. There is a substantive pragmatic element influencing public policy decisions. For example, the Thatcher Government's economic policies no longer approximate – even loosely – monetarist policy prescriptions. The Government continues to evoke general economic and political principles but it is quite capable of changing its policies on specific issues as the theoretical principles breakdown.

Riddell's analysis has considerable appeal: public policy suggests that while lip service may have been paid to New Right liberal ideas, their impact upon policy outcomes was marginal. Public rhetoric may include a commitment to liberal economics but radical changes take place in the realm of policies and not of rhetoric. Conservatism has also been more a part of the Thatcher Government rhetoric than its policies. The major caveat which must be appended to this interpretation is that the 1979 Thatcher Government undoubtedly had a commitment to liberal free market economics even if this has been dissipated by the difficulties of implementing public policy. And, as discussed earlier in this chapter, this Government has pursued a consistently hostile policy toward trade unions since 1979.

Authoritarian Populism

The central ideas   Stuart Hall (1983) has characterised the Thatcher Government as authoritarian populist. Hall places the phenomenon of the Thatcher government within the declining economic conditions of the 1960s and 1970s (noted in Chapter 4), and the consequent disintegration of 'consensus politics'. By the mid-1970s there was a general shift to the right, Hall contends: it was under the 1976 Labour Government that monetarist principles were formally adopted and inroads into public expenditure began. The 1979 Conservative Government furthered these developments, in conjunction with conservative objectives such as reviving the family's welfare role. As Hall (1983) writes: 'Thatcherism has given these elements (that is, anti-collectivism and anti-statism) of the neo-liberal doctrine within conservative "philosophy" an extensive rejuvenation. At the level of theoretical ideologies, anti-statism has been refurbished by the advance of monetarism as the most fashionable economic credo' (p. 28). Monetarism became the new accepted economic doctrine for the British economy. The long years of propagating by the Institute of Economic Affairs paid off as the Conservative Party leadership consolidated their position within the doctrines of monetarism, anti-statism and anti-collectivism. In the political arena these ideas were joined with a commitment to the liberal values of the market and individual liberty. The successful articulation of these principles is the work of the populist dimension of the Thatcher Government. As Hall (1983) writes, 'Thatcherite populism is a particularly rich mix. It combines the resonant themes of organic Toryism – nation, family, duty, authority, standards, traditionalism – with the aggressive themes of a revived neo-liberalism – self-interest, competitive individualism, anti-statism' (1983, p. 29). The ideas and policy objectives informing the Thatcher leadership of the Conservative party thus stand in sharp contrast to those of the preceding decades. But, for Hall, it is the contradiction between a free market and strong state that defines 'Thatcherism': in this 'contradictory point . . . neo-liberal political economy [is] fused with organic Toryism, the authentic language of "Thatcherism"' (Hall, 1983, p. 30). As observed in Chapter 2, Hall correctly identifies a set of elements found in New Right ideas but largely fails to analyse their differential importance and seems to assume an ideological homogeneity in the conception and pursuit of policies which does not exist. Hall (1985) has qualified this latter issue in response to criticisms: 'I have *never* advanced the proposition that Thatcherism has achieved "hegemony" . . . Thatcherite politics are "hegemonic" in their conception and project' (p. 119). Margaret Thatcher and her supporters call for the unleashing of the market economy (consistent with liberal political economic principles) while taking a populist stance on issues such as law and order, immigration, strikes, trade unions, taxation and bureaucracy. Combined, these themes are strikingly anti-statist and pro-market. But under the Thatcher Government they have become contradictory: its anti-statism does not actually mean the minimal state of liberal economics. To revert to the language of Chapter 2, the policies of the Thatcher Government embody elements of both liberalism and conservatism. From the authoritarian populist perspective, this contradiction constitutes the essence of this Government. The Tory concern with authority and order has been systematically linked with an advocacy of free market economics.

Problems with the authoritarian populist interpretation   There are some difficulties with the authoritarian populist argument. Proponents of this interpretation impute too great a homogeneity to the beliefs promulgated by the Thatcher Government: simply because liberal economic principles are linked to conservative concerns about authority and state power in public statements does not negate their intrinsically contradictory relationship. Further, the Thatcher Government's policies and rhetoric have not remained static: as Jessop *et al.* (1984) warn 'style should not be confused with substance. Thatcherism changes continually in the light of circumstances. The authoritarian populist approach demonstrates how Thatcherism has attempted to establish a chain of equivalences among themes such as monetarism, the strong state, law and order, the family, etc. But it also tends to reify these linkages and to ignore their changing emphases and contexts' (p. 42). Thus the ideas and principles attributed to the Thatcher Government are less homogeneous than the concept of authoritarian populism seems to allow; rather 'Thatcherism must be seen . . . more as an alliance of disparate forces around a self-contradictory programme' (Jessop *et al.* , 1984, p. 38). This can be seen in the Government's 1985–86 programme as spelled out in the Queen's Speech at the beginning of Parliament (November 1985), where a concern with survival dominates rather than a drive to implement electoral commitments.

Jessop *et al.* (1984) argue also that the weakness of the Keynesian welfare state institutions made it an easy target for the Thatcher Government's liberal policies. This is part of a common argument advanced by members of the left that the post-war consensus was not really socialist and therefore not worth defending. But, as Hall (1985) rightly notes, this trivialises the accomplishments embodied in the Keynesian welfare state: the latter 'achieved something in a reformist direction for the working class . . . Why else should anyone on the left be now campaigning for the restoration of the cuts in the welfare state if it did *nothing* for the working class?' (p. 123; see also Jessop *et al.*'s (1985) reply to Hall, 1985). The post-war consensus did fail to alter the position and influence of the City which facilitated, to some degree, the attack mounted by the Thatcher Government upon Keynesian policies. But, as outlined above, Keynesian policies were abandoned before the Thatcher Government entered office. Also, the Thatcher Government has not remained simply subservient to the City, especially given its electoral support: Thatcher has won support from the middle and working classes who have no natural affinity with the City. On the other hand, the Thatcher Government's drive to extend the number of shareholders in Britain (as in its campaign for selling British Telecom) serves only to reinforce the role of the City.

The Thatcher Government's electoral base must be treated carefully. The Conservative Party has always won support from the working class – the so-called 'angels in marble' phenomenon (see Table 7.4) – but it did increase its support from manual voters in 1979 and 1983 over previous elections at the expense of the Labour Party. It is also important to note the role of the third party (Liberal – SDP Alliance) in 1983 which increased its attraction to the manual and non-manual vote at the expense of the Labour Party; in 1983 the Conservative Party's manual vote remained constant while its non-manual support actually fell by 5 per cent, which gives some indication of the importance in this instance of the third party for

TABLE 7.4
Manual and non-manual support for the political parties since 1945 (%)

	1945		1950		1951		1955		1959		1964	
	NM	M	NM	M	NM	M	NM	M	NM	M	NM	M
Conservative	63	29	68	32	75	34	70	32	67	30	62	28
Liberal	9	9	9	9	3	3	6	6	12	13	16	8
Labour	28	62	23	59	22	63	23	62	21	57	22	64

	1966		1970		Feb 1974		Oct 1974		1979		1983	
	NM	M	NM	M	NM	M	NM	M	NM	M	NM	M
Conservative	60	25	64	33	53	24	51	24	60	35	55	35
Liberal	14	6	11	9	25	19	24	20	17	15	28	22
Labour	26	69	25	58	22	57	25	57	23	50	17	42

NM = non-manual; M = manual.
Source: Heath *et al.* (1985).

the Conservatives success. The Thatcher Government's populist support, considered in electoral terms, is quite modest.

The authoritarian populist interpretation of state bureaucracy, especially welfare services, requires addressing. Hall (1985) argues that the Thatcher Government, and its New Right supporters, were able to exploit popular dissatisfaction with the general experience of the post-war Keynesian welfare state and its services:

> the actual experience which working people have had of the corporatist state has not been a powerful incentive to further support for increases in its scope. Whether in the growing dole queues or in the waiting-rooms of an overburdened National Health Service, or suffering the indignities of the Social Security, the corporatist state is increasingly experienced by them not as a benefice but as a powerful bureaucratic imposition *on* 'the people'. The state has been present to them, less as a welfare or redistributive agency, and more as the 'state of monopoly capital'. (pp. 33–4)

The institutions of the Keynesian welfare state have been closely associated with the Labour Party, Hall contends. Indeed, the Labour Party has a very statist conception of socialism: ' "statism" is not foreign to the trajectory of Labour socialism: it is intrinsic to it' (Hall, 1985, p. 33). The Conservative Party, under the Thatcher leadership, have successfully made the 'state' the object of popular discontent and it is perceived as the source of the 1970s' economic and political problems.

Thus the authoritarian populist analysis identifies flaws in the Keynesian welfare state institutions which have been skilfully exploited by the Thatcher Government. There is some accuracy in such an analysis. For example, Hoggart (1957) argues that the working class dichotomy between 'them' and 'us' places state officials in the former category, deriving from their role in administering means-tested state benefits: in other words, hostility to state benefits centres upon selective benefits as opposed to universalistic benefits, and it is this which has alienated some voters from the Labour Party. The present Conservative Government has exploited this by pursuing a policy aimed at creating the experience of alienation from state benefits. For example, in the case of the

National Health Service the Government has created a language, and focused debate, around inadequacy of services, an assertion reinforced by the left and Labour Party's promise not to expand these benefits in terms of existing services. Where there is a perception of inadequacy – for example, in education – the Conservative Party has exploited this by advocating alternatives to public provision, and located the cause of problems in state services. This policy has succeeded, to some degree, in establishing a perception that public provision of services is undesirable – a perception which the opposition parties have reinforced rather than challenged. As Hall (1985) observes, the Thatcher Government has 'steadily *used* the unpopularity of some aspects of trade union practice with their own members to inflict massive wounds on the whole labour movement . . . [and] has steadily not only pursued the "privatization" of the public sector but installed "value for money" at the heart of the calculations of *every* Labour council and every other social institution – health service, school meals, universities, street cleaning, unemployment benefit offices, social services' (p. 119). In fact, oppositional discussion should centre on the issue of selective versus universal state benefits rather than on the inadequacy of public provision as an entire institutional – political practice. By focusing on the inadequacy of services and problems with state provision, critics of the Thatcher Government come dangerously close to confirming the latter's criticisms.

CONCLUSION: A LIBERAL GOVERNMENT?

The Thatcher Government entered office intent upon reducing the role of the state and the size of the public sector in Britain. Its theoretical rationale for these objectives came from liberal economics: monetarist theory promised an end to inflation, while freeing the market from state intervention and trade unions' power would generate economic prosperity. Reducing the welfare state would increase entrepreneurial drive in the economy, and replace notions of collective welfare protection with individualist and familial self-reliance and self-help. Public assistance should remain for the very needy but in general the negative microeconomic consequences of welfare services necessitated their abolition. To this extent, the Thatcher Government's policy objectives have reflected the liberal ideas reviewed in earlier chapters of this book.

However, the implementation of these policies has failed to generate the results anticipated by the Government – monetarist policy has neither been sustained nor successful economically, and aggregate public expenditure has continued to rise; to accommodate the resultant hardships the Thatcher Government has evoked conservative arguments about social order, authority, self-reliance and the dangers of 1960s' values to justify the difficulties endured by members of society. The Government's active role – which is obviously contrary to the precepts of liberal theory – derives from conservative arguments. Liberal theory encourages the Thatcher Government to withdraw the state from the economy and to retrench the social citizenship rights institutionalised in the welfare state; conservative arguments provide the basis for an activist policy pursuing these aims. As Hall (1985) rightly observes, 'Thatcherism deliberately – and from its viewpoint, correctly – eschews all reference to the concept of citizenship' (p. 123). The liberal and conservative arguments underpinning the Thatcher Government share a common opposition to social citizenship rights. In this respect the authoritarian populist interpretation is of value. It is accurately grounded in the tension between liberal and conservative thought which are presented by this Government. And its name rightly stresses the break with previous Conservative Party administrations: the Thatcher Government's distinct style of populism (the kinds of issues it chooses to emphasise) and the underpinning faith in authority structures – whether of the state, the family, the Church or the economy – have been linked in a unique configuration. The resultant assault upon the Keynesian welfare state and the striving for a strong state is certainly quite unique in post-war British political experience.

New Right liberal and conservative theories have certainly not been the exclusive determinant of Thatcher Government policy; but they have been important. Liberal economic arguments shaped the 1979 Government's economic strategy while conservatism has informed the assault upon social citizenship rights. Both strategies have been altered and adjusted, pragmatically in many cases, as policies have failed to produce anticipated results or as hardship (for example, unemployment levels) has required some evidence of

Government concern. The theoretical contradiction between liberal minimalism and conservative activism has never been resolved intellectually but its success electorally and programmatically is sufficient for the Government.

8

The Reagan
Administration

INTRODUCTION

The Reagan Administration openly claims New Right influence upon its economic and social policies. However, there is no simple equivalence with the experience of the Thatcher Government, except at a very general level. Both Administrations have drawn upon 'radical' economic doctrines – monetarism for the Thatcher Government, and supply-side economics in the American case. While these two economic doctrines have important differences, this chapter stresses similarities, since the emergence and influence of New Right economic and political theories is significant for political developments in both countries. New Right liberal ideas flourished in the United States and Britain during the mid- to late 1970s reflecting the economic difficulties confronting each country; the 1973 oil price shock heralded in a decade of serious economic difficulty, symbolised by 'stagflation' – the concurrence of inflation and unemployment. Treating both the Reagan and Thatcher Administrations – however briefly – is a useful comparative exercise which advances analysis of their separate experiences.

As in Chapter 7, the main aim here is to assess the influence of New Right liberal theory upon the policies pursued by the Reagan Administration. These concern implementing supply-side economics prescriptions, reducing public expenditure on non-defence programmes, increasing defence spending and deregulating the economy. The chapter begins with the emergence of the Reagan candidacy in the Republican Party.

The policy-making process in the United States differs from that in Britain. The recruitment of politicians to the key decision-making and leadership positions is different. In Britain the political party remains all-important: parliamentary majorities are created and governments formed on the basis of disciplined parties. The Prime Minister heads the government, which is directly based on the majority party in the House of Commons. This majority enables the government to pass its legislation. In the United States political parties are loose, decreasingly well-organised, coalitions waiting for politicians with presidential ambitions to harness them. Political parties are more tightly organised at the local level in the United States; it is the national organisations which are particularly loose. The candidate's affiliation with his or her political party conveys only a general ideological and political orientation. And party affiliation for the newly elected President certainly does not translate into automatic legislative majorities in Congress. Rather, each President must forge his own relations with members of the House of Representatives and the Senate (through duly appointed delegates) to translate his campaign pledges into legislative content and ultimately into law (see Bowles, 1987, for an account of White House–Capitol Hill relations). Another important institutional contrast between the two countries is their political systems: the United States has a federal system, while Britain's is unitary. This has important consequences for the implementation of policy. In the United States, federal legislation may face problems of implementation by the regional states and local governments; in Britain such regional or locally-based resistance is less consequential. These are some of the significant differences between the American and British political systems aside from the two countries' varying political culture and history. Such differences are central to any full account of the two political systems; they serve as a contextual warning against casual generalising. But they do not preclude useful comparisons between the two systems or between the two current Governments.

RONALD REAGAN AND THE REPUBLICAN PARTY

Ronald Reagan has been a prominent member of the Republican Party since the mid-1960s, that is, for almost the last twenty-five years. At the 1964 Republican Party Convention, the job of introducing the Party's Presidential candidate – Senator Barry Goldwater – fell to Ronald Reagan. A television speech delivered by Reagan for Goldwater was considered by Republicans as one of the few achievements in an otherwise dismal campaign. In 1967 the Lyndon Johnson White House anticipated Reagan as the 1968 Republican Presidential nominee; in the event, that honour went to Richard Nixon. In 1976 Reagan came extremely close to defeating the incumbent President Gerald Ford for the Republican Party's Presidential nomination – an unprecedented event if it had succeeded. However, ever persistent, Ronald Reagan was successful in vying for the Republican Party's nomination in 1980, in the subsequent election and in the 1984 re-election. His 1980 victory was accompanied by a substantial swing toward the Republican Party in Congress also, increasing the potential support for his ambitious, not to say radical, legislative programme.

Prior to his nomination for the Presidency, Ronald Reagan spent two terms (1966–74) as Governor of California, during which many of the policies he later pursued as President were initially formulated and implemented. Despite California's reputation as a progressive state, it had in the period of Reagan's Governorship an extremely conservative gubernatorial record. In California, Reagan developed his general principles for politics: his opposition to big government, especially that emanating from the federal level; the need for taxes to be kept to a minimum (a belief that went back to Reagan's experience as an actor during the Second World War, subjected to a huge tax on earnings); the general undesirability of the welfare state; the rejection of Keynesian deficit-induced demand-management in favour of a balanced budget; the desire to limit government regulation of industry to a minimum; and the need for a large defence budget as the basis for negotiation with the Soviet Union. The last originates with Ronald Reagan's strong antipathy toward Communism, both domestic and external. These themes informed Reagan's 1980 electoral stance, proving very attractive to American voters. As Peele (1984) notes:

> there could be little disguising the extent to which the brand of Republicanism which Ronald Reagan offered the American electorate in 1980 was a radical conservatism which involved an explicit rejection of many of the assumptions of the liberal Welfare State and the limited collectivism which had pervaded in America since the New Deal. In the eyes of some commentators it was designed to be a counter-revolution. (p. 146)

Just as the Conservative Party under Margaret Thatcher in 1979 offered a set of policies opposed to the dominant post-war consensus, so Ronald Reagan and the Republicans sought to reverse the trends toward collective welfare provision and state intervention, documented in Chapter 2. Reagan and Thatcher share an antipathy to a large state role either in the provision of welfare or in management of the economy. The context of these administrations differed but their independent commitment to reversing the trends of the post-war interventionist period overlapped. They share a faith in New Right political and economic theories: both leaders seek to reduce the welfare state because of its adverse affects on beneficiaries, unfair tax burden and displacement of market processes (see Chapters 2, 3 and 5 above); and both seek to minimise the role of government in economic activity because of their faith in the strength of undistorted market processes. As in Britain, this commitment to minimal government is contradicted in non-economic matters, where an active government is approved. In addition, Ronald Reagan wanted to increase the fifty regional states' control of their own jurisdictions, which he believed had been gradually mitigated by federal intervention: he is a staunch supporter of states' rights in the federal system. And Reagan also paid lip service to the conservative social and moral movement of the right in the United States (Peele, 1984) which sought the outlawing of abortion, the reinstatement of school prayers in public schools and a general restoration of the role of the family; (Reagan did endorse constitutional amendments on the first two of these issues but has not initiated specific legislation concerning these topics). Thus, the Reagan Administration has sought to retrench the size and role of the federal government, to engender economic prosperity through tax cuts, and to revive traditional beliefs about the importance of family, religious and moral values in the American polity. The Reagan Presidency's legislative initiatives were concerned initially with economic policy, the size of the state sector, and national defence. The first two are the main concern here since these are most derivative of liberal theory.

Just as the 1979 electoral success for the Conservative Party reflected, in part, disillusionment with the incumbent Callaghan Government, so in 1980 there was deep dissatisfaction with the performance of President Jimmy Carter in economic policy, and in foreign policy after the perceived humiliation of American strength in Iran. Thus the electorate's mandate for the radical policy proposals of either the 1980 Reagan Administration or the 1979 Thatcher Government is ambiguous: clearly the attraction of these proposals was equalled in both countries by deep dissatisfaction with the incumbents. In both countries the main Opposition party – the Democrats and the Labour Party – presided over much of the 1970s economic crisis and were associated with these problems by voters. In Chapter 7, the Labour Party's image as a 'statist' party was noted. In the United States, Democrats were the party of state expansion and public spending. Writing during the 1984 re-election campaign, Democrat Senator Paul Tsongas (1984) reaches a similar conclusion:

> before 1980, we Democrats had a reputation as 'tax and spend' enthusiasts. We failed to set priorities among social programs. Business was regarded with suspicion. Government was considered omniscient. The country rebelled against that mind-set, and Ronald Reagan was there to catch the falling apple. The notion that government is the solution to all our problems has been rethought. The president has received credit for restoring respect for the private sector. (p. 8)

The conservatism of Ronald Reagan's Presidential candidacy provided a unifying theme for Republican Party candidates in 1980. Reagan's conservative electoral programme – particularly the objectives of reducing the federal government's role in welfare and the economy, cutting taxes, strengthening defence and his stated social conservatism – constituted an appealing platform for Republican Congressional candidates. The agreement between the Presidential candidate and the congressional party candidates was not absolute but in that the Reagan programme accurately predicted the prevailing mood amongst the electorate, Republican candidates were only too pleased to be associated with it. By linking congressional and presidential electoral prospects Reagan also hoped to increase his governing capacity upon election: he hoped that his common ideology and party to those of successful congressional candidates could be the basis for legislating. This unity was manifested by the joint appearance of presidential candidate Reagan with 285 Republican congressional candidates at Capitol Hill before the election, and promulgated in the 'Capitol

Compact' (see Bowles, 1987, ch. 9). This programme embodied New Right liberal policy objectives, though not social conservative aims; these latter had to wait until the 1984 Presidential election to be included in the official Republican Party statement.

Against this background of agreement between the Republican presidential and congressional candidates, each did exceptionally well in the elections. Reagan received a solid electoral mandate and overwhelming support in the electoral college, while the Republicans gained thirty-three seats in the House of Representatives reducing the Democratic majority there to fifty-one; the Republicans acquired twelve new seats in the Senate giving them a majority of fifty-four to forty-six Democrats, an unusually powerful position. These results augured well for the Reagan Administration's radical policy objectives.

THE POLICY OBJECTIVES OF THE REAGAN ADMINISTRATION

Supply-side economics

The phenomenon of stagflation challenged the continuing utility of Keynesian economics during the 1970s. In Britain monetarism was flaunted as a more viable guide to national economic policy. In the United States, this role was taken by supply-side economics. And just as monetarism implied a substantially reduced economic role for the state, so did the doctrine upon which Ronald Reagan based his economic proposals. Supply-side economics gained the wide publicity in the 1980 campaign which monetarism received in Britain during the late 1970s. David Stockman (1986), subsequently Reagan's Budget Director, refers to the 'new supply-side gospel' (p. 42) and viewed it as a panacea for the 'central global economic failure of the late 1970s' (p. 43) which Keynesian policies were incapable of resolving. Stockman recounts the development and dissemination of supply-side economics in the late 1970s. The key figure was Congressman Jack Kemp: 'Kemp's office became a kind of postgraduate seminar in supply-side economics. Kemp was our political guru, (*Jude*) Wanniski and (*Arthur*) Laffer our chief theoreticians. Ceaselessly and happily we hammered out counter positions to every statist proposal or initiative Carter or Congress came up with. It was exciting. Our ideas could change history . . . I began to feel as if I were part of a movement' (p. 42). Wanniski (1979) had expounded supply-side economics, while Laffer's curve is discussed below.

Like monetarism, supply-side economics is a conservative economic doctrine which views capitalism as a natural economic form, deriving from the individualist nature of society. Individualism is kernel to humanity, and capitalist economic activity allows it to be manifested most purely. In the capitalist free market, entrepreneurs pursue profit opportunities based on expanded knowledge and innovation – the creative element of capitalism. This mirrors Hayek's conception of capitalist economic activity, as will be recalled from Chapters 2 and 4. Supply-side economics concentrates upon the level of taxes levied by the government, and the consequences of those levies for economic activity. Its advocates believe individuals respond to one key incentive – the money return upon their labour and efforts. All individuals are considered to be calculating utility-maximisers; therefore, they will work harder for higher pay and lower taxes; and the lower tax rates are, the fewer will work in the black economy. Stockman (1986) recounts his absorption of this principle while campaigning for the House of Representatives in 1975: 'My encounters with the workaday citizens of Southern Michigan had a profound effect on my quest for the ideological truth . . . I began to see a profound principle that was to prove crucial in the final, impending phase of my own odyssey: before the state can redistribute wealth, the society must first produce it. If incentives and morale among the more enterprising citizens are weakened too much, the resulting economic shortfalls will make the attainment of social justice impossible under any circumstance' (p. 37).

Supply-side economics entered into popular consciousness during the 1980 presidential campaign; it became associated particularly with the 'Laffer curve'. This is named after a Californian economist, Arthur Laffer (mentioned above in Stockman's memoirs), who argued that the United States' current levels of taxation had damaging incentive effects: that is, taxes were of such a magnitude that they were discouraging potential entrepreneurial activity. Laffer argued also that reducing taxes to a certain level would not alter the revenues accruing to government, since the positive incentive consequences of reduced taxes would be such as to result in greater economic activity and hence new revenues. Given that individuals and entrepreneurs respond to monetary incentives, government taxes are of vital importance according to supply-side economists. Such taxes determine individuals' choices between work and leisure; likewise factor costs determine how entrepreneurs set their production levels. In both instances, if taxes are raised beyond a certain level, individuals will choose leisure over work while entrepreneurs will set lower production levels. This is harmful for the aggregate level of economic activity. If taxes have reached an excessive level – as the Reagan Administration argued – reducing taxes will increase output without damaging the level of tax revenues accruing to the state.

For supply-side economists, taxes are not the only negative activity of government: government regulation of industry and provision of welfare benefits are also judged to be harmful to microeconomic incentives. The clear policy implication is for government withdrawal from these activities. Once again, Stockman (1986) articulates these arguments: for him:

> the central idea of the Reagan Revolution . . . was minimalist government, a spare and stingy creature, which offered even-handed public justice, but no more. Its vision of the good society rested on the strength and productive potential of free men in free markets. It sought to encourage the unfettered production of capitalist wealth and the expansion of private welfare that automatically attends it. It envisioned a land the opposite to the coast-to-coast patchwork of dependencies, shelters, protections, and redistributions that the nation's politicians had brokered over the decades. (p. 9)

Elsewhere, Stockman blames government intervention and regulation for the poor economic growth of the 1970s: 'our capitalist economy's natural capacity to expand and generate new wealth, and societal welfare was being badly hobbled by the sweeping anti-supply and incentive-destroying policies of the modern state. The marketplace had become riddled with sumps of waste in the form of subsidies and protectionism' (1986, p. 43).

As noted in the discussion of the market in Chapter 5, there are serious problems with an economic doctrine such as supply-side economics which assumes that individuals and entrepreneurs respond to monetary incentives only: many other social factors will influence decisions about work and leisure, while entrepreneurs are as concerned about sales levels as about factor costs in their production decisions. But Stockman's book demonstrates that supply-side arguments about taxes, incentives and excessive government were influential amongst the policy-makers shaping President Reagan's legislative initiatives; whether empirical evidence warranted this influence is a different issue, of little concern to these decision-makers. Accordingly, New Right liberal ideas influenced this Administration, just as monetarist arguments initially influenced the Thatcher Government. Throughout his book, Stockman (1986) refers approvingly to Hayek's ideas, which we have considered in earlier chapters: Stockman wielded a 'sword forged in the free market smithy of F. A Hayek' (p. 41), an influence complemented by the supply-side arguments of Laffer and Kemp. Hayek's name may not have instant public recognition but in the early 1970s his ideas and arguments did influence leading decision-makers in the Reagan and Thatcher Administrations (see, for Britain, Bosanquet, 1981).

Supply-side economics implemented

The Reagan Administration's economic strategy, based in part upon supply-side economics, had five key elements (compare Thurow, 1983, p. 129). Since they include more objectives than are usually implied by the term 'supply-side economics', these key elements have correctly been daubed as 'Reaganomics'. The five elements are:

  (i)   a large across-the-board cut in tax rates to stimulate economic activity by increasing monetary incentives;
 (ii)   government control of the rate of growth of the money supply to tackle inflation;
(iii)   a large reduction in non-defence (mainly welfare) public spending by the state;
 (iv)   an expansion of state defence expenditure;
  (v)   an extensive deregulation of the economy by the government.

Tax cuts and monetary policy   Implementing large across-the-board tax cuts is the policy imperative of the Laffer curve. Figure 8.1 depicts this theory diagrammatically. The assumptions behind

FIGURE 8.1
Laffer Curve

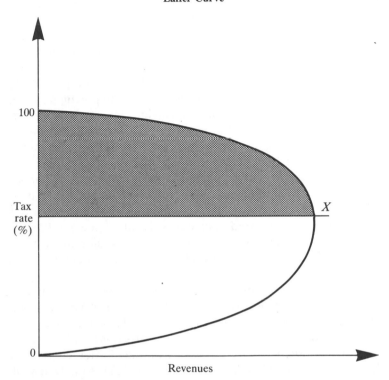

Source: Wanniski (1978) p. 50.

the theory about the relationship between tax rates, government revenues and economic production are relatively straightforward. If the tax rate is 100 per cent, production in the money economy will cease since the benefits of any product are absorbed in their entirety by the state in taxes. If the tax rate is zero, productive individuals can keep the entire proceeds of their transactions from the money economy. Incentives to production are at their highest and economic production should consequently be maximised. But the government receives no revenues when taxes are zero. It is the possibilities between these two extremes which concern economists: in particular, their aim is to identify the point at which revenues and production are maximised. If the government sets the tax rate below the shaded area in Figure 8.1, there will be greater output but decreased revenues accruing to the Treasury. Alternatively, if the government raises the tax rate into the shaded area, output will fall, as will revenues. Government tax rates must avoid entering the shaded area since they will lead to a decline in output and revenues (Wanniski, 1978). Accordingly, the policy problem is to identify the apposite point at which to set the tax rate, maximising both output and revenues (Thurow, 1983, pp. 133–4). Tax cut proponents maintain that new revenues would be sufficient to preclude a cut in government expenditure from its current levels; however, to achieve a balanced budget along with tax cuts and increases in defence spending, significant reductions in non-defence spending would be unavoidable: 'the Reagan Revolution, as I had defined it, required a frontal assault on the American welfare state. That was the only way to pay for the massive Kemp–Roth tax cut' (Stockman, 1986, p. 9). But without concurrent reductions in public spending, a huge, supply-side inspired, tax cut will inflate the public debt massively; this is exactly what has occurred under the Reagan Administration, which now presides over unprecedentedly large deficits.

Evaluation of the 'Laffer curve' must centre on the consequences of tax cuts for work efforts, that is, how much of an additional incentive is created by cutting taxes? The evidence is mixed: while tax cuts can contribute to greater work efforts this is unlikely to be as great as anticipated by advocates of the 'Laffer curve' (see Thurow, 1983, pp. 134ff). Thurow concludes that the likely benefits have been overestimated by supply-side advocates. Alt and Chrystal (1983) dispute the likely boost in economic activity and subsequent increase in revenues from a cut in taxes: 'this cannot generally be true as it would mean that the economy is unstable, for successive reductions in tax rates would produce unbounded growth' (p. 71). Despite such doubts, Reagan's policy-makers – directed by David Stockman as Director of the Office of Management and Budget – formulated a legislative proposal for large across-the-board tax cuts. Their model was the Kemp–Roth proposal for an immediate tax cut of 30 per cent to all categories of tax, a measure which for Stockman was 'not a negotiable part of the [Reagan] revolution' (1986, p. 183); however, through the legislative process this was watered down to a 25 per cent tax cut implemented over three years, included in the Economic Recovery Tax Act of 1981.

The Reagan Administration's economic strategy also sought a tight monetary policy to control the rate of growth of the money supply, somewhat analogous to the Thatcher Government's monetarist policy. The rationale for this policy was concern with inflation, as well as a preference for a limited government role in economic management. As Thurow (1983) observes, the novelty of adopting monetarism lay not in its implications for inflation but rather in suggesting that 'if tight money policies were yoked to strong supply-side policies, the tight money would stop inflation, without at the same time stopping the economy' (p. 129). That the Reagan Administration policy-makers believed such a scenario is evident from Stockman's (1986) memoirs: 'the heart of the supply-side synthesis rested on the notion of a 'push–pull' economic dynamic. Hard money policies would 'pull-down' the rate of inflation and nominal GNP growth. The tax cut and whole range of supply-side economic policy changes would 'push-up' the rate of real output and employment expansion. Both effects would occur in a *simultaneous time frame*' (p. 76, emphasis added). Monetarism and supply-side economics share similar premises about the nature of economic activity and the workings of the economy. Both doctrines imply giving market forces as much scope as possible in preference to state management of the economy. The Reagan Administration's strategy assumed that controlling the money supply, while cutting taxes to increase work incentives (thereby stimulating greater economic activity), were compatible policy initiatives. In fact, the policy was supposed to generate considerable economic activity:

> the only difference between this view (i.e. supply-side economics) and the one held by the monetarists is that the short-run recession that would be predicted by the monetarists became in the views of the supply-siders so short as not to exist. The predicted speed of reaction may be different for the two schools of economists, but the theory is identical (Thurow, 1983, p. 131).

Thus there is overlap between the policy implications of monetarist and supply-side economics. The serious economic difficulties of the first three years of the Reagan Administration, however, suggest that the prediction regarding a non-existent short-run recession by supply-siders was inaccurate. Table 8.1 summarises some economic

TABLE 8.1
Economic indicators for the Reagan Administration

	1978	1979	1980	1981	1982	1983	1984	1985
Foreign public debt/GDP (%)	8.11	6.73	8.03	8.31	9.72	9.09	7.64	9.35
Real GDP (%)	5.0	2.8	−0.4	2.1	−1.9	3.7	6.8	2.2
Consumer prices (%)	7.6	11.2	13.5	10.4	6.1	3.2	4.3	3.5
Money supply growth (%)	8.3	6.7	6.9	6.4	8.8	9.7	5.7	12.1
Budget deficit/ GDP (%)	−2.1	−1.2	−2.7	−2.5	−3.6	−5.8	−4.8	−5.5
Unemployment	6.0	5.8	7.0	7.5	9.5	9.5	7.4	7.2

Sources: International Economic Statistics (Craig Gardner/Price Waterhouse, in association with the International Economic Appraisal Service of The Economist Publications Ltd, June 1986); for unemployment see *Statistical Abstract of the United States* 1986 (US Department of Commerce, Bureau of the Census) table No. 658.

indicators for the United States under the Reagan Administration. Real GDP has fluctuated but is growing steadily during the latter years of the Reagan Administration, consumer prices have decreased as in Britain, money supply growth has been greater than anticipated and the public debt has increased steadily.

Cutting public social expenditure and increasing defence

The Reagan Administration sought a massive reduction in the American welfare state. Stockman (1986) is littered with allusions to the waste and abuse of social welfare in the United States. For Stockman, and for the Reagan Presidency, the welfare state symbolises state intervention – or 'statism' as Stockman terms it – at its most perverse. Stockman wants to cut the 'umbilical cords of dependency that ran from Washington to every nook and cranny of the nation' (1986, p. 11), to mount a 'frontal assault on the American welfare state' (p. 9) and to achieve a 'substantial retraction of welfare state benefits that people had come to feel "entitled" to receive' (p. 95). Neither Stockman nor the Administration employing him express concern about the needy or poor and believe that social hardship should be relieved privately through the market or through family networks. In particular, an undefined class of 'able-bodied poor' (p. 12) must be removed immediately from government welfare rolls. Destroying the welfare state and abrogating any tendency toward state intervention are central to Stockman's conception of the Reagan revolution: for him statism started with the New Deal, exploded during the Great Society and was completely ingrained in politics by the Carter Presidency when solutions to policy problems were automatically defined in terms of positive state action. The New Right liberals entering office with the Reagan Administration wanted to return the American polity to a pre-New Deal non-interventionist era when public welfare provision was minimal and interest-group politics controlled. For the Reagan Administration, therefore, retrenching the social citizenship rights incorporated in welfare institutions was central to their policy objectives.

The precepts of the 'Laffer curve' imply that cutting taxes increases the incentive to work, for both employees and employers. A logical corollary of this argument is that public provisions offsetting the hardship of economic life distort market processes, thereby altering people's conception of work and savings. Chapter 2 has alluded to this issue. Under the Reagan Administration the imperative to cut social welfare expenditure became pronounced. The White House policy-makers viewed the provision of welfare and unemployment benefits as equivalent to insurance policies in their impact upon individual incentives. If an individual's welfare and unemployment needs are met by the state, they contended, then the pressure upon that same individual to search for and keep full-time employment is reduced. Further, if health, social welfare and old age benefits are provided by the state, the pressure upon the individual to prepare for these him or herself is significantly diminished. This has important consequences for the level of savings and investment in the economy, it is maintained. Further, the public provision of welfare and social benefits opens up the potential for free-riding: 'knowing that others will work to provide the resources necessary to insure you against the hazards of life, you reduce your work effort and let others carry the load. But when everyone makes what is individually a rational decision to work less, the result is collective irrationality – an economy with too little work and output' (Thurow, 1983, p. 138).

Other New Right supporters linked the emergence of the welfare state to the breakup of the family and the destruction of traditional social values. Advocating Reagan's candidacy during the 1984 re-election campaign, Gilder (1984) gave his account of the harmful effects of welfare policy: 'because of the fivefold rise in the value of welfare benefits, these families (that is, with children), white and black, have faced increasing incentives to break up, and teen-age girls face rising inducements not to marry the father of their children. The result has been a plague of family breakdown and despair among the American poor and illegitimacy rates near 80% in inner cities. This is not a racial problem. It is a crisis of the welfare state . . . The government must adopt programs that keep families together rather than drive them asunder' (p. 10; see also Peele, 1984 and David, 1986). Such arguments were shared by some Administration decision-makers.

However, Lester Thurow disputes this alleged correlation between welfare provision and reduced savings: there is little empirical demonstration of the negative impact of public social welfare provision upon savings levels – in fact, just the opposite can be held. But this was of little interest to members of the Reagan Administration who saw supply-side economics as a universal panacea for the problems of the American economy irrespective of the absence of supporting evidence. Arthur Laffer, for example, has produced no evidence to support his claims about the beneficial consequences of large tax cuts. Both Britain and the United States were ripe for the emergence and promotion of a conservative economic doctrine. Britain got monetarism; the United States, supply-side economics. In both instances the successful doctrine was linked to other conservative social and moral positions held by the relevant politicians. It is not coincidental that economic doctrines advocating a minimal state involvement in the economy should be promoted in unison with an attack on the negative and undesirable affects of the welfare state. To implement New Right liberal doctrines required retrenching the welfare state; conservative arguments about the latter's harmful moral and social effects complemented such economic policies. That the evidence for either argument was, to say the least, debatable could be quietly ignored in the rush to find a doctrine that reflected the chosen ideological position in each country. As Alt and Chrystal (1983) observe, there is a 'close relationship between the choice of economic perspective and political values' (p. 173). Economics and politics are not synonymous but they are related in important respects.

Supply-side economists also argue that government expenditure is inherently inefficient and diverts resources from the private sector, which would use them more productively and efficiently. This proposition is frequently referred to as the 'crowding out' thesis, whereby public sector resource use forces a reduction in private sector activity and production. If the public sector activity is financed by borrowing, this is argued by supply-side economists to force up interest rates, which has a negative impact upon investment in the private sector. Alt and Chrystal (1983), amongst others, remain sceptical about the accuracy of the 'crowding out' thesis, but for an Administration influenced by liberal economics it provided a further rationale to retrench government spending.

The Reagan Administration's budget initiatives proposed cuts in the aggregate size of welfare expenditures as a percentage of GNP, and increased spending on defence. The initial proposed cuts focused upon the fixed-dollar programmes which funded education, employment, social services and health – usually provided by state and local authorities. Entitlement benefits to the low-income, such as Aid to Families with Dependent Children (AFDC), food stamps, housing assistance and child nutrition were targeted also. Less seriously affected were social security, Medicare and other social insurance federal benefits, protected by members of Congress during legislative debate on the budget proposals (see Palmer and Sawhill, 1984). Thus the March 1981 budget proposal (operative for the fiscal year 1982) set out a 20 per cent reduction in non-defence public expenditures; the vast burden of these cuts were to fall upon federal funds to state and local authorities and means-tested welfare entitlements; Stockman's 'able-bodied poor' were to be severed from collective funding. The steady expansion in the provision of welfare benefits by the American state to its less well-off citizens, outlined in Chapter 4, was precisely what the Reagan Presidency sought to halt, and where possible, reverse. In Nathan's (1983) judgement, 'the long cycle of growth in the role and activism of the national government in domestic affairs that began with FDR's New Deal ended with Reagan's New Federalism' (p. 49). This view was shared by the President, who said in 1982: 'I believe that we have started government on a different course, different from anything we've done in the last half century since Roosevelt began with the new deal' *Financial Times*, 24 July 1986).

The Reagan Administration failed to push through Congress all these cuts but agreement was reached to reverse much of existing policy. Congress proved more resistant after the first year (fiscal year 1982) to the level of cuts sought by the White House. However, the agreed changes included excluding the long-term unemployed, early retirees and some categories of disabled from benefits. The Administration argued that these groups – the 'able-bodied poor' – were perfectly capable of working and should be forced to do so. Higher-income beneficiaries were also excluded from certain benefits, such as student aid. At the lower end of the income scale, eligibility requirements for benefits were tightened, resulting in the withdrawal of food stamps rights from some recipients and funds from AFDC. Palmer and Sawhill (1984) conclude that 'the safety net is less effective than it was' (p. 14) as a consequence of these measures. A serious reversal of the welfare state rights steadily established during the preceding decades has occurred under the Reagan Presidency. Entitlement (food stamps, AFDC, Medicaid) and annually financed (education, housing, nutrition and health care) policies have borne the brunt of these welfare spending cuts; Medicaid and Supplemental Security Income programmes have been the least affected by the cuts. The distributional pattern of the spending cuts have been most severe for the working poor, reinforcing the distributional impact of the Administration's tax cuts. But the Reagan Administration has added significantly to the defence budget, as Table 8.2 reports. The combination of increased defence spending, large tax cuts but less-than-sought non-defence spending cuts has been greater government spending than revenue intake; this in turn has generated an enormous budget deficit.

Table 8.2 reveals that as a percentage of GNP, aggregate public sector outlays increased from 23.1 in 1981 to 24.7 by 1983 in the United States. In part this reflects the impact of recessionary pressures upon the public purse as in Britain: thus, although the Reagan Administration was able to make significant cuts in social welfare provision the pressures for the same were such as to constitute a strong counter-tendency in the early 1980s. As Table 8.2 shows, expenditure on unemployment compensation rose almost 0.5 per cent during the first three years of the Reagan Presidency, while that on Medicare/Medicaid increased by almost 1 per cent. Allowing for shifting economic circumstances – mainly recessionary pressures – then expenditures upon welfare programmes were lower by 1985 than would have been the case if the 1981 targets had been retained. But it is public assistance

TABLE 8.2
Public expenditure under the Reagan Administration (billions of current $:)

	1978	1979	1980	1981	1982	1983	1984	1985
Aggregate outlays:	458.7	503.5	590.9	678.2	745.7	808.3	851.8	959.1
Disaggregated:								
Defence	104.5	116.3	134.0	157.5	185.3	209.9	227.4	253.0
Income security	61.5	66.4	66.5	99.7	107.7	122.6	122.7	127.2
Unemployment insurance	11.8	10.7	18.0	19.7	23.7	31.5	18.4	16.8
Food and nutrition	8.9	10.8	14.0	16.2	15.6	18.0	18.1	18.7
Health	18.5	20.5	23.2	26.9	27.4	28.6	30.4	33.9
Social security	93.9	104.1	118.5	139.6	156.0	170.7	178.2	191.1
Medicare	22.8	26.5	32.1	39.1	46.6	52.6	57.5	66.3
Education, training, employment and social services	26.7	30.2	31.8	33.7	27.0	26.6	27.6	30.4
Training/ employment	10.8	10.8	10.3	9.2	5.5	5.3	4.6	5.3
Social services	5.6	6.6	6.1	6.9	6.0	6.1	7.2	7.0
Expenditures as percentage of aggregate outlays:								
Defence			23.2	24.0	25.4	26.4	27.8	
Income security			15.0	15.1	14.7	15.4	13.2	
Health			4.0	4.1	3.8	3.6	3.6	
Education, training and employment			5.3	4.8	3.6	3.3	3.4	
Social security and medicare			26.1	27.2	27.8	28.0	28.1	
Constant (1972) dollars (% in parentheses):								
Aggregate outlays	300.2	304.4	324.4	337.1	346.1	360.1	366.3	397.0
Defence	67.2	69.5	71.3	74.2	80.2	86.5	90.0	96.8
	(22.4)	(22.8)	(22.0)	(22.1)	(23.2)	(24.0)	(24.6)	(24.4)
Non-defence	233.0	234.9	253.1	262.5	266.0	273.0	276.2	300.2
	(77.6)	(77.2)	(78.0)	(77.9)	(76.9)	(76.0)	(75.4)	(75.6)
Payments to individuals	141.7	144.0	156.1	166.4	172.2	183.7	179.6	185.5
Net interest	23.6	26.1	29.6	35.2	40.6	41.3	49.2	55.7

Source: Statistical Abstract of the United States 1985, 1986 (US Dept of Commerce, Bureau of the Census) table 492 (1985) and tables 493, 494 (1986).

programmes (that is, means-tested) rather than social insurance programmes (universal in application) which have been most affected. Of the latter, Medicare has almost doubled since 1981 whereas expenditures upon training and employment programmes have been cut by almost 50 per cent (Hanson, 1987). The impact of the Reagan Administration upon the public provision of health, welfare and unemployment benefits has been significant, resulting in real hardship.

Overall, the Reagan Administration's impact upon public expenditure is similar to that of the Thatcher Government. Both Governments have failed to reduce the aggregate size of the public sector – mainly because of the pressures upon the public sector resulting from economic recession. However, both Governments have induced a significant shift within public spending away from social welfare spending toward defence and law and order. This is likely to be a lasting affect of the Reagan Administration: supporters of the Administration proudly note that no new social programmes have been enacted since 1980. The Reagan Administration has altered the terms of debate about economic strategy: supply-side issues dominate debate amongst Republicans and Democrats; economic proposals are now justified according to their impact upon savings, investment and incentives rather than upon consumer demand. The massive federal deficit has reinforced this shift away from demand-management in economic policy debate. As in Britain, budget-cutting rather than expansion has been elevated by the Reagan Administration into the principal task of government; the federal deficit will make it difficult for future Administrations to abandon this course. In non-defence expenditures, the activist role of the federal government, established during the New Deal, has been halted; Congress and the judiciary have forced the maintenance of some protection for the least advantaged groups in society. But in defence expenditures the same budget-cutting Reagan Administration has pursued enormous increases in federal outlays paid for by an ever-expanding federal budget deficit.

The Reagan Administration has also created serious difficulties for trade unions in the United States. Although this Administration did not wage war against union organisations as intensely as did the Thatcher Government, its policies have affected these labour institutions. Shortly after assuming office, the Reagan Administration was confronted with a strike by the nation's air traffic controllers. The outcome of this dispute was decimation for the union and a major victory for the Presidency, which sacked all the controllers, substituting military and newly trained workers. A recruitment and training programme of new air traffic controllers was speeded up, which weakened the striking workers' power. A similar pattern has occurred in other industrial disputes. More generally, as in Britain, the economic climate of the Reagan Administration – certainly during the early years – reduced the militant power of American trade unions, as Shefter and Ginsberg (1985) observe: 'by driving up real interest rates and the value of the dollar, it [the Reagan administration] has eroded the competitiveness of many American industries, increasing unemployment and reducing labor's bargaining power' (p. 21, see also Davis, 1986).

The Reagan Administration and deregulation

Enhancing the forces of the market and reducing government intervention in the economy requires an end to federal regulations. The Reagan Administration came to office committed to do just this, though the outgoing Carter Presidency had already initiated important measures of deregulation – for example, in the airline industry. But the process of deregulation was given a sharp prod under the Reagan Administration. For Stockman (1986) 'sweeping deregulation was another pillar of the supply-side platform' (p. 109).

Supply-side economists are highly critical of government regulation. They argue that since the private economy would not choose to pay for regulation, it should not be undertaken by the state. Further, regulatory bureaucracies must be financed; this requires increased taxation which in turn has disincentive effects on production levels and output. That cars are safer because of statutory regulations on production or the air cleaner because of pollution controls is of little consequence to supply-side economists: they contend that since private citizens would not pay for these things directly there is no gain to society through the state doing so. It might be countered that the very point of government intervention and regulation is to provide those goods and services which will not be provided by the market but which most people would consider desirable. However, for the Reagan Administration, most government regulation is seen as an excessive burden upon entrepreneurs and producers which requires taxes to be levied for its financing. These constituted powerful rationales for the Reagan Administration to deregulate the American economy. The Administration has sought especially deregulation in the economic sphere. But the Reagan Administration is also eager to reduce the regulatory roles assumed by the federal government in social and welfare spheres, such as environmental control and the safety standards of work-places (see Quick, 1984 for this distinction). Both areas are considered in turn.

Economic deregulation   In the economic sphere, the Reagan Administration has been reluctant to enforce anti-trust legislation (that is, laws limiting the size of corporations), despite the inconsistency of monopolies or oligopolies with the liberal economic principle of freely competing firms. Thus, a thirteen-year pending lawsuit against IBM was resolved in 1982, while objection to mergers between huge corporations has been somewhat muted. In the IBM case, the Justice Department advanced the novel argument that a corporation could be efficient and large without being monopolistic. New merger guidelines were formulated by the Administration in 1982 and 1984; the 1982 measures specified a primary criterion for challenging mergers – whether the proposed merger would decrease competition in the market affected by the merger. This has made 'vertical' mergers (for example, manufacturing concerns taking over a retail business) less vulnerable to anti-trust measures (*The Economist* 23 August 1986). On gaining office, President Reagan cancelled the oil price controls and allocation quotas implemented by his Democratic predecessor.

Anti-trust legislation has not, however, been abandoned wholesale as the striking decision to break up the Bell Telephone monopoly on telecommunications demonstrates. Here, careful calculations about the likely benefits of encouraging entry into this business by other companies was judged most beneficial to national economic growth. Telecommunications are at the cutting edge of contemporary economic restructuring and the Reagan Administration sought to ensure that its full potential would be enhanced within the American economy. Restrictions upon other areas of economic activity have also been removed or loosened: for example, in domestic aviation, railroad transportation, broadcasting, and in the oil and natural gas industries (Shackleton, 1985). The

Federal Communications Commission has initiated significant deregulation in television and radio broadcasting and in telecommunications, especially computer-based, services.

The Reagan Administration has other deregulatory bills under scrutiny by Congress. These include ending restrictions on interlocking directorships of competing corporations, limiting the power of American courts to impose anti-trust laws outside the United States on foreign trade matters, and making it easier for firms to merge – the essence of anti-trust concerns!

Social and environmental deregulation In the social sphere, deregulation reflects also the New Right influence upon the Reagan Administration. Such deregulation breaks with preceding administrations, including that of Carter. Two areas of deregulation stand out: (i) that concerning safety in the work-place; and (ii) environmental control. The former is controlled by the Occupational Safety and Health Administration (OSHA), administered by field inspectors who make spot checks on work-places to ensure their compliance with safety requirements for their employees. The Reagan Administration altered OSHA's powers mainly by weaker enforcement. Quick (1984) writes that under the Reagan Administration OSHA 'has restricted the discretion of field enforcement personnel with respect to site violations, given them strong incentives not to issue citations that are likely to be challenged, and ordered them to target their inspections more narrowly on firms with high recorded rates of injuries. Beyond these changes, the clear direction of new enforcement policy is to have personnel perform the role of 'consultants' rather than 'cops', in an effort to create a new environment of co-operation between the agency and regulated firms' (p. 306). OSHA has always been subject to criticism and prior to the Reagan Administration some of its provisions were considered too difficult to implement. But the Reagan Administration has gone beyond such criticisms since it believes the government's role in the work environment should be minimised.

In environmental policy, deregulation has been less successful in part because of the personality of Reagan's first appointee to the position of Secretary of the Environment, James Watt. Watt's proposals, such as selling off national parks for coalmining and extensive oil mining along the American coasts, have been enormously controversial and diversionary from the Administration's aims. But the Environmental Protection Agency's (EPA) effectiveness has been eroded through the appointment of personnel sympathetic to the Reagan position, notably Anne Burford; these appointees have been lax in enforcing environmental controls. The EPA's budget has suffered a 50 per cent reduction (with Burford's support), further curtailing its regulatory capacity. The controversies of both Watt and the EPA appointees convey a strong disregard for the importance of environmental protection on the Reagan Administration agenda, though its actual success in rescinding legislation has been small. As Quick (1984) observes, 'the administration failed notably ... to achieve fundamental changes in the legislative framework of social regulation. Not one of the important pieces of social regulatory legislation was successfully altered, even though several (such as the Clean Air and Clean Water Acts) came up for reauthorization during the administration's first year'(p. 307).

The Reagan Administration's deregulation policies have revealed the influence of New Right arguments about the free market and minimal government reviewed in earlier chapters. For one analyst, a Reagan enthusiast, economic deregulation constitutes the 'first major victory for free market economics in American public policy, and it sets an important precedent. Since the New Deal, economic advances in the United States have been equated with bold government initiatives. The spectacular benefits of deregulation have shown the progress that can come from reducing government's role rather than enlarging it. By liberating price controls and permitting competition, the deregulation revolution has allowed entrepreneurs to find the most profitable ways of serving customers' (Okun, 1986, p. 65). The drop in airline ticket prices and in petroleum rates are given as beneficial examples of deregulation. But deregulation has significant costs, rarely mentioned by the Reagan Administration. For example, the environment is less well protected than it was prior to 1980; the Administration's willingness to lease much of the United States coastline for oil exploration without regulatory precautions indicates its priorities in this regard. Deregulation of the telephone industry and of banking has produced considerable hardship for the poor. While deregulation increases market forces, consumers need the appropriate funds to participate effectively in those markets.

Many poor Americans have insufficient resources for such participation. For example, local telephone rates have risen rapidly since deregulation, restricting use by the poor and elderly (Horwitz, 1985). Deregulation does not result in universal benefit; freeing market forces serves to reinforce inequality of participation when this is based on private resources.

The Reagan Administration has introduced considerable deregulation in the private economic sphere through either abrogation of regulatory requirements or half-hearted enforcement of extant stipulations. It has been less successful in implementing social deregulation. But it has changed the climate about the suitability of regulation by the state. As in welfare policy, the Reagan Administration has made a concerted and determined effort to reverse trends which are the culmination of several decades of government expansion. Privatisation will be a significant legacy of the Thatcher Government in Britain; likewise, in the United States, reversing the Reagan Administration's deregulation policies will be a considerable task for future administrations. In this sense, privatisation and deregulation are some of the most consequential aspects of these New Right-influenced Thatcher and Reagan Administrations.

CONCLUSION: ENDING STATE INTERVENTION?

Relations between the White House and Capitol Hill are critical to the success or failure of Presidential policy objectives. For the Reagan Presidency's first year of office this relationship was exceptionally favourable, facilitating a sizeable tax cut, considerable reductions in social welfare spending and an increase in defence spending. None of these objectives have been as extensive as the White House sought but they have been greater than many commentators believed possible. It is evident also that New Right liberal economic theories – specifically supply-side economics – influenced the formulation and execution of these policy objectives. This is amply illustrated in Stockman (1986). So, like Britain under the Thatcher Government, New Right liberalism has influenced government policy. Further, the huge deficit which has accrued during the Reagan Administration makes the implementation of new social programmes politically very difficult. It is a proud boast of Reagan supporters, such as George Gilder, that no non-defence legislative initiatives have been undertaken since 1980. At least in the areas of non-defence state expenditure and regulatory programmes the Reagan Administration has marked the end of state intervention. What are the implications of these developments?

The institutionalisation of liberal priorities

The policies pursued by the Reagan Administration have not only advanced their ends but have also limited the scope for their opponents, principally the Democratic Party. Most obviously, by making budget-cutting rather than budget-spending the main priority of government (with the obvious exception of defence, considered below) the New Deal and Great Society role of the Democrats has been seriously tarnished. For the Democrats to resume this traditional interventionist role, in the context of a huge national deficit, would require some increase in taxes; they seem loath to make this commitment. More practically, the non-defence spending cuts of the Reagan Administration has severed the financial link between the Democrats and their constituents. Blacks, Hispanics, inner city residents, the elderly, the poor and other Democrat supporters have been most affected by the cuts in social welfare spending. Those insurance programmes which apply to all citizens have been less affected than selective assistance programmes, whose recipients are less obviously Republican voters. The cuts have also intensifed cleavages within the Democratic Party, for example between urban and suburban residents and between blacks and whites; the latter conflict is evident especially in conflicts between Black Democratic mayors and their fellow Party members running state legislatures and gubernatorial offices. And the Administration's current tax reform proposals seek to eliminate the deduction of local and state taxes; this will create major problems for the fiscally weaker municipalities – that is, those in the North-east associated with the Democrats – who may have to raise taxes and lay off thousands of public sector workers (Shefter and Ginsberg, 1985).

Thus, through welfare spending cuts and other measures, the Reagan Administration has weakened the Democrats' links with their traditional voters and made it difficult for them to promise restoration of the abrogated programmes. At the same time, defence spending by this Administration, like tax cuts, has favoured Republican supporters. The 1984 presidential election also drew support to the Republicans from traditional Democrat voters such as Southerners, Catholics and blue collar workers, though this trend was less apparent in congressional results. The Reagan Administration will have a long legacy in domestic American politics, and its liberally-inspired welfare cuts and deregulation will not easily be overturned because of the structural deficit which its policies has generated. A future Administration which drastically cut defence spending would still need to be cautious in expanding non-defence social programmes while this deficit persists.

Attacking social citizenship rights

Implementing these liberal minimal state objectives has required an activist government – a paradox familiar from the British New Right experience reviewed in Chapter 7. This paradox is especially apparent in the Reagan Administration's support of conservative issues: school prayer and anti-abortion, for example, and opposition to affirmative action or the rights of minorities. For New Right liberals such as David Stockman, the Moral Majority and associated social conservatism was unattractive; he records his reaction to learning Jack Kemp's decision to support the Reagan candidacy thus: 'in the process, he [Kemp] was aligning himself with Jerry Falwell, the anti-gun control nuts, the Bible-thumping creationists, the anti-Communist witch-hunters, and small-minded Hollywood millionaires to whom "supply-side" meant one more Mercedes' (1986, p. 52). For President Reagan, as for Prime Minister Thatcher, there was some personal empathy for such social conservatives; and presidential candidate Reagan's conservative attitude toward these issues paid electoral dividends; but in order to maintain 'Yuppie' support the Reagan Administration has done almost nothing to further directly 'family'-type issues; the same is true in Britain. In both countries liberal economic arguments were the primary electoral attraction: social conservatism has provided useful explanations and rationales for the consequences of liberal economic policies, but this is a secondary role.

While the Reagan Administration may have done little directly by way of legislative initiative to advance conservative causes, other activities of the Administration are less benign in this regard. Thus the Administration has had an enormous influence upon the federal judiciary, appointing half of all serving judges in the federal courts. The Administration has consistently sought out and pressed ideologically conservative candidates who are opposed to abortion, affirmative action and judicial activism, and who support states' rights and tough crime measures (including capital punishment). The institutionalisation of a conservative federal judiciary will potentially prolong Reagan policies on social issues. For example, in July 1986 the Supreme Court declared it illegal to engage in oral or anal sex in private, a decision interpreted widely as an infringement of homosexual rights. On the other hand, in the same month, the Supreme Court reaffirmed the legality of affirmative action, which is quite contrary to the New Right position of the Reagan Administration. However, federal appellate courts below the Supreme Court may be more active in reaching conservative judgements. Making these judicial appointments has, of course, required an active state policy. In other areas, the Reagan Presidency had appointed candidates sharing his ideology: Ann Burford at the EPA is one example. A more recent one is the Education Secretary, William Bennett, who has advocated religious teachings in schools. But the Reagan Administration is unlikely to pursue this, or comparable policies, through Congress.

Taken together, the cuts in welfare support and advocacy of conservative social positions by the Reagan Administration has weakened social citizenship rights in the United States. These have never had more than a tenuous status when compared to Western European countries. But, as outlined in Chapter 4, the welfare state institutions established by the New Deal, Great Society and related policies did afford important protection and rights to the least privileged members of American society. For Stockman, the Reagan Revolution may be a failure because of its proposed spending cuts which did not succeed; but for those affected by such welfare cuts, the Reagan Revolution is more real. These citizenship rights have now been greatly eroded – considerably more so than in Britain. In this sense New Right liberalism has been more consequential in the United States than in Britain, where the stronger tradition of the welfare state has ensured a more effective defence of its institutions. The next chapter considers this contrast in more detail. In both countries, however, these Administrations have forced budget-cutting rather than spending on to the political agenda to a degree which dictates how oppositional parties formulate their strategies.

9

Social Citizenship Rights in the Welfare State

INTRODUCTION

The first eight chapters of this book have examined the content and influence of New Right political and economic theories. The book now looks beyond these arguments and Chapter 10 concentrates upon the likely role of markets in post-New Right public policy, specifically the formulation of labour market policy to combat unemployment and how this relates to expanding citizenship rights. This chapter examines the concept of citizenship rights and their incorporation in the institutions of the welfare state. While New Right arguments have affected civil and political citizenship rights, reducing the welfare state (and hence social rights) has been a central objective of those governments influenced by New Right ideas. It is this aspect of citizenship which is of primary concern here. This chapter further considers how welfare rights have been integrated into the British and American political systems. It is argued that the welfare state is now so central to Britain that a diminution of its scope (as sought by New Right advocates) is difficult to achieve; by contrast, the weaker American welfare state makes its retrenchment somewhat easier, though not unproblematical. While social citizenship rights do not face extinction, these two Governments have had harmful consequences for them in their respective countries.

Social citizenship rights and the welfare state

Chapter 1 introduced the notion of 'citizenship rights' to refer to the extension of civil, political and social rights in Western industrial

164

societies during the last two hundred years. Each applies to a different sphere: civil citizenship rights refers primarily to individual legal rights; political, to democratic participatory rights; and social, to those post-war economic and welfare rights embodied in the Keynesian welfare state. As one scholar observes, 'welfare statism is the twentieth century's response to the demand of citizens – however articulated – for material protection from contingencies that are beyond their privately organized capacity to avoid' (Friedman, 1981, p. 15). The welfare state directly counters market processes by providing citizens with a minimum income, a basic standard of social services (health and education, for example), and respite against economic uncertainty.

Throughout the preceding chapters it has been stressed that the ideology of New Right liberals and conservatives implies the retrenchment of these rights, particularly social citizenship rights. For a variety of economic and political reasons, outlined in Chapters 2 to 6, New Right advocates want to make people less dependent upon public welfare provision and more self-reliant, or dependent upon familial support and the vagaries of market forces. For New Right theorists, the welfare state is an undesirable bureaucratic apparatus, which not only reduces the incentive for individuals to work but is also harmful to the economy and social order. The welfare state generates a bureaucratic class responsible for its operation and committed to its perpetuity, if not its expansion, according to New Right critics. A market-based political movement emphasises how state welfare provision interferes with 'natural' economic processes, not its amelioration of hardship. This is why New Right advocates want to destroy social citizenship rights and to return people to the mercy of market processes.

The work of T. H. Marshall

The contemporary concept of citizenship rights derives from the work of the sociologist T. H. Marshall. In his formulation, Marshall (1964) recognised that such rights did not adhere to some absolute standard; rather, they are the product of a process of social development extending the scope of legitimate citizenship within a society. The establishment of citizenship rights usually occurs as a result of conflict and organised protest by those groups in society excluded from existing rights. Social groups engage in systematic protest (sometimes including violent conflict) to realise a fuller degree of social participation (Turner, 1986). Class conflict (that is, conflict between employers and workers) has been central historically to the granting of political, civil and social citizenship rights. And extensions in citizenship rights frequently occur in the context of major social change – for example, following a war or migratory movements. Thus the origins of citizenship rights lie in the formation of contemporary society. As such, citizenship rights are difficult to retract: having been created through struggle, and integrated into a country's political culture, it is not easy for a new administration to demolish them. Marshall (1964) writes as follows:

> citizenship is a status bestowed on those who are full members of a community. All who possess the status are equal with respect to the rights and duties with which the status is endowed. There is no universal principle that determines what those rights and duties shall be, but societies in which citizenship is a developing institution create an image of an ideal citizenship against which achievement can be measured and towards which aspiration can be directed. The urge forward along the path thus plotted is an urge towards a fuller measure of equality, an enrichment of the stuff of which the status is made and an increase in the number of those on whom the status is bestowed. Social class, on the other hand, is a system of inequality. And it too, like citizenship, can be based on a set of ideals, beliefs and values. It is therefore reasonable to expect that the impact of citizenship on social class should take the form of a conflict between opposing principles. (p. 84)

Citizenship rights are established through struggles frequently in the wake of social change. The last includes industrialisation which unleashes enormous change upon society, challenging hierarchical social values, emphasising merit over traditionally based status, and stressing universal rather than selective standards. As Turner (1986) summarises: 'modern citizenship presupposes some notion of equality, an emphasis on universalistic criteria and a secular system of values to reinforce claims and obligations. Societies organised on this principle emphasize contract over status, the dominance of secular reality over the sacred, the importance of universalism over locality and particularity, and the importance of extending citizenship rights to women and children so as to call into question the dominance of patriarchy' (p. 22). The establishment of citizenship rights reduces the authority and power of previously dominant groups and institutions in society: those groups benefiting through the exclusion of others from citizenship rights will resist initially the granting of these rights and seek their reversal in the future. This last objective becomes increasingly difficult the longer citizenship rights persist and are incorporated into a society's core values. Thus, as Miller (1976) argues, the meaning of 'social justice' changed significantly between the nineteenth-century market capitalism era and the twentieth-century regulated capitalism period. In the first, a person's desert was determined exclusively by market values; but in the later period this concept of desert has been broadened to reduce the importance of market estimations in its calculation and 'the better-off can show their own rewards to be just by meeting the just claims to their services made by those in need' (1976, p. 309). Through the establishment of an ever-widening conception of citizenship rights, societal values change to reflect shifting patterns of power and the development of new values.

The citizenship rights embodied in the welfare state are based on principles and beliefs different from those informing New Right arguments. Proponents of social, political and civil citizenship rights desire a more egalitarian society than do New Right liberals and conservatives, who assert the value and necessity of inequality. It is not surprising, therefore, that liberals and conservatives consider the reduction of social citizenship rights important since such rights conflict with market-based ones. As Rustin (1985) observes, 'the reaction of the radical right in America, Britain and elsewhere in the West is to be understood as in its own way a rational response to the severe pressures stemming from democratization and mass access to the political, economic and cultural arenas. Arguments for the restoration of market forces, for strong government, and for a re-establishment of traditional values in the areas of the family and sexual life, were moved by real anxiety about the threats which the prosperity and characteristic claims of the post-war era posed to the prerogatives of property and to the minorities associated with its rule' (p. 5).

However, neither the Thatcher Government nor the Reagan Administration have reduced social welfare spending to the level they wanted, particularly in the case of Britain, though their policies have altered priorities within these allocations. This outcome reflects the strength of welfare state institutions as well as public support for the social citizenship rights they embody. Such support derives from the origins of these social citizenship rights and from their integration into society. 'Integration' here refers to the assimilation of the welfare state and attendant social citizenship rights into the political culture of advanced industrial countries; the growth of interests within the welfare state's administrative and organisational structures defending it; the growth of interests outside the welfare state, including both welfare state claimants and professional, middle class, groups; and the routinisation of life experiences given extensive and, until the 1970s, expanding welfare state provision. British and American experiences offer a useful contrast: welfare rights are more extensive in the former political system than in the latter, which has consequences for the Thatcher and Reagan initiatives against them.

THE NATURE OF THE WELFARE STATE

The welfare state is the most important institutional embodiment of social citizenship rights: that is, rights to economic security, minimum standards of health and welfare and guaranteed access to education for all members of society. Social scientists have emphasised a variety of factors in the welfare state's development: these include the dynamics of industrialisation, the diffusion of liberal values supporting higher levels of public provision of welfare, the strength of working-class organisations, and innovations undertaken by members of government and the bureaucracy (Orloff and Skocpol, 1984). A full account of the nuances of these competing perspectives would require a separate chapter: suffice it to note that elements of each are relevant to a complete explanation of the welfare state's origins. Industrialisation resulted in major social, economic and political change, making inequalities both more extreme and the object of organised working class protest, particularly through the trade union movement in Britain. Central objectives of this protest were the alleviation of hardship and the achievement of egalitarianism through state policy. The resultant welfare state constitutes the creative response of society (varying by country) to these demands: it is a manifestation of the transformative capacity of individuals and society to new conditions and the contradictions these changes generate (Holmwood and Stewart, 1987).

The persistence of the welfare state generates public support for it: public provision of welfare and social services is an integral component of state intervention in Western industrial societies. The establishment and consolidation of welfare state policies contributes to the diffusion of a supportive ideology. Stephens (1979) has argued that the lengthy tenure in office of left-wing political parties enables them to influence the character of the political culture, rendering it more favourable to welfare state institutions. In Britain ideological support for the welfare state provides resilience against Thatcher Government attacks: empirical evidence indicates a wide commitment amongst the public to the appropriateness of collective provision against hardship (Taylor-Gooby, 1985). This contrasts with the experience of the American welfare state. In the United States, welfare state provisions are less extensive than in most other Western democracies, including Britain (Furniss and Tilton, 1977): a powerful example of this is the absence of a comprehensive national health system in the United States. America's smaller welfare state means it is a weaker part of the political culture there. This is reinforced by the weakness of the federal government and the fragmented nature of the American polity: it is notable that federal government employment has hardly changed over the last twenty-five years despite the increase in government activity. Financially, many regional state and local governments in the United States face serious problems in underwriting welfare programmes, especially means-tested public assistance policies; those subnational governments legally required to balance their annual budget frequently find it difficult to provide public welfare. The welfare tax-backlash symbolised by California's Proposition 13 reinforces these financial restrictions upon local authorities. Thus American federalism has been a significant institutional influence upon the nature of the welfare state there; for the most part, an influence which has limited the expansion of welfare programmes.

Culturally, welfare state institutions must compete with the strong American individualistic tradition and with the low status accorded welfare state recipients. A recent article by Lane (1986) concludes that Americans prefer market justice to state or political justice: 'even where the market's methods are thought to be unfair to certain groups, such as blacks or women, the intrusion of the government into the sacred market precincts is often regarded with suspicion, for the government's program of rectification trespasses on the evaluation of persons by the market's process of revealed contribution' (p. 397). It is not easy for American welfare programmes to overcome this strong cultural support for market processes.

Marginal versus institutional welfare states

The contrast between American and British public provision experiences can be treated systematically with Korpi's (1983) useful distinction between 'marginal' and 'institutional' welfare state models. Each is an ideal-type, representing extremes in possible welfare state forms, the former a minimal welfare state commitment, the latter a fuller set of state welfare responsibilities. Korpi distinguishes between them by the proportion of national income spent on welfare policy, the proportion of the population affected, whether social policies are universal or selective, the progressivity of the taxation system, the importance of full employment programmes and so on: 'we would expect universalistic measures, directed towards large sections of the population, to be important in the institutional model of social policy. Selective policies directed towards subgroups of the population with specific needs will be relatively more important in the marginal model'(Korpi, 1983, p. 192).

The two extremes are well represented by the United States (marginal) and Scandinavian countries (institutional), though Britain approximates to the second ideal-type. Korpi (1983) argues, analogously to the position advanced here, that the implementation of these two models result in different levels of public support for the welfare state: 'generally, we would expect that a marginal type of these two models results in different levels of public support for institutional type of social policy in generating coalitions in its defence. A marginal type of social policy, predominant for example in the United States, explicitly or implicitly draws a poverty line in the population and thus separates the poor and relatively small minority from the better-off majority of the population' (p. 193). A marginal welfare state has a more limited impact upon the polity than has an institutional welfare state in generating support bases and its integration into the political culture is weak: this is reinforced by the demarcation in welfare policy between those benefiting, and those not receiving benefits, which creates distinct barriers from those found in systems with universalistic welfare states.

The adoption of a marginal or institutional welfare form depends critically, Esping-Andersen and Korpi (1985) argue, upon the presence of a socialist working class organisation during the formation and maturation of the welfare state: 'cross-national comparisons indicate that the balance of political power is closely related to the extent to which the boundaries of social citizenship have been expanded' (p. 202); Chapter 4 noted the greater strength of the working class in Britain relative to the United States. Such an expansion requires the implementation of an institutional rather than a marginal welfare state form: Britain's welfare state approximates to the former while the United States fits the second category, which is important for the defence of welfare state policy and institutions against New Right critics. A universal and expanding welfare state gathers support: where taxes are perceived as resulting in generalised, rather than selective, benefits support will be broader; where taxes result in particularistic benefits, societal support will be weaker. And a universal system of welfare influences social routines and everyday life experiences more than does a marginal system, and is more likely to affect the political culture positively. The welfare state has not displaced the market system but it has become equally integral to ideological and everyday experiences in Britain; this is less true of the United States.

Thus whether welfare policies are selective or universal is important for their level of support in both countries; they should be differently resistant to New Right attacks. In the United States, social insurance programmes, which are not means-tested and universal in eligibility, have withstood the Reagan Administration's attack; but the public assistance entitlement programmes, which are means-tested and selective in eligibility, have been most seriously affected by the Administration's retrenchment programme, as reviewed in Chapter 8. Public assistance entitlement programmes, because selective in application, have a weaker support base in American society. There is less scope for broadly-based social resistance to their retrenchment, unlike social insurance programmes which affect most groups in society. In Britain, a similar pattern is evident. Universal welfare programmes like those for education and health have been less subject either to privatisation or to retraction, which reflects the wide support in society for these policies (see Rustin, 1985; Rosenberry, 1982).

Aside from political cultural accommodation to the welfare state, some other factors facilitate its persistence. One is support for the welfare state within the institutions of the state. In the adoption of welfare policies, Orloff and Skocpol (1984) emphasise 'both the autonomous actions of officials and politicians and the ways in which state structures and their transformations affected the policy preferences of politically influential social groups' (p. 745). In addition to the needs articulated by social groups and generated by economic change it must be recognised that 'welfare policies are also directly grounded in the logics of state-building, in the struggles of politicians for control and advantage, and in the expectations groups have about what states and parties with specific structures and modes of operation could or should do' (p. 746). In the development of the welfare state some state officials, whether elected or bureaucratic, or together, became committed to implementing policies judged socially and/or politically desirable. Heclo (1974) documents this process in relation to Swedish and British unemployment and old-age assistance, where state officials analysed social problems and devised policy responses. This created a framework within the state's institutions premised upon public welfare provision (see also Dryzek and Goodin, 1986). It is public officials who must respond to environmental pressures – be these derived from class conflict, increasing social complexity or industrialisation – with effective public policy. They restructure the political system by the introduction of major innovations. As a consequence of this role, public officials acquire programmatic commitments to policies such as those associated with the welfare state and seek to protect them when challenged (Gurr and King, 1987; King, 1986). This may mean conflict between elected and bureaucratic officials, the second group defending long-cherished policies. But it relates also to how the maturation of the welfare state leads to the development of group interests both within and outside state institutions.

Welfare state producers and consumers

The welfare state not only provides an institutional base for public officials but also creates a focus for a whole plethora of professional middle-class groups; it spawns also a class of welfare state clients or dependants who are likely to share a commitment to defending these institutions and policies. The first group includes professionals such as doctors, teachers and social workers who now have important interests in the defence and preservation of the welfare state. But the welfare state has not simply expanded the institutions of the state; it has also expanded citizenship rights to groups not traditionally associated with the state. This is in addition to administrators in these and other welfare policy areas such as the social services and local government. These groups' interests are not based on conventional class and economic categories of differentiation. As Alan Cawson (1982) has observed, 'sectoral interests which emerge from the activities of the state, especially those grounded in the various branches of the state itself, are not so deeply entrenched in class relations and may, in certain circumstances, be seen as being more significant than class divisions' (p. 76).

Public sector employees and professionals are highly unionised (Dunleavy, 1980; Gough, 1979) which makes them powerful groups available for mobilisation to protect the welfare services they helped initiate and now maintain. High public sector unionisation is a general phenomenon in advanced industrial societies, including the United States (in contrast to the nationally low unionisation levels there), and not one restricted to Britain. Of course, there is no necessary unity or shared affinity between different professional and unionised groups within the public sector and they suffer differentially from cuts in welfare spending. Solidarity between lower level public employees and senior policy-making bureaucrats is not intrinsically high, but in practice there is likely to be some shared interest in maintaining the welfare state. However, in Britain, measures pursued by the Thatcher Government seek to undermine potential solidarity. The Government is introducing currently pay differentials, within civil servant categories, to the British bureaucracy. And, many lower-level public sector employees are women, frequently employed on a part-time basis – highly vulnerable to redundancy. Thus, high levels of public-sector unionisation may be a less effective mechanism for defending welfare state institutions than might be anticipated, at least in the lower ranks of the bureaucracy; at higher levels a stronger defence can be expected.

There is a second group with vested interests in the persistence of the welfare state and its policies: those receiving benefits, for whom it was originally created. A significant proportion of the population is in some way economically dependent upon welfare state spending for basic necessities. With steady increases in unemployment levels in Britain, the proportion of the population receiving social security has continued to expand. In some senses, this group constitutes a 'dependent class', whose life experiences and routines are fundamentally shaped by their relationship to the welfare state and its patterns of benefits. But without this state income, their lot would be very precarious. For those suffering unemployment under the Thatcher Government's liberal economic policies, the social citizenship rights to welfare services, social security and minimum health standards are critically important.

DEFENDING CITIZENSHIP RIGHTS

The maturation of the welfare state and its integration into society has had profound consequences for social structures and relationships: it has altered production and consumption positions within society in the process of creating a complex set of new interests and dependencies. These interests constitute a protective force for the welfare state in the face of Government efforts to reduce its size. The expansion in state employment and in the number of welfare state recipients have both facilitated the integration of welfare state institutions in the political economy, though more so in Britain than the United States. These two groups – producers and consumers of welfare services – thus have major interests in the current welfare state.

However, middle-class professionals and working-class recipients have different relationships with the state (Dunleavy, 1979), which has consequences for the protection of welfare programmes against proposed retrenchment. Officials and professionals both produce *and* consume welfare state services; welfare state dependents are exclusively consumers of these services and programmes. This is apparent in Britain and in the United States. Two implications follow. First, those programmes which are consumed by both groups should have potentially greater support than those consumed by one group only. But, second, those policies and services with which middle-class professionals are mainly concerned might be expected to be better protected against cuts than those focused on welfare state dependents: either because of electoral power or because of their position as producers of these services, professional groups might be expected to exercise greater force in defending services. There is evidence that such factors have influenced the policies of the Thatcher and Reagan Administrations. For example, the Thatcher Government's recent concern to emphasise its *increase* in expenditure upon health and internal Cabinet divisions about increasing public spending, even if this means exceeding stipulated expenditure targets. More systematic evidence comes from the policies which have survived the Thatcher and Reagan attacks: as noted above, in the United States, it is the universally-applied social insurance programmes which have suffered least from Administration cuts, whereas means-tested entitlement programmes, such as food stamps and AFDC, consumed primarily by the working class, have suffered the greatest retraction. Likewise, welfare programmes for employment and training – predominantly consumed by the working class – have shrunk since 1981. In Britain, the Thatcher Government's privatisation programme has been most successful in those areas of least concern to the professional middle class; thus, to date, no progress toward privatisation in the medical sphere of the National Health Service has occurred (unlike the laundry services, or local council cleaning responsibilities); and the Thatcher Government's objective of introducing education vouchers never got off the ground (Le Grand and Winter, 1987). Undoubtedly, these outcomes cannot be explained exclusively by their relationship to middle-class professionals; none the less, this is an important factor underlying their persistence.

The welfare state embodies a set of social citizenship rights which have become integral to the political culture of Britain; comparable rights exist in the United States but their narrower scope and selective nature has necessarily made them less central, though not insignificant, to American political culture. The difference between the two countries in this regard concerns how universal welfare policies are: Britain has a fuller welfare state in this sense and hence a stronger public notion of social citizenship. That these citizenship rights have become integral to British society helps explain the failure of the Thatcher Government to implement the range of cuts in the welfare state which it initially sought. And in the United States the Reagan Administration's proposed Draconian cuts in federal welfare benefits were thwarted by a Congress aware of public support for such measures; despite the increasing costs of social insurance policies to the American taxpayer, they remain intact. Public support for social citizenship rights is less firmly rooted in the United States than it is in Britain and less identified with welfare state institutions; but it is much stronger for social insurance than public assistance policies. Britain and the United States are following a general trend here; as Therborn (1984) correctly notes, welfare state institutions and policies have become integral to all advanced industrial democracies: 'the predominant everyday state routine – as indicated by patterns of public expenditure and public employment – has centred on social security, public welfare and public education' (p. 28).

In sum, there is ideological and institutional support for the welfare state in Britain and, more weakly, in the United States, and it is not easily undermined. The welfare state is integrated into the structure of society and its consumption and production patterns. The Thatcher and Reagan Administrations can attack successfully those less popular aspects of welfare services providing selective benefits; retrenchment of universally held rights in either country is much more difficult. However, the cuts in selective benefits (and linked with privatisation in Britain) have influenced the terms of political discourse within which these issues are debated, but this is less significant than the destruction of the welfare state sought by New Right theorists. There are no grounds for complacency about the attack upon public welfare provision pursued by the Thatcher and Reagan Administrations: their consistent criticisms in the public arena weakens the welfare state's structural position in contemporary societies; and neither administration has allowed any new welfare policies to be initiated. This in turn has placed the emphasis upon justification for such proposals presented by other political parties. What the experience of these two New Right-influenced administrations suggests is that fuller welfare states – those approximating Korpi's (1983) 'institutional' model – should be established for social citizenship rights to become firmly entrenched in the political economy.

CONCLUSIONS

Citizenship rights are dynamic rather than static: such rights evolve in contemporary societies, enlarging the range of issues and categories affected. Marshall (1964) traced the sequential establishment of civil, political and social citizenship rights, while Miller (1976) has argued that the concept of social justice has widened from the nineteenth to the twentieth century. And it is to be expected that citizenship rights will continue to expand. Two areas in particular are ripe for such expansion in Britain and the United States: the right to full employment through an active labour market policy; and women's rights, which requires a significant change in existing values in society as well as in the way social citizenship rights have been conceptualised. These issues are the subject of Chapter 10.

10

Markets and Citizenship: A New Agenda

INTRODUCTION: MARKETS VERSUS PLANNING – A NEW DEBATE?

This chapter's central argument is that the future development of national economic policy in Britain, which has a short history of Keynesianism challenged by New Right liberalism, will combine elements from each. Such a pattern is likely to characterise the late 1980s and persist into the 1990s. The influence of New Right liberals has not extended to a complete dismantling of the Keynesian welfare state consensus but their arguments and policies have been sufficiently influential to force future administrations to retain elements of liberalism. In particular, New Right liberals have forced markets on to the political and intellectual agenda – requiring socialists and social democrats to modify their policy proposals as a consequence. The long-standing debate about the appropriate role of markets and planning in public policy has been revived under New Right influence. In this chapter the sort of market policy to be pursued by future Governments is discussed. The main premise for this discussion is the social citizenship right embodied in the Beveridge Report in Britain and the 1946 Employment Act in the United States: the right to work, which requires the government to pursue full employment strategies (though see Stein, 1969 on the 1946 Act).

The emphasis here is upon an active labour market policy. However, discussions about the apposite balance of planning and market in the post-New Right period raise broader issues. Most importantly, what kind of state, responsible for planning and public policy, should be strived for? The appropriate response, it is advanced here, is a state whose values reflect social citizenship rights. But these rights must be more widely conceived than in the post-war consensus; most importantly, gender assumptions must be changed, since those informing the post-war consensus reinforce existing gender roles and biases in the political economy rather than challenging them. These are the topics for this final chapter. The discussion will draw mainly upon British experience, where debates about future policy have been more extensive than in the United States. American Democrats offer either a set of traditional Democrat policies (like Walter Mondale, for example) or a watered down version of New Right liberalism (Gary Hart, for example); both accepted many Reagan Administration cuts in the welfare state and supported arms spending, though they did advocate a more active economic role for the state (see Davis, 1986). For potential Presidential Democratic candidates in 1988, there is as yet no clear position; however, within the Party 'the majority view is that the party should move to the centre – particularly if it is to win the conservative south, which is widely seen as the key to victory in 1988. The challenge is to develop new policies that are slightly more conservative but still distinguishable from the Republicans' " (Dale, *Financial Times*, 16 August 1986). Such uncertainty makes it more profitable to examine British political developments for these issues.

Markets and Consumption

New Right politicians, including members of the Thatcher Government, have successfully emphasised consumption issues such as education, health care, social services and housing: this emphasis has been to denigrate public provision of such goods and services in favour of competitive, market-based production. New Right politicians have created, or at least exploited, public dissatisfaction with the capacity of the state to meet these consumption needs; as noted in Chapter 7, dissatisfaction with welfare services (dole queues, hospital waiting lists and so on) existed by the 1970s. For New Right theorists and politicians the source of this discontent is their public provision; because of the absence of competition and choice, these services are inferior and forfeit consumer sovereignty. To remedy this, New Right advocates have sought to introduce market forces into the provision of consumption goods and services. This is manifested in the Thatcher

Government's privatisation programme and in its efforts to contract-out other state activities. The combination of New Right criticisms of state services with such policies has revived the question of the role of markets in contemporary advanced industrial societies.

That this reappraisal has influenced socialists and social democrats is plain (see Hodgson, 1984; Nove, 1983 and Panitch, 1985/86). One vivid example is provided by Saunders (1985): after a personal reappraisal of socialist objectives, he concludes that the right to house ownership through the market should be extended to other areas: 'the argument over home ownership was for me clear-cut. More problematic was the implication for what I was arguing for other consumption services supplied by the state. Gradually, and not without considerable discomfort, I came to realise that if it was right and desirable for people to participate in the market in order to accommodate themselves so too it was right and desirable for them to assume more control in other parts of their lives wherever possible in the sphere of consumption' (p. 167). This resurgence of interest in markets reflects New Right influence. A more fundamental influence is the discontent articulated by socialists and social democrats both with the Eastern European model of socialism and with conventional public ownership as the key litmus test of socialist practice. Nationalisation can no longer be presented uncritically as the basis of public policy (as policy debate in both the Labour and Social Democratic – Liberal Alliance parties makes clear); nor can consumer interests be ignored in the provision of state services. However, despite the efforts of New Right liberals during the last decade, it is inconceivable that Britain (or the United States) will revert to a pure nineteenth-century market economy (for accounts of the market versus planning debate see von Mises, 1935; Hayek, 1935; Lané, 1985; Alt and Chrystal, 1983); and post-1945 experience completely undermines Hayek's (1944) claim that public planning necessarily results in a totalitarian society. Rather, a new ethos is being forged which absorbs aspects of New Right liberalism with a reconstructed Keynesian macroeconomics.

MARKETS AND ECONOMIC POLICY

The achievement of economic growth remains a key priority for all shades of political opinion: Conservative, Labour and Social Democratic–Liberal Alliance. In Chapter 4, the importance of steadily expanding economic growth to the success of the Keynesian welfare consensus was stressed. But economic growth must be the basis for guaranteeing full employment – a key social citizenship right – rather than an end in itself. National economic policy – and, indeed, all state intervention – now exists in a critical environment as a result of New Right arguments. This is quite evident in Britain from the Labour Party's cautious approach to public ownership (Jones, 1986). But while New Right liberal economic arguments must require caution about policy proposals, and a more favourable attitude toward market processes, the problems of the latter should not be neglected. Citizenship rights are necessary to protect and regulate market interactions; for those least well-placed, it is uncertain that freedom and democracy are guaranteed under a market system. This is why post-New Right policy must seek to maximise social citizenship rights, even if this is combined with a more benign view of markets in public policy.

All proposals for future macroeconomic policy in Britain confront serious problems. The British economy has undergone economic deindustrialisation during the last two and a half decades (some would suggest for even longer). To some extent, this process is part of a restructuring of the British economy which may result in long-term buoyancy – the development of new technology industries being an important component of this process. But the short term is bleak: historically unprecedented unemployment levels, concentrated in specific regions and urban areas of the country. A North–South division has developed in Britain reflecting different economic conditions – the North being economically destitute compared to the South-east of Britain. Unemployment has affected particular age groups: young school leavers and middle-aged long-term unemployed whose skills in traditional heavy industry are redundant. Minority groups are especially adversely affected by unemployment. Discussion of economic policy must be placed against this background.

A REVIVED KEYNESIANISM?

New Right liberals berated the failure of Keynesian economic policy: by the 1970s the combined problems of unemployment and inflation reflected the inadequacy of this economic doctrine and indeed the mere pursuit of Keynesian policies were interpreted as contributing to the economic problems of that decade. Can Keynesianism be recovered in this setting and is it worth reconstructing?

There are good reasons for reformulating Keynesian economic policies. The central intellectual object of this theory is the alleviation of unemployment, which remains highly pertinent; the theory also seeks to reduce the uncertainties of market processes and glaring inequalities which these create. The success of Keynesianism as a policy response to crisis in the 1930s and 1940s provides little basis for its wholesale abandonment in the 1980s. During that period, Keynes's imperative for sustained investment, if implemented over the long run, 'would create abundance, eliminate that part of the profits which was simply a return on monetary wealth, and lead to substantially greater social and economic equality. And since the strategy of investment made immediately for high levels of employment and was compatible with major redistributive and welfare reforms, it was the perfect basis for the emerging compromise' (Grahl, 1983, p. 20). The economic difficulties of the 1970s in Britain and in the United States made such Keynesian prescriptions vulnerable to attack by New Right liberals such as Hayek, Friedman and Buchanan, obsessively seeking an increase in the scope of the free market regardless of the affect upon individual freedoms and life-chances; that the post-1945 period has seen a strengthening of social citizenship rights is ignored.

A further reason for retaining elements of Keynesianism, is the record of success which this policy can claim in certain countries. Therborn (1985, 1986) argues that the advanced industrial countries best able to minimise the economic crisis of the 1970s were those most committed to Keynesian policies, reflected in an institutionalised commitment to full employment. Austria, Japan, Norway, Sweden and Switzerland all fit this pattern, according to Therborn. However, these Keynesian policies have concentrated upon investment rather than on stimulating consumer demand, and they have been linked to low interest rates and labour market policy: 'the general argument for and against Keynesianism has often been conducted in mistaken terms. The most effective expansive policies have been directed not so much towards stimulating consumer demand as directly towards investment. Secondly, the effectiveness of fiscal expansion crucially depends on whether or not it is supported by an expansive monetary policy, mainly of low real interest rates and, in some but not all cases, by a deliberate cheap currency policy. Thirdly, successful Keynesianism has, in the current crisis, always been accompanied and reinforced by selective state intervention, and sometimes also by private business not following the dictates of short-term market rationality' (Therborn, 1986, p. 29). Thus, Keynesian policies do have utility in very different countries and are worth retaining in national economic policy. Not all of Therborn's examples are equally relevant to British and American experience but neither are all irrelevant (see Rowthorn, 1986 on Therborn's arguments about Japan and Switzerland). Obviously, no one policy blueprint can be devised to apply to all cases. But elements of these policies can be combined to meet the conditions of individual countries. In particular, the commitment to full employment, manifested institutionally, is very important for those countries suffering high unemployment.

If it is accepted that Keynesian economic policy is worth reviving, how should this be accomplished? The principal response of Keynesian advocates is that its economic policies must be combined with a national policy which takes greater account of the power of trade unions than did the original precepts. To tackle unemployment, Keynesians propose pursuing an expansionary monetary and fiscal policy which will stimulate demand in the economy and increase employment. In order to avoid inflation it is necessary to combine these policies with an incomes policy which constrains wage increases. Without an incomes policy, Keynesian measures will result in substantial inflation. The increased power of trade unions in the 1960s and 1970s relative to earlier decades meant that wages kept rising in accord with profit increases. But in the 1980s and 1990s, such wage pressure in the context of Keynesian policies will generate inflation. Therefore, an incomes policy must be implemented by the national government. However, implementing such a policy requires corporatist institutions – that is, a set of union and employer organisations which can negotiate on behalf of their members and ensure their members' agreement to policy decisions reached, in this case some form of wage restraint.

Such corporatist institutional arrangements are absent in Britain and attempts to achieve incomes policy have been wholly unsuccessful, the last being Callaghan's social contract in the mid-1970s. Schott (1984) spells out the implication of this absence: in the Keynesian model of economic policy the 'route to success depends intimately on whether or not an incomes policy can be successfully mounted. If it cannot be, then there is no Keynesian solution to the dual problems of inflation and unemployment' (p. 184). Schott goes on to advocate the fostering of corporatist institutions in Britain to facilitate incomes policy in the long run. This is rather wishful thinking, however, and unlikely to materialise – certainly not in the short run, though this does not prevent some commentators from promoting incomes policy. Writing in the magazine of the Social Democratic Party, the economist James Meade (1985) argues that to avoid inflation in the wake of expansionary policies, an incomes policy must be operated: if increased demand is to generate expanded employment and output rather than higher wages, an incomes policy is central, Meade argues. A key part of the proposed solution for Meade is the 'removal of all the special trade union legal immunities and privileges' combined with a 'right for workers to take a wage claim to an impartial pay board' (1985, p. 14). One development which might lend credence to this position is the weakening of trade unions since 1979; as Bassett (1986) records in his study, strike-free agreements are gaining acceptance amongst many union leaders and members (strike-free agreements have been accepted by the EETPU and AUEW unions), as has balloting for strike decisions and leadership elections. Overall, trade unions are in a far weaker position as a consequence of the Thatcher Government's policies, which may make them more ready to agree upon incomes policy aimed at increasing employment. For Meade, it is imperative that the problem of how to ensure expanded demand results in a drop in unemployment is critical and he believes some sort of incomes policy will be necessary.

Meade's position needs to be broadened. If Keynesian policies are to be pursued in conjunction with an incomes policy, the latter, to be implemented, will have to offer substantive distributive benefits to workers. A social contract between capital and labour which is intended to attain wage control must provide attractive incentives to unions for their participation, incentives not simply in terms of salary increases but also regarding income distribution and increased industrial democracy: in other words, citizenship rights need to be included in any incomes policy package. And such a policy must restore the employee rights abrogated or weakened since 1979 under the Thatcher Government. Wage bargaining needs to be combined with agreements to greater worker participation in industrial decision-making throughout all sectors of the economy; such measures are already under way following pressure from the European Community; and also in investment, research and development policy as the Lucas Aerospace Shop Stewards Combine (Wainwright and Elliott, 1982) project attempted. Worker participation requires influence decisions about what goods to produce, according to socially useful needs rather than simply market imperatives: the conventional 'split between the industrial and the political sphere is challenged implicitly by the Workers' Plan movement. Both by seeking influence over the disposition of capital, and by seeking to impose value-criteria on the definition of needs and products, the Lucas Shop Stewards Combine raised issues of economic policy normally reserved for the State' (Rustin, 1985, p. 183). If Keynesian economic policies are to be reconstructed this will require some type of incomes policy, which bases its appeal on more than wage restraint; rather, innovative plans for greater worker control of production, employee rights and redistribution. Such proposals seem infinitely preferable to the harshness of unregulated market forces, the New Right alternative.

A policy that approximates these objectives has been developed by the now-defunct Greater London Council in its London Industrial Strategy (Greater London Council, 1985). The LIS's central aim is the revitalisation of the London economy, through the creation of jobs which meet the needs of groups especially affected by economic crisis – minorities, women, long-term unemployed and the handicapped, for example – and through greater worker control of the design and production of goods. Through the Greater London Enterprise Board and the London Training Board, the GLC attempted to stimulate and to restructure the London economy but with the interests and needs of workers in mind rather than just those of capital and employers. The LIS recognises the market economy, and the advantages which can accrue to market processes; but it seeks to combine market use with public intervention: 'restructuring should be achieved in ways consistent with the interests of workers in secure and well-paid employment, whilst prioritizing the usefulness of products and their relation to social need' (Rustin, 1986, p. 77). The LIS document claims to reject both New Right monetarism and Keynesianism, developing an alternative strategy which has a much clearer conception of workers' needs, socially useful production and state intervention other than at a Keynesian macroeconomic level. Thus the LIS seeks to provide jobs for all who want them, but in accordance with social and political criteria other than simply those of the market. This relates to issues discussed below. First, labour market policy needs to be addressed.

LABOUR MARKET POLICY

The persistence and scale of unemployment means that improving employment opportunities and increasing labour market flexibility must be central to future economic policy. The neglect of labour market policy is a major weakness of the way in which Keynesian policies were formulated in Britain after 1945. Labour market policy must feature prominently in the future absorption of markets into national economic policy. In this area, Britain has a poor record – for example, in comparison with Sweden (Mukherjee, 1972; Therborn, 1986). A labour market policy has a number of purposes. Most importantly, it should seek to maintain full employment, which in turn reduces the incidence of hardship in the economy. Such a policy should aim to match the skills of the labour force with the needs of the economy, through extensive training and retraining schemes; these should not be confined to periods of economic crisis in the economy. Labour market policy can also encompass large-scale public employment to absorb those workers unable to find work in the economy, especially during economic recessions.

Labour market policy contributes to the realisation of the vital social citizenship right of a job for those who seek one. A central feature of social citizenship rights is the right to employment. Like other social citizenship rights, the right to work was incorporated into the Beveridge Plan (see Chapter 4) upon which the welfare state was based. The economic growth and subsequent full employment of the post-war years allowed this right to be assumed rather than persistently pursued in systematically-based and institutionalised public policy. Labour market policy received little formal attention in Britain or the United States in contrast to those countries – Sweden, Norway and Austria – which Therborn (1985, 1986) rightly identifies as most effective in responding to the 1970s' economic crisis. That labour market policy has not been formulated in detail reflects the way in which welfare state institutions have been constructed as well as limitations in the conception of social citizenship. As Rustin (1985) writes, 'the contrast between the legally enforceable rights to certain kinds of social and welfare provision, and the absence of any enforceable right of the individual to work, represents a major division within the fabric of welfare capitalism between the sector dominated by the market and by economic contract, and the sector regulated by the state through the universal provision of various services or income entitlement' (p. 149). As a consequence of this division between public welfare and private sector labour markets the experience of social citizenship has been poorer than it might have been. Labour market policy is an aspect of social citizenship which cannot be overlooked in the future, if the utility of state planning and intervention is to be demonstrated. A reconstructed Keynesianism cannot rely on market criteria alone for employment. State policy must address the imperfections of the labour market and its consistent incapacity to clear in the 1980s. As Aberg (1984) observes, social citizenship rights are enhanced by an effective labour market policy: the latter 'contribute to an allocation of labour power which is less dependent on wage differentials, and therefore contribute to the basis for trade-union wage policies aimed at satisfying conceptions of justice and equality' (pp. 220–1). Labour market policy is integral to the full institutional welfare state identified in Chapter 9.

An active labour market policy has been followed most closely by Sweden where, since the 1950s, the National Labour Market Board (AMS) has implemented labour market training and co-ordination of employee skills with employer needs, and addressed the problems of the long-term unemployed. For the Swedes, labour market training constitutes a type of training 'specifically designed to bring the skills available within the current manpower stock into line with those which the economy requires because of shifts in demands for products, and changes in the technology or production processes. This concept of labour market training is a dynamic approach to changes in the structure of employment' (Mukherjee, 1972, p. 10). The result has been a very substantial adult training policy by the AMS approved of by the trade unions and employers alike. There is also an emphasis upon the creation of jobs and the preclusion (as much as possible) of lay-offs. And during the 1970s and 1980s unemployment was notably lower in Sweden (between 2 and 3 per cent) than in most comparable advanced industrial democracies, certainly Britain: by 1984 unemployment was 13.2 per cent in Britain and 3.1 per cent in Sweden (Therborn, 1986). The Swedish labour market policy emphasises also the morale of the unemployed: 'in all its dealings with the public, the Swedish employment exchange system concentrates on protecting and enhancing the client's individual self-esteem' (Mukherjee, 1972, p. 49).

Sweden's institutionalised commitment to maintaining high employment levels and countering the vagaries of market forces gave it a firm base with which to respond to the economic problems of the 1970s. Where business rationalisation and economic restructuring occurred, state grants ensured proper training and retraining for affected workers. Retraining programmes made mobility between growing and declining sectors of the economy a less painful process for workers than if they had been left to the mercy of market forces, as New Right liberals propose. Since the mid-1970s the Swedish labour market policy has placed most emphasis upon the protection of jobs and maintenance of local employment patterns. There are opportunities for recurrent education in Sweden, education is linked with employer needs, and positive discrimination for women and the disabled have been incorporated into Sweden's labour market policy. As Brown and Fairley (1987) observe, the Swedish 'response to the crisis is in marked contrast to the experience in the UK where the cost of re-structuring, flexibility and mobility is being met by the unemployed... Sweden's response to the crisis has been to give further security to individuals and restrict the power of employers; in contrast the UK government's proposal is to free employers from regulation and decrease their costs and taxes at the expense of individuals who are paying the cost of the re-structuring process through unemployment' (p. 7). It is a grim contrast in national policy, and one which serves to increase the hardship of the unemployed in Britain.

A labour market policy of sorts has developed unavoidably under the Thatcher Government, given the enormity of unemployment. The main Government agency responsible for organising training schemes is the Manpower Services Commission (established in 1973) which has grown substantially since 1978 (see Brown and Fairley, 1987). In 1981 the MSC set up a New Training Initiative, which is the main instrument of Government labour market policy; its brief is the modernisation of skills and organisation of training programmes to assist school-leavers and unemployed adults. The NTI has established the Youth Training Scheme, Community Programme and Adult Training Strategy. While such measures are better than nothing, they have difficulties. Employers often view these schemes as short-term substitutes for hiring permanent and more costly labour, and few of the training measures offer skills or useful qualifications. Individuals on such schemes are excluded from normal employment protection legislation, a measure with which trade unions have agreed, and there is insufficient effort to pursue positive discrimination for those groups consistently discriminated in the labour market; in fact, these schemes appear to reproduce existing discrimination. Assessment of the effectiveness of these schemes is difficult but the continuing upward trend in unemployment suggests that it has been an insufficient response. It has not resolved the needs of long-term unemployed skilled adults whose place of employment has closed down. To some degree a 'dole culture' has developed around this group and the young, with many school-leavers fatalistically concluding that they may never work in the traditional sense of regular-houred and structured employment. Beechey (1985) has documented changes in work patterns: a steady decline in full-time employment and concurrent increase in part-time labour, both of which are linked to the growth of service industries in place of manufacturing. She argues that this growth in part-time employment reflects discriminations against women, since they predominant in such work; however, Britain is 'almost alone in having such a strong association of part-time working with women's employment' (Beechey, 1985, p. 13). Beechey maintains that the dynamic responsible for part-time employment growth is job flexibility; but this flexibility has in turn been structured to female employment since this has certain advantages for employers; part-time employment also reduces workers' rights and increases worker insecurity. To reverse the trend toward increased youth and adult employment will require concerted government policy. The consequences of increased female part-time work are considered later.

Overall, existing labour market measures and policies are inadequate and must be formulated more systematically in future policy and given a central role in establishing social citizenship rights. Markets are likely to remain important instruments of public policy in the post-New Right political configuration: but this cannot mean free and indiscriminate markets. Rather, there must be careful planning of the use of markets: existing economic policies (including the desire to maximise market processes) have proved strikingly insufficient and inefficient in tackling unemployment. While it is beyond the brief of this volume to offer specific policy proposals, some of the more plausible possibilities for such a labour market policy can be noted. First, training must be incorporated systematically into the British economy – paralleling the Swedish practice, for example. Many firms face skill shortages and this should be remedied. Such training must aim at the long-term adult unemployed, school-leavers, minorities and young adults in their twenties who may have already exhausted government youth training schemes. Of the latter type, a new two-year scheme for school-leavers is in operation, but this precludes those beyond school-leaving age. Further, some consideration must be given to the desirability of labour mobility and, if desirable, what role government funding and subsidies should have.

Finally, a recent proposal by the economist Mario Nuti (1985/86) should be mentioned. Nuti discusses what sorts of activities should be undertaken by the state, as economic planner, in market economies. He advocates intervention in three separate spheres – employment, investment and balance of payments – to address the respective problems of unemployment, low economic growth and external deficits, with the establishment of a new state institution in each area. For employment, Nuti seeks the creation of a National Employment Corporation which 'would hire workers at the minimum national wage for each skill and occupation and rent them out to firms at the best competitive rate (whether lower, or temporarily higher) they can obtain in the market; if there is no demand for the services of some of its workers it can rent them out free of charge to Local Authorities' (1985/86, p. 380) (see Rustin, 1985, ch. 7 for a similar scheme). This is an admirable strategy which combines use of market processes with some selective state intervention. Combined with a labour market policy centred on training and education, Nuti's proposal (and Rustin's) points toward the shape of future public policy: it retains elements of Keynesian macroeconomic planning and state intervention but with reliance upon market forces as liberals advise. Such a combination should yield long-term benefit to the economy and work-force alike, particularly since labour market policy goes logically hand-in-hand with the types of social citizenship rights reviewed in Chapter 9.

CONCLUSION: MARKETS AND CITIZENSHIP

For some socialists, the weakening of the Keynesian welfare state represents an opportunity for a complete reformulation of objectives which transcend the post-war consensus. For example, Panitch (1985/86) argues that 'the strength of the monetarist assault should not have become the occasion for a knee-jerk defence of the Keynesian/welfare state with all its ambiguous and constricted reforms, but rather treated as the occasion for proposing – for insisting on – the fundamental restructuring of the state and its relationship to society so that the communities it is supposed to serve and the people who labour for it together have great involvement in the public domain. Rather than leave the issue at "less state" versus "more state", socialists must recognise that popular antipathy to the state can also be addressed in terms of speaking *of a different kind of state*' (p. 92).

For Leo Panitch, the Keynesian welfare state consensus should not be assiduously reconstructed (see Hall, 1986, as noted in Chapter 7 for a different view). Rather, the nature of state intervention – whether in social rights or economic policy – needs fundamental rethinking. New Right attacks upon the post-war consensus provide an opportunity to consider 'what kind of state' is most desirable for socialist objectives. The type of response to the challenges of New Right arguments indicated by Panitch is important. In many ways, it is appropriate to question the value of state institutions which were the source of such deep dissatisfaction in the 1970s, ably exploited by the Thatcher Government. As the discussion of the London Industrial Strategy above suggests, future state intervention or state planning needs to be premised on a carefully formalised conception of its apposite role: there must be a clear social rationale shaping market intervention. If markets are to be utilised in public policy it must be in order to accomplish clearly stated social objectives. The traditional debate of plan versus market has to be recast in terms of 'what kind of state' should be responsible for planning? Panitch's criticisms should not encourage an easy abandoning of the social citizenship rights institutionalised in the post-1945 welfare state, but they do allow an evaluation of the adequacy of these rights. The two areas most vulnerable to Panitch's criticisms are women's rights and worker participation in production.

The preceding chapter has already noted the weakness of social citizenship rights regarding gender: as institutionalised in the Keynesian welfare state, existing gender roles were reinforced rather than challenged. There is a serious danger of reconstructing Keynesian policies without altering gender roles. This point is well made by Phillips (1983) in her observations on the labour movement's alternative economic strategy: 'it is a strategy for restoring Britain to the economic growth and relatively full employment that characterised the best of the post-war years . . . As a programme for economic expansion it has relegated women's issues to a separate sphere. Under the guise of a supposedly neutral strategy for all working people, it has presented a vision which fits most with the needs of working men' (p. 6). Both the changing nature of employment and the continuing importance of domestic circumstances make it vital that future public policy incorporate clear propositions to alter existing gender roles. As Phillips (1983) argues elsewhere, 'no strategy can work today if it focuses exclusively on either house or work. Women span both worlds, and in doing so they demand a strategy that embraces both. It is no good just dealing with one or the other' (p. 21).

Gender must be addressed not only because of its neglect in the Keynesian welfare state and its definition of social citizenship rights, but also because the Thatcher Government has had serious effects upon women's rights (David, 1985, 1986). Most obviously, the economic theories of New Right liberals have a traditional conception of the nuclear family and of women's roles. The

Thatcher Government's economic objectives have consequences for the position of women – socially conservative consequences. These liberal objectives imply a private nuclear family, untrammelled by government intervention, in which men work and women mind children and undertake unpaid domestic work, which keeps women from competing in the market-place for jobs with men. This nuclear family and domestic division of labour is reinforced by the Government's failure to provide adequate childminding services which would allow women to seek employment. As stressed in Chapter 2, the electoral appeal of New Right advocates has been pitched in terms of liberal economic arguments; the associated conservative arguments supplement and justify outcomes of these liberal policies. Thus, the Thatcher Government (and the Reagan Administration in the United States) want married women to remain in the home for economic reasons; conservative arguments support this economic rationale. Further, in Britain, women are the main source of part-time employment; obviously their commitment to a nuclear family and unpaid domestic responsibilities suits the requirements of part-time employers: employers want a flexible workforce but 'the desire for flexibility takes a gendered form, and in Britain today, it is almost exclusively women's jobs which have been constructed on a part-time basis' (Beechey, 1985, p. 12). Economic reasons contribute to the persistence of traditional gender roles and sexual divisions of labour in Britain.

Thus, the whole thrust of the Thatcher Government's liberal economics is oppressive to women. Aside from this, the last ten years have seen the destruction of 2 million full-time jobs occupied by women (mainly in declining manufacturing industries) and their substitution with part-time employment. Women's right to work has also been threatened. The 1980 Employment Act weakened rights for maternity leave and increased the danger of dismissal because of pregnancy. For those women in full-time employment they now need two years' length of services to qualify for these rights; and five years for part-time employees. Women with an earning husband have been deemed ineligible for the Government's community programme; and women's protection of pay and work conditions has been weakened by the ending of the Fair Wages resolution and the undermining of the wages councils. These specific measures consolidate the harmful implications of New Right liberalism for women's rights in Britain and the United

States. Liberal economics defines out of the economy 'much of what women are supposed to do with their time' (Phillips, 1983, p. 1). The Thatcher and Reagan Administrations have operationalised this assumption in their public policy.

So what can be done? The pursuit of social citizenship rights in the post-New Right era must seek consciously to transcend the traditional sexual division of labour, and state planning must reflect this aim. The London Training Board emphasised the needs of women and funded childcare places, interventions which 'challenge and change the boundaries between domestic work and the private and public economies' (Fairley, 1985, p. 12). Small steps, perhaps, but indicative of possibilities – though such forms of state intervention imply the importance of local decision-making bodies, abolished by the Thatcher Government (see Gurr and King, 1987, ch. 5). In contrast, the traditionally based alternative economic strategy largely ignores women, as Phillips (1983) correctly notes: its conception of employment, industrial democracy and the different positions of manufacturing and services in the economy all reflect male assumptions. The gender composition of work is changing (Beechey, 1985; Therborn, 1986) and the balance between part-time and full-time employment is shifting. For industrial democracy to affect women positively it has to be more widely based than simply the workplace: 'if industrial democracy becomes the only mechanism for popular involvement in planning, it will affect men and women unequally . . . If planning is to be for all, we need more than workplace democracy. We need other opportunities for popular involvement' (Phillips, 1983, p. 31). This book does not develop precise policy proposals regarding these issues since that would require a separate study. But one change capable of fostering women's equality is the introduction of shorter working hours; this creates opportunities for greater domestic equality and should expand the range of employment available to women (see Beechey, 1985; Phillips, 1983; Rustin, 1985). And it contributes to the objective of reducing unemployment.

To conclude, the criticisms of the Keynesian welfare state raised by Panitch (1985/86) and others are not without some validity. The post-New Right era will revert to some sort of interventionist state – probably of a Keynesian hue. But such an interventionist state should not reconstruct the post-war consensus and maintain existing welfare institutions. It must have a wider brief, which deliberately defines social citizenship rights with reference to gender equality in work and the home; Keynesian economic policies must include a systematically formulated labour market policy informed by the needs of the young and old unemployed, minorities and the disabled. This is not a short-term solution but a long-term strategy. New Right liberals have exploited failures in state institutions embodying social citizenship rights. If these rights are to enjoy full public support they must be defined and guaranteed in a way which will generate such wide support.

Epilogue: Citizenship Against Markets

The 1980s are an exciting time in politics. Old orthodoxies are being challenged and new configurations shaped. The diffusion of New Right ideas in Britain and the United States is a manifestation of this turbulence. But political debate occurs within a historical and institutional context – the accumulated experience of a political system and its people as well as that system's institutions. New Right advocates have attempted to radically reshape accepted practices, charging them with inadequacy in the face of economic crisis. Rather than recognising the important role of the post-war consensus in resolving the profound economic and political crisis of the 1930s, New right proponents have demanded a reversion to an arcane nineteenth-century model of political economy with little applicability to the late twentieth century. But New Right ideas have been articulated within existing institutions many of which embody Keynesian social democratic principles resistant to attack. The post-war welfare state is an expression of social citizenship rights established by the less powerful as a counter to market uncertainties: politics facilitates the establishment of citizenship rights *against* the dominance of market processes. As Esping-Andersen (1985) has observed recently, 'social citizenship may alleviate pressing needs, but it also provides a means of "social democratizing" capitalist society' (pp. 224–5); the extent of this 'social democratization' will depend on the nature and scope of the welfare state implemented in each society. Even where the social democratisation process has been least developed, it still has an important affect upon political institutions and culture: these become a defence against retrenchment and regressive change. Social citizenship rights are institutional expressions of deeply held beliefs and ideas which cannot easily be abrogated by New Right enthusiasts.

But the capacity of existing welfare institutions to withstand the challenge of New Right ideas and politicians depends on how extensively they have been formulated and implemented in the political system. While the British welfare state is more extensive and deeply ingrained than its American counterpart, it is less impressive than those of Norway and Sweden. There the process of social democratisation has been more extensive and consequently less vulnerable to New Right offensives: 'the effectiveness of the New Right in both Britain and Denmark cannot be explained by the circumstance that the labor movements there had been exceptionally successful in altering the political economy, but rather by the incompleteness of their accomplishments' (Esping-Andersen, 1985, p. 245). I have argued that in Britain New Right arguments have had some influence with the public and upon Government policy: the attack upon state provision of consumption goods and services has struck a chord with the electorate, to which all political parties have had to respond. If the process of social democratisation in Britain had been more extensive and successful this might not have occurred; but it has, and future political strategies must take account of this. The Labour party must not abandon its commitment to social citizenship. It must remember that citizenship rights are a fundamental means of redress against markets, important to large segments of society. But its future strategy will most likely retain some elements of the New Right liberal challenge. New Right ideas are more transient than Keynesianism but they will continue to influence public policy.

There is an obvious danger of giving too much significance to ideas in politics: the discussion of Keynesian and New Right principles may accord each an undue independence of political processes and calculations. This is not my intention. But the experience of British and American politics in the last decade is that debate over ideas and policy proposals is far from irrelevant to the content of political practice. Ideas do not determine politics, but they certainly influence political debate. That they do not determine policy is apparent from the experience of the Thatcher Government and Reagan Administration in pursuing selected New Right objectives: some changes have been effected but rather less than sought. This can be explained, to some degree, by the institutional context within which ideas are discussed and translated into public policy. In particular, the Thatcher Government's liberal- and conservative-inspired attack upon social citizenship rights has been thwarted by the welfare state institutions expressing those rights. The extent to which this attack has been successful (as in its criticisms of state provision of consumption goods and services) reflects the relative weakness of those institutions. In the United States a similar attack by the Reagan Administration has had even more success because the process of social democratisation is weaker there. But resistance to the Reagan initiative has come also from Congressional representatives conscious of constituency concerns about social need: citizenship rights have been a less significant buffer against New Right objectives, but not inconsequential.

Both the British and American opposition parties must renew their commitment to citizenship, specifically including a commitment to gender equality, and to the process of social democratisation. Markets should be incorporated in policy proposals through a commitment to a labour market policy aimed at achieving and sustaining full employment combined with redistributive policies. This is the surest means of maintaining and extending citizenship rights and controlling indiscriminate market forces.

Bibliography

Aberg, Rune (1984) 'Market-Independent Income Distribution: Efficiency and Legitimacy', in John Goldthorpe (ed.), *Order and Conflict in Contemporary Capitalism* (Oxford: Clarendon Press).

Addison, Paul (1975) *The Road to 1945* (London: Cape).

Alt, Jame E. and Chrystal, K. Alec (1983) *Political Economics* (Brighton: Wheatsheaf Books).

Anderson, Malcolm and Fairley, John (1983) 'The Politics of Industrial Training in the United Kingdom', *Journal of Public Policy*, no. 3, pp. 191–208.

Arblaster, Anthony (1984) *The Rise and Decline of Western Liberalism* (Oxford: Basil Blackwell).

Arrow, Kenneth (1951) *Social Choice and Individual Values* (New York: John Wiley and Sons; 1963, revised edn Yale University Press).

Ashford, Nigel (1984) *Consensus and Conflict within Neo-Liberalism* (Strathclyde Papers on Government and Politics) no. 34.

Ashford, Nigel (1985) 'The Bankruptcy of Collectivism', in Arther Seldon (ed.) *The 'New Right' Enlightenment* (London: Economic and Literary Books).

Barry, Brian (1970) *Sociologists, Economists and Democracy* (London: Collier–Macmillan).

Barry, Brian and Hardin, Russell (eds) (1983) *Rational Man and Irrational Society* (London and Beverly Hills, Calif: Sage).

Barry, Norman P. (1983) 'Review Article: The New Liberalism', *British Journal of Political Science*, vol. 13, pp. 93–123.

Bassett, Philip (1986) *Strike Free: New Industrial Relations in Britain* (London: Macmillan).

Bator, Francis M. (1960) *The Question of Government Spending* (New York: Collier Books).

Bean, Philip, Ferris, John and Whynes, David (1985) *In Defence of Welfare* (London and New York: Tavistock).

Becker, Lawrence C. (1977) *Property Rights: Philosophic Foundations* (London: Routledge & Kegan Paul).

Beechey, Veronica (1985) 'The Shape of the Workforce to Come', *Marxism Today*, vol. 29, no. 8, pp. 11–17.

Beer, Samuel H. (1964) *British Politics in the Collectivist Age* (New York: Vintage Books)

Bell, David S. (ed.) (1985) *The Conservative Government 1979–84* (London: Croom Helm).

199

Berlin, Isaiah (1969) *Four Essays on Liberty* (Oxford: Oxford University Press).

Beveridge, Sir William (1942) *Social Insurance and Allied Services* (London: HMSO) Cmnd 6404.

Birch, Anthony H. (1984) 'Overload, Ungovernability and Delegitimation: The Theories and the British Case', *British Journal of Political Science*, vol. 14, pp. 135–60.

Black, D. (1958) *The Theory of Committees and Elections*. (Cambridge: Cambridge University Press).

Blake, Robert (1970) *The Conservative Party from Peel to Churchill* (London: Collins).

Bonner, John (1986) *Politics, Economics and Welfare* (Brighton: Wheatsheaf Books).

Bosanquet, Nick (1981) 'Sir Keith's Reading List', *The Political Quarterly*, vol. 52, pp. 324–41.

Bosanquet, Nick (1983) *After the New Right* (London: Heinemann).

Bowles, Nigel (1987) *The White House and Capitol Hill* (Oxford: Clarendon Press).

Brittan, Samuel (1975) 'The Economic Contradictions of Democracy', *British Journal of Political Science, vol. 5.*

Brittan, Samuel (1979) *Participation without Politics* (London: The Institute of Economic Affairs).

Brown, Alice and Fairley, John (1987) 'A Scottish Labour Market Board', *The Scottish Government Yearbook.*

Brus, Wlodzimierz (1985) 'Socialism – Feasible and Viable', *New Left Review*, no. 153.

Buchanan, James M. (1975) *The Limits of Liberty: Between Anarchy and Leviathan* (Chicago, Illinois: University of Chicago Press).

Buchanan, James M. and Tullock, Gordon (1962) *The Calculus of Consent* (Ann Arbor, Michigan: University of Michigan Press).

Buchanan, James M. and Wagner, Richard E. (1977) *Democracy in Deficit* (New York and London: Academic Press).

Buchanan, James M. *et al.* (1978) *The Economics of Politics* (London: The Institute of Economic Affairs Readings 18).

Carnoy, Martin (1983) *The State and Political Theory* (Princeton, New Jersey: Princeton University Press).

Carter, Neil (1986) 'Co-operatives – The State of Play', *Political Quarterly*, vol. 57, no. 2, pp. 182–87.

Cawson, Alan (1982) *Corporatism and Welfare* (London: Heinemann Educational Books).

Carr-Saunders, A. M., Florence, P. Sargant and Peers, Robert (1938) *Consumers' Co-operation in Great Britain* (London: George Allen & Unwin).

Congdon, Tim (1985) 'Public spending – the reality', *The Times*, 11 June.

Cowling, Maurice (ed.) (1978) *Conservative Essays* (London: Cassell).

Crosland, C. A. R. (1956) *The Future of Socialism* (London: Cape).

Crawford, Alan (1980) *Thunder on the Right: The 'New Right' and the Politics of Resentment* (New York: Pantheon Books).

Crouch, Colin (1982) *The Politics of Industrial Relations*, 2nd edn (London: Fontana).

Crouch, Colin (1985) 'Can socialism achieve street credibility?' *Guardian*, 15 February.

Crozier, Michael J., Huntington, Samuel P. and Watanuki, Joji (1975) *The Crisis of Democracy* (New York: New York University Press).

Dale, Reginald (1986) 'US Democratic Party: The Missing Leader', *Financial Times*, 16 August 1986.

Dalton, George (1974) *Economic systems and society* (Harmondsworth: Penguin Books).

David, Miriam (1985) 'Motherhood, Child Care and the New Right', Paper presented to the annual meeting of the British Association for the Advancement of Science, August, Strathclyde University.

David, Miriam (1986) 'Moral and Maternal: The Family in the Right', Ruth Levitas (ed.) *The Ideology of the New Right* (Oxford: Polity Press).

Davis, Mike (1985) 'Reagonomics' Magical Mystery Tour', *New Left Review*, no. 149, pp. 45–65.

Davis, Mike (1986) 'The Lesser Evil? The Left and the Democratic Party', *New Left Review*, no. 155, pp. 5–36.

Dean, James W. (1981) 'The Dissolution of the Keynesian consensus', in Daniel Bell and Irving Kristol (eds) *The Crisis in Economic Theory* (New York: Basic Books).

Deaton, David, (1985) 'The Labour Market and Industrial Relations Policy of the Thatcher Government', in David Bell (ed) *The Conservative Government 1979–84* (London: Croom Helm).

Douglas, James (1976) 'Review Article: The Overloaded Crown', *British Journal of Political Science*, vol. 6, pp. 483–505.

Downs, Anthony (1957) *An Economic Theory of Democracy* (New York: Harper and Row).

Dryzek, John and Goodin, Robert E. (1986) 'Risk-Sharing and Social Justice: The Motivational Foundations of the Post-War Welfare State', *British Journal of Political Science*, vol. 16, pp. 1–34.

Dunleavy, Patrick (1979) 'The Urban Bases of Political Alignment: "Social Class", Domestic Property Ownership, or State Intervention in Consumption Processes', *British Journal of Political Science*, vol. 9.

Dunleavy, Patrick (1980) *Urban Political Analysis* (London: Macmillan).

Dunleavy, Patrick (1983) 'Analysing British Politics', in Henry Drucker, Patrick Dunleavy, Andrew Gamble and Gillian Peele (eds) *Developments in British Politics* (London: Macmillan).

Dunleavy, Patrick (1985) 'Bureaucrats, Budgets and the Growth of the State: Reconstructing an Instrumental Model', *British Journal of Political Science* vol. 15, pp. 299–328.

Dunleavy, Patrick (1986a) 'Explaining the Privatization Boom: Public Choice Versus Radical Approaches', *Public Administration*, vol. 64 pp. 13–34.

Dunleavy, Patrick (1986b) 'Theories of the State in British Politics', in Henry Drucker, Patrick Dunleavy, Andrew Gamble and Gillian Peele (eds) *Developments in British Politics 2* (London: Macmillan).

Dunleavy, Patrick and Husbands, Christopher T. (1985) *British Democracy at the Crossroads* (London: George Allen & Unwin).

Durham, Martin (1985) 'Family, Morality and the New Right', *Parliamentary Affairs*, vol. 38, no. 2, pp. 180–91.

Economist, The (1986) 'Too much trust in antitrust', 23 August.

Edgar, David (1984) 'Bitter Harvest' in James Curran (ed.) *The Future of the Left* (Cambridge: Polity Press/New Socialist).

Edgar, David (1986) 'The Free or the Good', in Ruth Levitas (ed.) *The Ideology of the New Right* (Cambridge: Polity Press).

Eisenstein, Zillah R. (1981) 'The Sexual Politics of the New Right: Understanding the "Crisis of Liberalism" for the 1980s', in N. O. Keohane, M. Z. Rosaldo and B. C. Gelpi (eds) *Feminist Theory: A Critique of Ideology* (Brighton: Harvester Press).

Elliott, Brian (1985) 'Response to "The Values of the New Right: Theory and Practice"', *Edinburgh University Centre for Theology and Public Issues* (New College, The Mound: Edinburgh).

Elliott, Brian and David McCrone (1985) 'Class, Culture and Morality: a sociological analysis of neo-conservatism' (Paper presented at annual meeting of the British Political Studies Association).

Eltis, Walter (1976) 'The Failure of the Keynesian Conventional Wisdom', *Lloyds Bank Review*.

Esping-Andersen, Gosta (1985) 'Power and Distributional Regimes', *Politics and Society*, vol. 14, no. 2, pp. 223–56.

Esping-Andersen, Gosta and Korpi, Walter, (1985) 'Social Policy as Class Politics in Post-War Capitalism: Scandinavia, Austria and Germany' in John Goldthorpe (ed.) *Order and Conflict in Contemporary Capitalism* (Oxford: Oxford University Press).

Fairley, John (1985) 'A Little Local Initiative', *Radical Scotland*, October/November, pp. 12–14.

Ferguson, Thomas and Rogers, Joel (1986) 'The Myth of America's Turn to the Right', *The Atlantic Monthly*, May, pp. 43–53.

Ferris, John (1985) 'Citizenship and the crisis of the welfare state', in Philip Bean *et al.* (eds) *In Defence of Welfare* (London and New York: Tavistock).

Feuchtwang, Stephan and Hussain, Athar (1983) *The Chinese Economic Reforms* (London: Croom Helm).

Frey, Bruno S. (1978) *Modern Political Economy* (Oxford: Martin Robertson).

Friedman, Kathi V. (1981) *Legitimation of Social Rights and the Western Welfare State: A Weberian Perspective* (Capital Hill, North Carolina: University of North Carolina Press).

Friedman, Milton (1962) *Capitalism and Freedom* (Chicago: University of Chicago Press).

Friedman, M. and Schwartz, A. J. (1963) *A Monetary History of the United States* (Princeton, N.J: Princeton University Press).

Furniss, Norman and Tilton, Timothy (1977) *The Case for the Welfare State* (Bloomington, Indiana and London: Indiana University Press).

Galbraith, John K. (1958) *The Affluent Society* (London: Hamish Hamilton).

Galbraith, John K. (1973) *Economics and the Public Purpose* (New York: Mentor Books).

Gamble, Andrew (1979) 'The Free Economy and the Strong State', *The Socialist Register*, pp. 1–25.

Gamble, Andrew (1985) 'Smashing the State: Thatcher's Radical Crusade', *Marxism Today*, June.

Gamble, Andrew (1985/86) 'Capitalism or Barbarism: The Austrian Critique of Socialism', *The Socialist Register*, pp. 255–372.

Gilder, George (1982) *Wealth and Poverty* (London: Buchan and Enright; originally published in 1981 in the United States).

Gilder, George (1984) 'A Vote for My Guy is a Vote for JFK's Legacy', *The Washington Post National Weekly Edition*, vol. 2, no. 2, 12 November, pp. 9–10.

Goodin, Robert E. (1982) 'Freedom and the welfare state: theoretical foundations', *Journal of Social Policy*, vol. 11, pp. 149–76.

Goodin, Robert E. (1985a) 'Self-Reliance Versus the Welfare State', *Journal of Social Policy*, vol. 14, no. 1, pp. 25–47.

Goodin, Robert E. (1985b) 'Vulnerabilities and Responsibilities: An Ethical Defense of the Welfare State', *American Political Science Review*, vol. 79, pp. 775–87.

Goodin, Robert E. (1986) 'Reasons for Welfare' (Unpublished paper).

Gough, Ian (1979) *The Political Economy of the Welfare State* (London: Macmillan).

Grahl, John (1983) 'The Liberal Revolutionary', *Marxism Today*, vol. 27, no. 6, pp. 18–24.

Grant, Wyn and Nath, Shiv (1984) *The Politics of Economic Policymaking* (Oxford: Basil Blackwell).

Gray, John (1984) *Hayek on Liberty* (Oxford: Basil Blackwell).

Greater London Council (1985) *London Industrial Strategy* (London: Greater London Council).

Gurr, Ted Robert and King, Desmond S. (1987) *The State and the City* (London: Macmillan; Chicago Illinois: University of Chicago Press).

Habermas, Jürgen (1975) *Legitimation Crisis* (London: Heinemann).

Hall, Stuart (1983) 'The Great Moving Right Show', in Stuart Hall and Martin Jacques (eds) *The Politics of Thatcherism* (London: Lawrence and Wishart).

Hall, Stuart (1985) 'Authoritarian Populism: A Reply', *New Left Review*, no. 151. pp. 106–13.

Hall, Stuart and Jacques, Martin (eds) (1983) *The Politics of Thatcherism* (London: Lawrence and Wishart).

Hansard (1977) *House of Commons Debates*, vol. 929, 29 March.

Hanson, Russell L. (1987) 'The Expansion and Contraction of the American Welfare State', in R. Goodin and J. Le Grand *et al.*, *The Middle Classes and the Welfare State* (London: George Allen & Unwin).

Harrington, Michael (1962) *The Other America: Poverty in the United States*. (New York, 1968: Penguin Special).

Harris, Lord (1985) 'The Morality of the Market', Edinburgh University Centre for Theology and Public Issues (New College, The Mound: Edinburgh).

Hayek, F. A. (ed.) (1935) *Collectivist Economic Planning* (London: George Routledge).

Hayek, F. A. (1944) *The Road to Serfdom* (London: Routledge & Kegan Paul).

Hayek, F. A. (1960) *The Constitution of Liberty* (London: Routledge & Kegan Paul).

Hayek, F. A. (1973) *Law, Legislation and Liberty Volume 1: Rules and Order* (London: Routledge & Kegan Paul).

Hayek, F. A. (1976) *Law, Legislation and Liberty Volume 2: The Mirage of Social Justice* (London: Routledge & Kegan Paul).

Hayek, F.A. (1978) *A Tiger by the Tail* (London: Institute of Economic Affairs).

Hayek, F. A. (1979) *Law, Legislation and Liberty Volume 3: The Political Order of a Free People* (London: Routledge & Kegan Paul).

Hayek, F. A. (1980) *1980s Unemployment and the Unions* (London: Institute of Economic Affairs).

Heald, David (1983) *Public Expenditure* (Oxford: Martin Robertson).

Heath, Anthony (1974) 'The Rational Model of Man', *European Journal of Sociology*, vol. 15, no. 2, pp. 184–205.

Heath, Anthony, Jowell, R. and Curtice, J. (1985) *How Britain Votes* (Oxford: Pergamon Press).

Heclo, Hugh (1974) *Modern Social Policies in Britain and Sweden* (New Haven, Conn.: Yale University Press).

Heller, Walter (1967) *New Dimensions of Political Economy* (New York: W. W. Norton).

HMSO (1980) *The Government's Expenditure Plans 1980–81 to 1983–84*, Cmnd 7841.

Hodgson, Geoff (1984) *The Democratic Economy* (Harmondsworth: Penguin Books).

Hoggart, Richard (1957) *The Uses of Literacy* (Harmondsworth: Penguin Books).

Holmes, Peter (1985) 'The Thatcher Government's Overall Economic Performance', in David Bell (ed.) *The Conservative Government 1979–84* (London: Croom Helm).

Holmwood, John and Stewart, Alexander (1987) *The Failure of Social Theory* (forthcoming).

Horwitz, Sam (1985) 'Telephones, Banks and "Lifelines" for the Poor', *The Washington Post National Weekly Edition*, vol. 2, no. 22, 1 April, pp. 9–10.

Huntington, Samuel P. (1975) 'The United States', in Michael Crozier, Samuel P. Huntington and Joji Watanuki *The Crisis of Democracy* (New York: New York University Press).

Hutchinson, T. W. (1981) *The Politics and Philosophy of Economics* (Oxford: Basil Blackwell).

Jencks, Christopher (1985) 'How Poor Are the Poor?', *New York Review of Books*, 9 May.

Jessop, Bob (1980) 'The Transformation of the State in Post-war Britain', in Richard Scase (ed.) *The State in Western Europe* (London: Croom Helm).

Jessop, Bob, Bonnett, Kevin, Bromley, Simon and Ling, Tom (1984) 'Authoritarian Populism, Two Nations and Thatcherism', *New Left Review*, no. 147, pp. 32–60.

Jessop, Bob, Bonnett, Kevin, Bromley, Simon and Ling, Tom (1985) 'Thatcherism and the Politics of Hegemony: a Reply to Hall', *New Left Review*, no. 153, pp. 87–101.

Jones, Doug (1986) 'Labour's Spending Plans – Why the Right is Wrong', *New Statesman*, 22 August.

Keegan, William (1984) *Mrs Thatcher's Economic Experiment* (Harmondsworth: Penguin Books).

Keynes, John Maynard (1936) *The General Theory of Employment, Interest and Money* (London: Macmillan).

King, Anthony (1975) 'Overload: Problems of Governing in the 1970s' *Political Studies*, vol. 23, pp. 284–96.

King, Desmond S. (1985) 'The New Right and the Public Sector in Britain and the United States' (Paper presented to annual meeting of the European Consortium for Political Research).

King, Desmond S. (1986) 'Public Sector Growth and State Autonomy in Western Europe: The Changing Role and Scope of the State in Ireland since 1950', *West European Politics*, vol. 9, pp. 81–96.

Klein, Rudolph and Michael O'Higgins (eds) (1985) *The Future of Welfare* (Oxford: Basil Blackwell).

Korpi, Walter (1983) *The Democratic Class Struggle* (London: Routledge & Kegan Paul).

Kukathas, Chandran (1985) 'Competition as a Voyage of Discovery', in Arthur Seldon (ed.) *The 'New Right' Enlightenment* (London: Economic and Literary Books).

Lachmann, L. M. (1973) *Macro-economic Thinking and the Market Economy* (London: Institute of Economic Affairs).

Lané, Jan. Erik (ed.) (1985) *State and Market: The Politics of the Public and the Private* (London: Sage).

Lane, Robert E. (1986) 'Market Justice, Political Justice', *American Political Science Review*, vol. 80, no. 2, pp. 383–402.

Laski, Harold J. (1936) *The Rise of European Liberalism* (London: George Allen & Unwin).

Lauber, Volkmar (1983) 'From Growth Consensus to Fragmentation in Western Europe', *Comparative Politics*, pp. 329–49.

Laver, Michael (1981) *The Politics of Private Desires* (Harmondsworth: Penguin Books).

Le Grand, Julian and Winter, David (1987) 'The Middle Class Defence of the British Welfare State', in R. Goodin and J. Le Grand *et al. The Middle Classes and the Welfare State* (London: George Allen & Unwin).

Leeman, Wayne A. (1977) *Centralized and Decentralized Economic Systems* (Chicago: Rand McNally).

Levine, David P. (1981) *Economic Theory Volume 2*. (London: Routledge & Kegan Paul).

Levitas, Ruth (ed.) (1985) *The Ideology of the New Right* (Oxford: Polity Press).

Lindblom, Charles E. (1977) *Politics and Markets* (New York: Basic Books).

Linton, Martin (1985) *The Swedish Road to Socialism* (London: Fabian Tract 503).

Loney, Martin (1986) *The Politics of Greed: The New Right and the Welfare State* (London: Pluto Press).

Lubasz, Heinz (1976) 'Marx's Initial Problematic: The Problem of Poverty', *Political Studies*, vol. XXIV, no. 1, pp. 24–42.

Mandeville, Bernard (1970) *The Fable of the Bees* (Harmondsworth: Penguin Books).

Mann, Michael (1985) *Socialism Can Survive* (London: Fabian Tract no. 502).

Mann, Michael (1985) 'Can Labour make social citizens of us all?', *Guardian* 4 March.

Marshall, T. H. (1964) *Class, Citizenship and Social Development* (New York: Doubleday & Co.).

Martin, Andrew (1973) *The Politics of Economic Policy in the United States* (Beverly Hills, Calif. and London: Sage).

McBride, Stephen (1986) 'Mrs Thatcher and the Post-war Consensus: The Case of Trade Union Policy', *Parliamentary Affairs*, vol. 39, pp. 330–40.

McLean, Iain (1986) 'Review Article: Some Recent Work in Public Choice', *British Journal of Political Science*, vol. 16, pp. 377–94.

Meade, J. E. (1985) 'We can conquer unemployment', *New Democrat*, vol. 3, no. 3, pp. 13–14.

Miller, David (1976) *Social Justice* (Oxford: Clarendon Press).

Moore, Robert (1985) 'Sociology, Social Change, and the Sociology of Race Relations', (Paper presented to annual meeting of British Association for the Advancement of Science August, Strathclyde University).

Moran, Michael (1985) *Politics and Society in Britain: An Introduction* (London: Macmillan).

Morgan, Kenneth O. (1984) *Labour in Power 1945–1951* (Oxford: Oxford University Press).

Mueller, Dennis C. (1979) *Public Choice* (London and New York: Cambridge University Press).

Mukherjee, Santosh (1972) *Making Labour Markets Work* (London: P.E.P.).

Murray, Robin (1985) 'Benetton Britain: The New Economic Order', *Marxism Today*, pp. 28–32.

Nathan, Richard P. (1983) 'The Reagan Presidency in Domestic Affairs' in Fred I. Greenstein (ed.), *The Reagan Presidency: An Early Assessment* (Baltimore, Maryland and London: The Johns Hopkins University Press).

Newman, Stephen (1984) *Liberalism at Wits' End* (Ithaca, New York: Cornell University Press).

Nisbet, Robert A. (1966) *The Sociological Tradition* (London: Heinemann).

Niskanen, William A. (1971) *Bureaucracy and Representative Government* (Chicago, Illinois: Aldine-Atherton).

Niskanen, William A. (1973) *Bureaucracy: Servant or Master?* (London: Institute of Economic Affairs).

Nove, Alex (1983) *The Economics of Feasible Socialism* (London: George Allen & Unwin).

Nozick, Robert (1974) *Anarchy, State and Utopia* (New York: Basic Books).

Nuti, D. M. (1985/86) 'Economic Planning in Market Economies: Scope, Instruments, Institutions', *The Socialist Register*, pp.373–84.

O'Connor, James (1973) *The Fiscal Crisis of the State* (New York: St Martin's Press).

Offe, Claus (1984) *Contradictions of the Welfare State* (London: Hutchinson).

O'Higgins, Michael (1985) 'Inequality, Redistribution and Recession: The British Experience, 1976–1982', *Journal of Social Policy*, vol. 14, no. 3, pp. 279–307.

O'Higgins, Michael and Patterson, Alan (1985) 'The Prospects for Public Expenditure: A Disaggregate Analysis', in Rudolph Klein and Michael O'Higgins (eds) *The Future of Welfare* (Oxford: Basil Blackwell).

Okun, B. Robert (1986) 'Let Markets be Markets', *Policy Review*, no. 35.

Olson, Mancur (1965) *The Logic of Collective Action* (Cambridge: Harvard University Press; 1968, New York: Schocken Books).

Olson, Mancur, (1982) *The Rise and Decline of Nations* (New Haven, Conn.: Yale University Press).

Orloff, Anne and Skocpol, Theda (1984) 'Why Not Equal Protection? Explaining the Politics of Public Social Spending in Britain 1900–1911, and the United States, 1880s–1920', *American Sociological Review*, vol. 49, pp. 726–50.

Oules, Firmin (1966) *Economic Planning and Democracy* (Harmondsworth: Penguin Books).

Palmer, John L. and Sawhill, Isabel V. (eds) (1984) *The Reagan Record* (Cambridge: Ballinger Co.).

Panitch, Leo (1985/86) 'The Impasse of Social Democratic Politics', *The Socialist Register* (London: Merlin Press).

Parsons, Wayne (1982) 'Politics without Promises: The Crisis of "Overload" and Governability', *Parliamentary Affairs*, vol. 35, no. 4, pp. 421–35.

Peele, Gillian (1984) *Revival and Reaction: The Right in Contemporary America* (Oxford: Clarendon Press).

Pickersgill, Gary M. and Pickersgill, Joyce E. (1974) *Contemporary Economic Systems: A Comparative View* (Englewood Cliffs, New Jersey: Prentice-Hall).

Pigou, A. C. (1929) *The Economics of Welfare* (London: Macmillan).

Phillips, Anne (1983) *Hidden Hands: Women and Economic Policies* (London: Pluto Press).

Plant, Raymond (1984) *Equality, Markets and the New Right* (London: Fabian Tract 494).

Plant, Raymond (1985) 'The very idea of a welfare state', in Philip Bean *et al.* (eds) *In Defence of Welfare* (London and New York: Tavistock).

Polanyi, Karl (1957) *The Great Transformation* (Boston, Mass.: Beacon Press).

Polanyi, Michael (1951) *The Logic of Liberty* (London, 1951).

Poulantzas, Nicos (1978) *State, Power, Socialism* (London: Verso).

Quick, Perry D. (1984) 'Business: Reagan's Industrial Policy', in John L. Palmer and Isabel V. Sawhill (eds) *The Reagan Record* (Cambridge, Mass.: Ballinger Publishing Co.).

Rand, Ayn (1957) *Atlas Shrugged* (New York: Random House).

Rand, Ayn (1964) *The Virtue of Selfishness: A New Concept of Egoism* (New York: New American Library).

Riddell, Peter (1983) *The Thatcher Government* (Oxford: Martin Robertson).

Robinson, Joan (1962) *Economic Philosophy* (Harmondsworth: Penguin Books).

Robinson, Joan (1971) *Economic Heresies* (London: Macmillan).

Robinson, Ray (1986) 'Restructuring the Welfare State: An Analysis of Public Expenditure, 1979/80–1984/85', *Journal of Social Policy*, vol. 15, pp. 1–21.

Rose, Richard and B. Guy Peters (1977 *Can Government Go Bankrupt?* (New York: Basic Books).

Rosenberry, Sara A. (1982) 'Social Insurance, Distributive Criteria and the Welfare Backlash: A Comparative Analysis', *British Journal of Political Science*, vol. 12, pp. 421–47.

Rothbard, Murray (1978) *For a New Liberty: The Libertarian Manifesto* (New York: Collier Books).

Rowthorn, Bob (1986) 'Unemployment: A Resistible Force', *Marxism Today* September, pp. 28–31.

Rustin, Michael (1985) *For a Pluralist Socialism* (London: Verso).

Rustin, Michael (1986) 'Lessons of the London Industrial Strategy', *New Left Review* no. 155, pp. 75–84.

Saunders, Peter (1985) 'Labour', in Arthur Seldon (ed.) *The 'New Right' Enlightenment* (London: Economic and Literary Books).

Schott, Kerry (1984) *Policy, Power and Order* (New Haven, Conn. and London: Yale University Press).

Schumpeter, Joseph A. (1950) *Capitalism, Socialism and Democracy*, 3rd edn (New York: Harper and Row).

Schweinitz, Karl de (1943) *England's Road to Social Security* (New York: Barnes).

Scruton, Roger (1980) *The Meaning of Conservatism* (Harmondsworth: Penguin Books).

Sen, Amartya (1982) *Choice, Welfare and Measurement* (Oxford: Basil Blackwell).

Shackleton, J. R. (1985) 'UK Privatisation – US Deregulation', *Politics*, no. 5, pp. 8–16.

Shapiro, Rose (1985) 'Britain's Sexual Counter-Revolutionaries', *Marxism Today*, February.

Shaw, Jane (1985) 'Breaking New Ground: Public Choice Economists Explain Why Government Doesn't Work', *Policy Review*, no. 33, Summer, pp. 77–80.

Shefter, Martin and Ginsberg, Benjamin (1985) 'Why Reaganism Will Be With Us Into the 21st Century', *The Washington Post National Weekly Edition*, 30 September, pp. 21–2.

Shonfield, Andrew (1965) *Modern Capitalism: The Changing Balance of Public and Private Power* (Oxford and New York: Oxford University Press).

Smith, Adam (1759) *The Theory of Moral Sentiments* (London).

Smith, Adam (1776) (1828) *An Enquiry into the Nature and Causes of the Wealth of Nations* (Edinburgh: Adam and Charles Black).

Sowell, Thomas (1981) *Markets and Minorities* (Oxford: Basil Blackwell).

Stein, Herbert (1969) *The Fiscal Revolution in America* (Chicago, Illinois: University of Chicago Press).

Steiner, Peter O. (1970) 'The Public Sector and the Public Interest', in Robert H. Haveman and Julius Margolis (eds) *Public Expenditures and Policy Analysis* (Chicago, Illinois: Markham Publishing Co.).

Stephens, John D. (1979) *The Transition from Capitalism to Socialism* (London: Macmillan and Atlantic Highlands, New Jersey: Harvester Press).

Stockman, David A. (1986) *The Triumph of Politics* (London: The Bodley Head).

Sugden, Robert (1981) *The Political Economy of Public Choice* (Oxford: Martin Robertson).

Sundquist, James L. (1968) *Politics and Policy: The Eisenhower, Kennedy and Johnson Years* (Washington DC: Brookings Institution).

Taylor-Gooby, Peter (1985) *Public Opinion, Ideology and State Welfare* (London: Routledge & Kegan Paul).

Taylor-Gooby, Peter (1986) 'Privatism, Power and the Welfare State', *Sociology*, vol. 20, no. 2.

Therborn, Goran (1984) 'The Prospects of Labour and the Transformation of Advanced Capitalism', *New Left Review* no. 145, pp. 5–38.

Therborn, Goran (1985) 'West on the Dole', *Marxism Today*, vol. 29, no. 6, pp. 6–10.

Therborn, Goran (1986) *Why Some Peoples Are More Unemployed Than Others* (London: Verso).

Thomas, Robert J. (1982) 'Citizenship and Gender in Work Organisation: Some Considerations for Theories of the Labor Process', in Michael Burawoy and Theda Skocpol (eds) *Marxist Inquiries* (Chicago and London: University of Chicago Press).

Thompson, Grahame (1984) ' "Rolling back" the state? Economic Intervention 1975–82', in Gregor McLennan, David Held and Stuart Hall (eds) *State and Society in Contemporary Britain* (Cambridge: Polity Press).

Thurow, Lester C. (1983) *Dangerous Currents: The State of Economics* (New York: Vintage Books).

Tobin, James (1986) 'How to Think About the Deficit', *The New York Review of Books*, vol. 33, no. 14, pp. 43–6.

Tsongas, Paul (1984) 'Vote for My Guy: Your Children Need Him', *The Washington Post National Weekly Edition*, vol. 2, no. 2, 12 November, pp. 8–9.

Tullock, Gordon (1976) *The Vote Motive* (London: The Institute of Economic Affairs).

Turner, Bryan S. (1986) *Citizenship and Capitalism* (London: George Allen & Unwin).

Turner, R. Kerry and Collis, Clive (1977) *The Economics of Planning* (London: Macmillan).

Viguerie, Richard A. (1981) *The New Right: We're Ready to Lead* (Falls Church, Virginia: The Viguerie Company).

Von Mises, Ludwig (1935) 'Economic Calculation in the Socialist Commonwealth', in F. A. Hayek (ed.) *Collectivist Economic Planning* (London: George Routledge and Sons).

Wainwright, Hilary and Elliott, Dave (1982) *The Lucas Plan* (London and New York: Alison & Busby).

Walker, Alan (1984) 'The Political Economy of Privatisation', in Julian Le Grand and Ray Robinson (eds) *Privatisation and the Welfare State* (London: George Allen & Unwin).

Wanniski, Jude (1978) 'Taxes, revenues, and the "Laffer curve"', *Public Interest*, no. 50, pp. 3–16.

Wanniski, Jude (1979) *The Way the World Works* (New York: Basic Books).

Webster, Trevor (1985) 'Profits of privatisation', *The Scotsman*, 19 January.

Whiteley, Paul F. (1985) 'Evaluating the Monetarist Experiment in Britain' (Paper presented to annual meeting of European Consortium for Political Research, Barcelona).

Whynes, David (1985) 'Markets and neo-liberal political economy', in Philip Bean *et al.* (eds) *In Defence of Welfare* (London and New York: Tavistock).

Williams, Philip (1979) *Hugh Gaitskell: A Political Biography* (London: Jonathan Cape).

Williamson, Oliver E. (1975) *Markets and Hierarchies: Analysis and Antitrust Implications* (New York: Free Press).

Wilson, James Q. (ed.) (1980) *The Politics of Regulation* (New York: Basic Books).

Woolley, John T. (1982) 'Monetarists and the Politics of Monetary Policy', *Annals of the American Academy of Political and Social Science*, no. 459, pp. 148–60.

Young, Stephen (1986) 'The Nature of Privatisation in Britain, 1979–85', *West European Politics*, vol. 9, no. 2, pp. 235–52.

Zukin, Sharon (1985) 'Markets and Politics in France's Declining Regions', *Journal of Policy Analysis and Management*, vol. 5, pp. 40–57.

Index